FARM WORKERS IN WESTERN CANADA

Injustices and Activism

Shirley A. McDonald and Bob Barnetson, Editors

The University of Alberta Press

Published by

The University of Alberta Press
Ring House 2
Edmonton, Alberta, Canada T6G 2E1
www.uap.ualberta.ca

Library and Archives Canada Cataloguing in Publication

Farm workers in Western Canada : injustices and activism / Shirley A. McDonald and Bob Barnetson, editors.

Includes bibliographical references and index.
Issued in print and electronic formats.
ISBN 978-1-77212-138-4 (paperback).—ISBN 978-1-77212-272-5 (epub).—
ISBN 978-1-77212-273-2 (mobipocket).—ISBN 978-1-77212-274-9 (pdf)

1. Agricultural laborers—Canada, Western—Legal status, laws, etc.
2. Agricultural laborers—Canada, Western—Social conditions.
3. Agricultural laws and legislation—Canada, Western. I. McDonald, Shirley Ann, 1953–, editor II. Barnetson, Bob, 1970–, editor

KE3196.A37F37 2016 344.71201'763 C2016-902850-X
C2016-902851-8

First edition, first printing, 2016.
First printed and bound in Canada by Houghton Boston Printers, Saskatoon, Saskatchewan.
Copyediting and proofreading by Brendan Wild.
Indexing by Stephen Ullstrom.

The University of Alberta Press is committed to protecting our natural environment. As part of our efforts, this book is printed on Enviro Paper: it contains 100% post-consumer recycled fibres and is acid- and chlorine-free.

This book has been published with the help of a grant from the Canadian Federation for the Humanities and Social Sciences, through the Awards to Scholarly Publications Program, using funds provided by the Social Sciences and Humanities Research Council of Canada.

The University of Alberta Press gratefully acknowledges the support received for its publishing program from the Government of Canada, the Canada Council for the Arts, and the Government of Alberta through the Alberta Media Fund.

Canada

Canada Council for the Arts   Conseil des Arts du Canada

Alberta Government

This book is dedicated to the many faceless and silent men, women, and children whose hard labour feeds a hungry world.

The farmer has been an independent fellow, able to get along without much help from anyone. He could always hire plenty of men, and there are machines for every need. So far as the farmer has been concerned, he could get along very well.

—Nellie McClung, *In Times Like These* (1915)

Contents

Acknowledgements

Shirley A. McDonald

The inception of this book was inspired by the activism of two Alberta farm workers, Darlene Dunlop and Eric Musekamp, who have, for 15 years, rallied public support for the rights of farm workers and lobbied members of the Alberta government, seeking to change the legislation to allow farm workers to unionize and collectively bargain for fair pay, safe working conditions, regulated hours, and the rest of the benefits that workers covered under the province's labour laws take for granted. The inception of this book was also inspired by my doctoral research; thus, I would like to thank University of Alberta professors Albert Braz, Christine Wiesenthal, and Sarah Carter for their generosity and patience as I endeavoured, regardless of the obstacles, to complete my PHD. Since the beginning of the book project, numerous other people have also provided valuable support. Bob and I sincerely appreciate the help and guidance of Peter Midgley, senior editor at the University of Alberta Press, whose unwavering, whole-hearted confidence in the book and reliance on Bob and me to bring the project to completion kept us going. We would also like to acknowledge the relentless work of MLA Dr. David Swann, who has lobbied Alberta's Legislature to bring farm workers under the protection of the labour laws. As well, we would like to acknowledge the contributions of our late colleague Kerry Preibisch, whose guidance helped us to shape the book's focus and who attracted the interest of several of the high-calibre scholars whose work appears in this volume. We are also indebted to the several anonymous reviewers whose comments shaped the final form of this book. Bob and I would also like to thank Walter Musekamp for generously donating his time and expertise in desktop publishing to format the chapters and other book components into a presentable manuscript. Thank you, too, to my colleagues in the Faculty of Creative and Critical Studies at the University of British Columbia Okanagan, for their generous financial support for this project. Special thanks go to Ramine Adl, my long-time friend and colleague, who encouraged me and offered his home as a writer's retreat many times over the past few years. I would also like to acknowledge the support of the kind folks at the Museum of the Highwood in High River, Alberta, and at the Bert Sheppard Stockmen's Foundation Library and Archives in Cochrane, Alberta. Bob Barnetson would like to thank his colleagues at Athabasca University, including Dr. Jason Foster, Dr. Alvin Finkel, and Dr. Bruce Spencer for their comments. Bob would also like to acknowledge the contributions of Doug Taylor (formerly of Alberta Agriculture), and the staff members at the Parkland Institute, at the Alberta Workers' Health Centre, and at the Alberta Federation of Labour for their assistance. He would also like to acknowledge the Alberta Federation of Labour's financial support for this project. Finally, Bob would like to thank his family (Jennifer and Jessica) for their patience while this collection was put together. And I thank Bob Barnetson for being the kindest and most diligent co-editor with whom anyone could possibly hope to work.

Introduction

Bob Barnetson and Shirley A. McDonald

On August 20, 1999, farm worker Terry Rash accidentally rolled a water truck into a ditch on Highway 36 near Taber, Alberta. The truck belonged to his employer Charles Henry Beauchamp, who, arriving at the scene and seeing the wreck, became enraged and stabbed Rash repeatedly, killing him. Beauchamp received a 14-month sentence with a recommendation for early release. On appeal, his sentence was extended to four years (*R. v. Beauchamp*, 2002). The workplace killing of Terry Rash is unusual, yet deaths of and injuries to farm workers are regular occurrences that reflect the fact that farm work is among the most dangerous jobs in Canada (Picket, Hartling, Brison, & Guernsey, 1999). Consider Kevan Chandler, an Alberta feedlot employee who was killed in a grain silo at Tongue Creek Feeders near High River, Alberta. On Father's Day, 2006, the 32-year-old father of two entered the silo in order to shovel out the grain. Because Silo 7 was not equipped with a mechanical sweeper to bring down the grain that clings high to the interior walls, Chandler had to use a pole to knock it down and, in the process, the grain fell on him and smothered him to death (Barley, 2008). His widow and young family were left without financial support because, in 2006, the Alberta government did not require feedlot owners to purchase workers' compensation insurance (Barnetson, 2015a).

Most farm workers do not lose their lives, but many sustain debilitating injuries, especially when farmers organize work in ways that exposes farm workers to hazardous conditions. Philippa Thomas suffered a debilitating injury when she received a cut on her thumb while employed at an equestrian centre near Cochrane, Alberta. The small cut became infected and Thomas developed complex regional pain syndrome (CRPS). This condition is a chronic progressive disease characterized by severe pain, swelling, and changes in the skin; CRPS ultimately rendered Thomas's right arm useless (Bachusky, 2012). Like most agricultural operators, Thomas's employer did not carry workers' compensation insurance, so Thomas and the taxpayer-funded health-care system have covered the costs caused by her injury. Why did the Alberta government—which had to pick up many of the costs of farm injuries—deny farm workers the rights guaranteed to labourers in all other sectors? At the time of writing, the Alberta government also excluded farm workers from most of the rights set out in the Employment Standards Code and from the entirety of the Occupational Health and Safety Act. The passage of the Enhanced Protection for Farm and Ranch Workers Act in 2015 made workers' compensation insurance mandatory, but whether farm workers will have the full spectrum of workplace rights remains to be seen.

Farm Workers in Western Canada: Injustices and Activism examines the social, political, and economic conditions that have shaped the organization of farm work in the western provinces, with particular attention paid to the effect such conditions have on farm workers. In order to provide both depth and breadth of coverage, the book has two focuses. It begins with a series of case studies of farm work in Alberta that complement the rich, albeit mostly historical, literature about labour in Alberta, such as that of Alvin Finkel (2012), Sandra Rollings-Magnusson (2009), and Cecilia Danysk (1995), as well as extend discussions of farm worker rights in Canada by scholars like Eric Tucker (2006) and Fay Faraday, Judy Fudge, and Eric Tucker (2012). Furthermore, the Alberta case studies explore conflicting interests found in agricultural employment, thereby extending existing research on rural Alberta by Ken Larson (2005), and Roger Epp and Dave Whitson (2001).

Subsequent chapters attend to the experiences of immigrant, migrant, and temporary foreign workers who produce, process, and distribute food in British Columbia, Alberta, and Manitoba. These chapters highlight how neoliberal agricultural and trade policies have intensified the international migration of workers seeking work in food production, processing, and distribution (Griffith, 2006; Martin, 2002; Rogaly, 2008). Neoliberalism embraces the assertion that human well-being can best be advanced by minimizing institutional constraints on individuals via public policy that emphasizes strong private property rights, free markets, and free trade (Harvey, 2005). Neoliberalism is evident in Canada's agriculture sector in the form of government policies that minimize state regulation and facilitate employers' increasing use of migrant farm workers to reduce the costs of production. The growing use of migrant farm workers in the agricultural sector reflects the fact that Canadian citizens have responded to deteriorating wages and working conditions in agriculture by abandoning that type of employment. The employment trend may also reflect agricultural employers' preference for migrant workers, whose precarious legal status makes them less likely than workers with full citizenship rights to resist employers' demands to work long hours and perform repetitive tasks under difficult and even unsafe working conditions (Brass, 2004; Schwartzmann, 2013; Stull & Broadway, 2004). Indeed, as Kerry Preibisch (2007) and Angela Stuesse (2010) observe, migrant workers constitute an important component in Canadian farms' continued competitiveness among producers in North American agriculture.

An important outcome of the cross-jurisdictional approach in *Farm Workers in Western Canada* is the authors' collaborative enumeration of the many and complex ways in which agricultural workers are vulnerable to ill treatment in the workplace. Farm workers across western Canada experience low wages, poor working conditions, and high rates of injury. There are, however, important differences in how provincial governments seek to manage these negative aspects of farm work. For example, the governments of both British Columbia and Manitoba require farm owner-operators to participate in their workers' compensation systems, thereby ensuring that injured farm workers receive wage-loss and medical benefits. In contrast, the governments of Alberta (until 2016) and Saskatchewan have made agricultural employers' participation in a compensation system voluntary, thereby leaving workers' financial security in the hands of those employers in the event of injury. The differences in provincial policies suggest that farm workers' degree of vulnerability to ill treatment in the workplace is mediated in important ways by the regulatory choices of policy makers.

Bob Barnetson's chapter, "Capitalist Farms, Vulnerable Workers: The Political Economy of Farm Work in Alberta," considers Alberta's longstanding exclusion of farm workers from virtually all workplace protections. It suggests that farmers (i.e., employers) have profoundly influenced this policy decision. The Progressive Conservative government (1971–2015) politically justified these exclusions as necessary to preserve the so-called family farm from bankruptcy. Barnetson's analysis of changes in Alberta's agricultural industry—including a shift toward physically and financially large farms that employ the majority of waged farm workers—raises questions about the validity of the family farm rationale. In its place, Barnetson asserts that the exclusion has been the product of a political quid pro quo between the Conservative government and rural voters, a mutually beneficial agreement by which rural voters, especially those with investments in agriculture, exchanged electoral support of the Tories for government programs and minimal regulation of farming operations.

In a chapter spawned by a class project in a University of Calgary clinical law course, Jennifer Koshan and her co-authors examine whether the pre-2016 exclusion of Alberta farm workers from most statutory employment laws was permissible under the Canadian Charter of Rights and Freedoms. Koshan and her co-authors conclude that these exclusions represented various violations of farm workers' freedom of association and rights to security of person and equality under the Charter. The authors also assert that these violations were unlikely to be saved as demonstrably justifiable limits in a free and democratic society under section 1 of the Charter. They suggest that constitutional litigation, mass litigation against farmers for injuries sustained in the workplace, consumer boycotts, and human rights complaints are potential means to generate policy change around these exclusions if the recently elected New Democratic government maintains Alberta's long history of farm worker exclusions. They caution, however, that simply to grant farm workers employment rights will not necessarily improve their lot. It may be necessary for farm workers to unionize to enable the creation of an environment within which they can effectively realize their rights.

Shirley McDonald's chapter examines the ideologies of farm owners during the settlement period in order to identify the historical roots of norms underlying contemporary agricultural employment. McDonald uses archival materials and unpublished private diaries of some of the first agriculturalists in Alberta to identify a long-standing (although not necessarily universal) sense of entitlement among farm owner-operators that fortifies and justifies their dominant positions over—and often aggressive treatment toward—hired farm workers. This sense of entitlement reflects deeply held agrarian myths that valorize farmers and encourage the maintenance of class and racial distinctions in Alberta today via their transmission by provincial institutions, such as regional museums, that guarantee agrarian settlers hallowed places in history. The poor treatment and limited opportunities for non-Anglo-Canadian settlers in Alberta's early days identified by McDonald remain relevant given the growing use of migrant workers in western Canadian agriculture.

Foreign migrant workers—including farm workers who come to Canada under the Seasonal Agricultural Worker Program, and meat-processing workers who come to Canada under the Temporary Foreign Worker Program—face different forms of vulnerability than farm workers who are permanent residents. While foreign migrant workers theoretically possess the same workplace rights as Canadian workers, in practice such workers are often unable to exercise these rights. The barriers migrant workers face include a lack of knowledge about their rights, physical and social isolation, and (perhaps most importantly) an extreme degree of reliance upon their employers for continued access to both employment and residency in the country.

Kerry's Preibisch's chapter, "BC-Grown: Examining the Place-Embeddedness of Managed Migration and Farm Labour Markets in British Columbia," examines fruit and vegetable producers' use of immigrant and migrant labour. British Columbia's late enrolment in Canada's Seasonal Agricultural Worker Program (SAWP) reflects the widespread availability of immigrant workers (primarily Indo-Canadians) during the latter third of the 20th century. Preibisch asserts, however, that as immigrant workers found opportunities in other sectors or became less productive due to aging, growers experienced labour shortages and pressured the government for access to migrant workers (predominantly from Mexico) under SAWP. Since 2003, British Columbia has seen an explosive growth in the number of workers employed under the program. Preibisch notes that the relative youth and precarious legal status of these migrant workers makes them hyper-productive workers; thus, the increased productivity of migrant workers more than offsets the additional costs associated with bringing migrant workers to Canada. Employers view these migrant workers as more reliable than locally available workers, because they are less likely to resist or refuse difficult and dangerous working conditions when such resistance may result in their immediate deportation. The precarious legal status of migrant farm workers in British Columbia, Preibisch concludes, is an important but often invisible factor in the continued economic competitiveness of the province's agriculture.

Focusing on the roles of migrant workers in agricultural production, processing, and distribution in BC's Okanagan Valley, Patricia Tomic and Ricardo Trumper identify the long-standing importance of (usually foreign) migrant workers to the region's agriculture. Yet, they argue, these workers are largely invisible in historical constructions of the Okanagan Valley; that is, employers' exploitation of migrant workers is obscured by political and economic representations of the valley as a bucolic region and a playground for a primarily white population. They explore the economic importance of unskilled Québécois youth in the late 20th century, and the current dependence of fruit growers on foreign workers participating in the Seasonal Agricultural Worker Program and Temporary Foreign Worker Program. While these migrant workers must cope with terms and conditions of work that Canadian workers will not accept, Tomic and Trumper reveal that they are largely excluded from public roles in the region's burgeoning food and wine tourism industry. In this way, agriculturalists in the Okanagan Valley are able to market the region as a "local food" destination while obscuring the global (and exploitative) nature of the agricultural labour necessary to its economy.

An important factor driving changing employment practices in western Canadian agriculture is the economic pressure placed on producers by global agro-food trends toward increasing concentration, integration, and international trade (Busch, 2010; McMichael, 1996). Many western Canadian farm owner-operators have responded to this pressure by increasing the size, specialization, and capitalization of their farms (Statistics Canada, 2012). While Barnetson asserts that some farm owner-operators who face increasing costs of farm production and decreasing revenue have sought to minimize wage and regulatory costs associated with hiring farm workers, Zane Hamm reveals that other owner-operators react to this cost-price squeeze (Mitchell, 1975) by engaging in off-farm employment, often in Alberta's oil-and-gas sector. Hamm's chapter examines farm operators' often gendered experiences of employment-related geographic mobility. In addition to documenting how Alberta's oil-and-gas sector affects the viability of and dynamics on farms, Hamm sheds light on the fact that there are many kinds of migrant workers and migrant work in agriculture.

It is also important to recognize the agency of farm workers. With editorial support from Shirley McDonald, farm worker and activist Darlene Dunlop offers an autobiographical narrative, a first-hand view of the conditions that hired farm workers experience. Dunlop begins by discussing her experiences working at the behest of bullying farm operators whose often angry demands for extreme efficiency pushed her and her co-workers beyond the limits of safety. She also reflects on her experiences working, at times, alongside children, whose lack of knowledge and skill put their safety at risk. Dunlop explains why the exploitation of farm workers, especially children, motivated her and her spouse, Eric Musekamp, to form the Farmworkers Union of Alberta. Dunlop documents her and Musekamp's 15 years of activism as they sought to change the attitudes of the members of the Progressive Conservative government toward farm workers and encourage them to allow farm workers basic employment rights, such as the right to unionize, which workers in other sectors take for granted.

The agricultural industry is, of course, broader than just farms, ranches, and orchards. The North American meat-processing industry is a compelling example of changes in employee-employer relationships in the agro-food complex. Michael Broadway reveals how the meat-processing industry has consolidated, relocated, and implemented new technologies and labour processes. To address the consequent difficulties meat processors faced in maintaining an adequate labour force, employers—including the owners of a plant operating in the southern Alberta town of Brooks—have increased their hiring of immigrant and migrant workers. In his chapter, Broadway explores the profound role played by the provincial government in the restructuring of Alberta's meat-processing industry and by the federal government in facilitating employers' access to an adequate workforce and to American markets. He also discusses the social impacts of rapid population growth and demographic change in Brooks, formerly a predominantly white community. Broadway discloses that both the federal and the provincial governments tend to leave it to municipal governments and community agencies to address these social impacts.

Broadway also elucidates the benefits that plant owners accrue from the precarious legal status of the migrant workers they employ. For example, he relates that employers benefit from federal immigration policies that bind migrant workers to specific employers. By limiting the labour mobility of workers, employers are able to reduce high levels of staff turnover. Yet, a problem that is endemic in the meat-processing industry is that labour constraints also restrict some migrant workers' access to public services or protections available to permanent residents, such as health care, education, unionization, and workplace rights. Consequently, the precariousness of migrant workers' employment and legal status means they are less likely to resist unpleasant or unsafe working conditions in meat-processing plants.

In a study that complements Broadway's chapter, Jill Bucklaschuk documents the experiences of migrant workers in the meat-processing industry in Manitoba, where plant owners and administrators have aggressively accessed the Provincial Nominee Program (PNP) in order to gain permanent residency status for many of their migrant workers. In this arrangement, migrant workers gain entry to Canada on temporary work permits and, later, acquire permanent residency status under the PNP. Like Broadway, Bucklaschuk finds incidences of work-related pain and injury among migrant workers and a predominance of reluctance among them to seek remediation of the workplace conditions that cause these injuries. Bucklaschuk notes that for migrant workers the prospect of achieving permanent residency status and gaining its benefits contributes to their willingness to tolerate unpleasant and injurious working conditions. The implication is that Manitoba's two-step immigration process may intensify migrant workers' vulnerability to employer demands in the short term.

Together, these chapters identify troubling aspects of agricultural work in western Canada. While employers have long kept farm work a poorly compensated and dangerous occupation, it is notable that they influence public policies that disallow farm workers (particularly those resident in Alberta) and foreign migrant workers from benefitting from the significant workplace protections that governments have made available to almost all other workers over the past 100 years. This collection extends the growing literature that gives voice to foreign migrant workers in agriculture and other occupations. It also serves a remedial purpose by filling the virtual absence of research about the workplace experiences of Canadian residents who are farm workers. Particular interests for future research are the motivating factors behind Canadian farm workers' decisions to undertake difficult and dangerous work and the strategies such workers adopt for coping with these challenges.

The ongoing vulnerability of farm workers in the workplace reflects federal and provincial policy decisions designed to ensure that farmers can access farm workers at the lowest possible cost. Although the exact policy arrangements and instruments have changed over time and have differed according to jurisdiction, the long-term effect of these policies has been to maintain farmers' access to cheap pools of labour. For example, while provincial governments have improved Canadian farm workers' workplace rights over time, the federal government has altered its immigration policies to allow employers to access vulnerable foreign migrant workers who have difficulty exercising their rights due to their precarious legal status.

The reasons for the existence of these federal and provincial policies are complex and warrant additional investigation. As the chapters in this volume will reveal, the statutory exclusion of farm workers from workplace protections subsidizes the capital accumulation process by transferring some of the cost of production and reproduction associated with food from, for example, employers to farm workers which, thereby, increases the profitability of all businesses. The orthodox belief among producers of consumer goods is that keeping the costs of food down reduces the pressure on middle-class consumers to cover their basic living costs and, thus, increases their disposable income, which, in turn, allows them to purchase items that are more profitable for consumer goods manufacturers to market than food. Yet, the degree to which policy makers consider such dynamics in their decision-making process remains unclear.

In the past, farm owner-operators and other agricultural employers have had significant power to shape these policies; however, we should be mindful that owner-operators do not constitute a monolithic group. Nor do all owner-operators in Alberta oppose mandatory workers' compensation coverage (Barnetson, 2015b). Some owner-operators do without waged labour while others are highly reliant upon it, and some are migrant workers themselves, who take off-farm employment to supplement their farm income or as a way to transit to forms of labour other than farming. There is relatively little research about employment-related geographic mobility by farm owner-operators. Of particular interest for further research are the factors that owner-operators must consider when deciding to engage in off-farm employment. Similarly, there is a dearth of research about the decision-making process when owner-operators determine whether or not they will hire waged labourers and the process by which they determine the nature of the working conditions for their employees. Thus, these topics would also be fruitful areas for further study.

An equally important area of study is the variety of employment practices that employers in different regions adopt. For example, employers in the Manitoba meat-processing industry have sought to "convert" migrant workers to permanent residents through the Provincial Nominee Program in order to build a stable workforce in rural Manitoba. While permanent residency appears to reduce migrant workers' vulnerability in the long term, in the short term, paradoxically, it intensifies their vulnerability by dramatically increasing the stakes and, consequently, their reluctance to resist their employer's demands. In contrast to the approach of employers in Manitoba, the managers of meat-processing operation in Brooks, Alberta, have responded to a shortfall of workers by bringing in successive waves of immigrant and migrant workers. Curiously, neither employer has altered the design of meat-processing systems to decrease the reluctance of Canadian workers to take on such employment; their apathy is due, perhaps, to government policy that grants them access to migrant workers who will accept the difficult and dangerous working conditions meat processors provide.

The chapters in this collection offer many compelling reasons, including those in the realm of social justice, to address agricultural working conditions. It is important to note, however, that improvements to the working conditions of farm workers entail broader social benefits. For example, reducing food producers' use of dangerous chemicals, such as pesticides, reduces the pesticide load found in food, on farms, and throughout the broader environment. Moreover, if meat processors were to slow the conveyor systems in their plants, they would reduce the risks of their employees developing repetitive strain injuries. Slowing production speeds would also enable their employees to work with increased care, thereby reducing the risk of bacterial contamination that causes food-borne illness when bacteria spreads to meat from animal hides and intestines during processing. In these ways, improving the working conditions of agricultural workers benefits us all.

References

Bachusky, J. (2012, Oct. 31). Alberta's farm workers seeking legislative equality. *Cochrane Eagle*. Retrieved Jan. 17, 2015 from http://www.cochraneeagle.com/article/20121031/coe0801/310319993/alberta-s-farm-workers-seeking-legislative-equality

Barley, P. (2008). *Report to the Minister of Justice and Attorney General, Public Fatality Inquiry by the Honourable Judge Peter Barley*. Okotoks, AB: Author. Retrieved June 28, 2013 from http://www.ufcw.ca/Theme/UFCW/images/en/harvestofdeath/Dir-Fatality%20Attachment-Jan%202009.pdf

Barnetson, B. (2012). No right to be safe: Justifying the exclusion of Alberta farm workers from occupational health and safety legislations. *Socialist Studies, 16*(1), 3–29.

Barnetson, B. (2015a) "Fortis et liber" unless you are a farm worker: Workers' compensation exceptionalism in Alberta, Canada. *Journal of Workplace Rights*, April–May, 1–13.

Barnetson, B. (2015b). *A dirty business: The exclusion of Alberta farm workers from injury compensation*. Edmonton, AB: Parkland Institute.

Brass, T. (2004). "Medieval working practices?" British agriculture and the return of the gangmaster. *Journal of Peasant Studies, 31*(2), 313–340.

Busch, L. (2010). Can fairy tales come true? The surprising story of neoliberalism and world agriculture. *Sociologia Ruralis, 50*(4), 331–351.

Danysk, C. (1995). *Hired hands: Labour and the development of prairie agriculture, 1880–1930*. Toronto, ON: University of Toronto Press.

Epp, R., & Whitson, D. (Eds.). *Writing off the rural west: Globalization, governments, and the transformation of rural communities*. Edmonton, AB: University of Alberta Press.

Faraday, F., Fudge, J., & Tucker, E. (Eds.). *Constitutional labour rights in Canada: Farm workers and the* Fraser *case*. Toronto, ON: Irwin Law.

Finkel, A. (Ed.). (2012). *Working people in Alberta: A history*. Edmonton, AB: Athabasca University Press.

Griffith, D. (2006). *American guestworkers: Jamaicans and Mexicans in the US labor market*. University Park, PA: Pennsylvania State University Press.

Harvey, D. (2005). *A brief history of neoliberalism*. Oxford, UK: Oxford University Press.

Larsen, K. (2005). Alberta's thirty year war against the family farm. In T. Harrison (Ed.), *The return of the Trojan horse: Alberta and the new world (dis)order* (pp. 190–212). Toronto, ON: Black Rose Books.

Martin, P. (2002). Mexican workers and US agriculture: The revolving door. *International Migration Review, 36*(4), 1124–1142.

McMichael, P. (1996). Globalization: Myths and realities. *Rural Sociology, 61*(1), 25–55.

Mitchell, D. (1975). *The politics of food*. Toronto, ON: James Lorimer.

Pickett, W., Hartling, L., Brison, R., & Guernsey, J. (1999). Fatal work-related farm injuries in Canada, 1991–1995. *Canadian Medical Association Journal, 160*(13), 1843–1848.

Preibisch, K.L. (2007). Local produce, foreign labor: Labor mobility programs and global trade competitiveness in Canada. *Rural Sociology, 72*(3), 418–449.

R. v. Beauchamp. ABCA 60 (2002).

Rogaly, B. (2008). Intensification of workplace regimes in British horticulture: The role of migrant workers. *Population, Space and Place, 14*(6), 497–510.

Rollings-Magnusson, S. (2009). *Heavy burdens on small shoulders: The labour of pioneer children on the Canadian prairies*. Edmonton, AB: University of Alberta Press.

Schwartzmann, K. (2013). *The chicken trail: Following workers, migrants, and corporations across the Americas*. Ithaca, NY: Cornell University Press.

Statistics Canada. (2012). *2011 Census of Agriculture*. Ottawa, ON: Author.

Stuesse, A. (2010). What's "justice and dignity" got to do with it? Migrant vulnerability, corporate complicity, and the state. *Human Organization, 69*(1), 19–30.

Stull, D., & Broadway, M. (2004). *Slaughterhouse blues: The meat and poultry industry in North America*. Belmont, CA: Wadsworth/Thomson Learning.

Tucker, E. (2006). Will the vicious circle of precariousness be unbroken? The exclusion of Ontario farm workers from the Occupational Health and Safety Act. In L. Vosko (Ed.), *Precarious employment: Understanding labour market insecurity in Canada* (pp. 256–276). Montreal, QC: McGill-Queen's University Press.

ONE

CAPITALIST FARMS, VULNERABLE WORKERS

The Political Economy of Farm Work in Alberta

Bob Barnetson

Until 2016, Alberta excluded farm workers from the employment rights and protections it accorded to virtually every other worker. For example, the government excluded farm workers from employment standards (including child labour) laws and health and safety laws, and prevented them from forming or joining unions. In addition, employers were not required to enrol farm employees in the workers' compensation system. The former Progressive Conservative government (1971–2015) justified these exclusions by claiming they were necessary to protect so-called family farms from bankruptcy. The concentration of paid farm workers on physically and financially large farms invites scepticism of this rationale.

This chapter identifies the political and economic factors that contributed to the regulatory exclusion of farm workers under the Progressive Conservative regime. One of these factors is the tendency of farmers to cope with increasing costs of production and decreasing profits by, in part, externalizing their production costs onto farm workers in the forms of long hours of labour for low wages and denial of benefits including coverage under workers' compensation. Government policy makers ignored these working conditions due to the presence of a political quid pro quo wherein the government exchanged favourable regulation (and other preferential treatment) for electoral support from voters in rural communities.

Both proponents and opponents of regulation use politically powerful but factually inaccurate terms such as "family farm" and "industrial farm" when discussing which farms should be subject to employment law. The view of those who oppose regulation is that the so-called family farm should not be governed by laws that seem more appropriate for regulation of farms that are best categorized as industrial operations. Yet, as this chapter demonstrates, neither term accurately describes the nature of farming activities that take place, nor do they delineate clear division between the two categories. Indeed, most farms in Alberta are family owned, including physically and financially large farms. As I intend to demonstrate, more analytically meaningful categories of farms are available, but their utility in politically charged debate has yet to be made clear.

Agro-industrialization, Capitalistic, and Capitalist Farms

Over the past 200 years, Canadian food production has transformed from a subsistence sector of the economy into one profoundly shaped by agro-industrialization. Agro-industrialization is characterized by the growth of commercial and off-farm processing, distribution, and input provisioning activities; changing relationships between producers and suppliers/distributors via vertical integration and contract-based procurement; and changes in product composition, technologies, and market structure (Reardon & Barrett, 2000; Troughton, 2005; Weis, 2010). The focus of this chapter is on paid employment in primary production, which entails farming, ranching, and fishing. Primary production is one of seven agro-food chains that constitute Canada's agro-food system. The other agro-food chains include food processing, wholesale and retail, institutional food services, inputs and servicing, state regulation, and higher education (Winson, 1993).

Within each agro-food chain there are often heterogeneous groups of actors, such as suppliers, producers, and processors, with differing interests and levels of influence. Due to concentration and conglomeration, individual firms may participate in multiple agro-food chains. Some chains are oligopolies, wherein a small number of firms set prices. For example, large retailers are the most powerful actors in the agro-food complex because they are able to exert significant economic pressure on small retailers and food processors (Konefal, Maccarenhas, & Hatanaka, 2005; Sommerville & Magnan, 2015). Similarly, processers have the power to coerce producers (Lopez, Azzam, & Liron-Espana, 2002). The implementation of neoliberal policies by governments has had a significant global effect on agriculture.

Key neoliberal agricultural policies include those that reduce state subsidies and regulation, and promote intra- and inter-state trade. As a result of these policies, there has been intensifying concentration, integration, and globalization of agro-food systems (Busch, 2010; Carton de Grammont & Lara Flores, 2010; Du Toit & Ewert, 2002; McMichael, 1996).

In spite of evidence of vertical integration that crosses various agro-food chains, executives of agribusiness corporations have been reluctant to invest in farming and ranching and, instead, deploy a more cost-effective strategy of externalizing production (and the attendant risks) onto producers. The continued existence of individual producers obscures fundamental changes in the composition and operation of the agro-food complex (Winson, 1993, 1996). In spite of these changes, some producers have carried on in the owner-operator tradition of physically and financially small operations on farms where the owner-operator and/or family members perform the majority of the work with the additional help of waged labourers during peak production periods. Other producers have responded to the pressures of agro-industrialization via concentration, intensification, and specialization (Qualman & Weibe, 2002; Smithers & Johnson, 2004; Stirling, 2001). These kinds of farms can be termed capitalistic operations in that they exhibit increasing accumulations of capital (e.g., land, machinery, money), but the owner-operator and family members continue to do much of the work with seasonal help supplied by waged workers. Capitalistic farms differ from capitalist farms because the latter rely heavily upon waged labour to complete work (Ghorayshi, 1987).

This trend toward capitalistic agricultural is evident in Canada's long-term transition toward the rise to dominance in the industry by a small number of producers who operate large farms. Expansion of farm size through consolidation has been the objective of a long-term federal policy designed to increase farm income without increasing the cost of food (Agriculture and Agri-Food Canada, 1981, 1993, 2009; Federal Task Force on Agriculture, 1969; Skogstad, 2007). These federal policies, which are designed to minimize food costs (the so-called "cheap food" policy), are examples of ways that the state subsidizes capital accumulation by allowing employers in all industries to transfer part of the cost of social reproduction (in this case, food) to farmers and ranchers and their employees (Basran &

Hay, 1988; Skogstad, 1979). Yet, regardless of increases in farm size, farm operators have remained subject to an intensifying cost-price squeeze, wherein the cost of production has risen faster than gross returns (Mitchell, 1975; Qualman & Tait, 2004).

A subset of Canadian farms can be characterized as capitalist enterprises. While they exhibit the concentration, intensification, and specialization seen on capitalistic farms, they are better termed capitalist farms due to the presence of waged labour in amounts that change the social relations of production. On these farms, farmers exchange their roles as labourers for those of managers. It is difficult to formulate a "bright-line" test to determine whether a farm is a capitalist enterprise (e.g., farms with X number of farm workers are capitalist farms). This difficulty is further compounded by seasonal changes in the number of farm workers and the labour contributions made by unpaid family members (Ghorayshi 1986, 1987; Winson 1993, 1996). These farms may be the kind of operations that Conservative politicians term "industrial farms," although this distinction has never been made clear; rather, politicians often use the term "industrial" as a proxy for physically and financially large operations, regardless of the relations of production the operation adopts.

Farm Consolidation, Capitalization, and Specialization in Alberta

Increasing size, capitalization and specialization—the indicators of capitalistic agriculture—are evident in Alberta. Between 1941 and 2011, the number of farms in Alberta decreased by 56.6% (from 99,732 to 43,234), while average farm size expanded by 169% (from 434 to 1,168 acres) (Alberta Agriculture and Rural Development, 2013a). There were particularly pronounced changes between 1981 and 2011 (see Table 1.1 in this chapter's Appendix). During this period, the number of farms with an area of less than 560 acres declined by 25.5%, while the number of farms between 560 and 1,119 acres declined by 48.2%. Comparably, during the same period, the number of farms with an area of between 2,240 and 2,879 acres increased by 28.9%, and the number of farms over 2,879 acres grew by 85%. Given that the area under cultivation remained relatively steady between 1981 and

2011, the fact that there are now fewer and larger farms than there were previously suggests significant consolidation of farms by Alberta producers. This pattern is consistent with trends elsewhere in Canada (de Avillez, 2011; Weston, 2007).

The significant growth of farm size is also evident in increases in real-dollar gross farm receipts (i.e., farm income before expenses). Between 1981 and 2011, the number of farms with annual gross receipts of $500,000 to $999,000 increased by 603.5%, the number of farms with annual gross receipts of $1 million to $1.999 million increased by 648.4%, and the number of farms with annual gross receipts of $2 million and up increased by 1,186.9%. In contrast, the number of farms with receipts under $100,000 per year shrank by 45.4% (Statistics Canada, 2007, 2012). There has also been a significant increase in farm capitalization. Between 1983 and 2012, total farm capital in Alberta (livestock and poultry, land and buildings, and machinery and equipment) rose from $34.985 billion to $107.261 billion (Alberta Agriculture and Rural Development, 2013a).

This rise to dominance of physically and financially large operations means that such operations, while few in number, account for the bulk of production. In 2006, farms grossing $250,000 or more accounted for 75% of gross farm revenue in Canada (Agriculture and Agri-Food Canada, 2009). Smaller farms make relatively little contribution to the overall food supply. According to retired Alberta Agriculture bureaucrat Doug Taylor (2013), farm growth and consolidation means that "based on the 80/20 principle, 90% of the enterprises labeled farms could disappear and [people] wouldn't notice much change in the food supply."

In addition to increasing in size, Alberta farms have also increased in specialization in terms of the crops they produce. Increasing farm specialization is evident in employment data: While overall agricultural employment (i.e., owner-operators plus waged labourers) declined from 92,000 in 1993 to 56,200 in 2011, almost all of this reduction occurred on mixed farming operations (i.e., operations that combined livestock and crop production, which is typical of traditional owner-operator farms). On mixed farming operations, the number of hired labourers dropped from 38,400 to 3,800. In contrast, the number of employees on farms engaged solely in crop production declined only from 27,700 to 22,000, while the number of hired workers employed on farms and ranches engaged solely in raising cattle and other livestock dropped only from 34,400 to 28,100 (Alberta Agriculture and Rural Development, 2013a). The trend indicates that mixed operations have given way to specialized operations.

Capitalistic trends are also evident in the processing agro-food chain. For example, Alberta's feedlot industry, which exhibits both concentration in the large number of livestock in small spaces and specialization in its focus on finishing animals for slaughter, saw rapid growth in both size and number of operations between the mid-1980s and mid-1990s with the support of federal and provincial subsidies (MacLachlan, 2005). Following the elimination of these subsidies in the 1990s, Alberta's livestock and feedlot industry exhibited increasing intensification as minor operators left the industry or were absorbed into the remaining major operations (MacLachlan & Townshend, 2010). A similar trend is evident in Alberta in hog production (Qualman, 2001) and meat processing (Troughton, 2005), as well as in these industries in other Canadian provinces (de Allivez, 2011; Weston, 2007; Weston & Scarpa de Masellis, 2003). Despite evidence of increasing size, capitalization, and specialization, food producers continue to face a cost-price squeeze.

Cost-price squeezes occur when the costs of production rise faster than gross revenues, which results in a decline in producers' net incomes (Mitchell, 1975). Between 1983 and 2012, Alberta producers saw their expenses and receipts steadily rise, while their realized net income remained almost the same (see Table 1.2 in Appendix). Furthermore, growth in expenses (such as fuel, fertilizer) has outpaced growth in receipts, which mirrors national trends (Agriculture and Agri-Food Canada, 2009). The resulting cost-price squeeze leaves producers with less profit (or greater losses) that they must manage. As Zane Hamm discusses later in this volume, some producers offset their losses by generating income from off-farm employment (see Chapter 6). The number of farm operators who assume off-farm employment in Alberta has increased. In 1991, only 40.1% of operators worked off-farm; in 2011, that percentage rose to 52.0% (Alberta Agriculture and Rural Development, 2013a). This data does not fully reflect spousal off-farm employment. Alternatively, some farm owners/operators manage financial pressure by engaging in self-exploitation by drawing little or no wages from their gross farm income or by exploiting family members. Research on off-farm employment and self-exploitation suggests that small farm owners use strategies that have negative physical and psychological consequences for them and, particularly, for their female family members (Heather, Skillen, Young, & Vladicka, 2005; Kubik & Moore, 2002).

Despite the substantial evidence of increasingly capitalistic operations, the majority of farms in Alberta continue to be owned and controlled by families (see Table 1.3 in Appendix). Family control of farms, regardless of the size and incorporation of these agribusinesses, maintains the appearance of an unbroken continuity in the cultural traditions of family farming and creates a façade that the contemporary agricultural industry comprises mostly so-called family farms. The "family farm" label obscures the increasingly capitalistic nature of operations and (as set out below) the capitalist nature of work on the largest farms. From a policy-making and regulatory perspective, what this observation suggests is that the presence and characteristics of waged labour on farms is more analytically useful than characteristics such as farm size and ownership, which have lent themselves to the creation of the misleading terms and non-existent divisions between "family farm" and "industrial farm."

Agricultural Employment in Alberta

While Alberta clearly exhibits an increasingly capitalistic agricultural industry, there is also evidence of increasingly capitalist agriculture. The key indicia of capitalist agriculture are the presence on farms of waged labourers over whom farmers increasingly undertake supervisory or managerial responsibility instead of performing work alongside them (Ghorayshi, 1986;Winson, 1996). Alberta has a long history of waged agricultural labour, including racialized labour. Between 1890 and 1929, waged labour constituted up to 30% of Alberta's agricultural workforce at harvest time; in 1921, that number was nearly 17,000 workers (Haythorne, 1933; Macpherson, 1953;Thompson, 1978). In the settlement period, temporary employment for waged agricultural workers who were also homesteaders allowed them to work their own land during non-peak periods (Danysk, 1995; MacPherson & Thompson,

1989; Parr, 1985). Farmers' need for workers to bring in the harvest was so great that railroads subsidized migrant worker fares and, by the 1920s, waged labour was farmers' single greatest expenditure (McGinnis, 1977).

In the early days of farming in Alberta, homesteaders employed Indigenous people as well as European and Asian settlers and often treated workers differently depending upon their ethnicity. Later, economic changes fostered a double bias, based on ethnicity and class. For example, until the 1930s, when prairie land was available for homesteading, farm owners acknowledged and showed respect for white farm workers, who sought through their labour to establish their own farms. In contrast, with the end of homesteading and the rise of land prices, farm owners demonstrated biases against workers whose class background precluded their establishment of farms. Moreover, depending on an employee's ethnicity, farmers often denied them names and labelled them by their ethnicity. Racially discriminatory British settlers referred to the Indigenous hired hands on their ranches as "some Indians" and to Chinese workers as "Chinamen" (McDonald, this volume). The low wages offered by farmers for such work meant that many workers came from ethnic minorities, thereby creating a racialized workforce. The trend of employers to think in racialized terms when hiring temporary farm workers continues to the present day. As Kerry Preibisch discusses in a later chapter, both federal and provincial governments have created policies to ensure that Alberta farmers have a numerically adequate workforce by utilizing the Seasonal Agricultural Worker Program (SAWP), which allows them to recruit workers from Mexico and Caribbean countries.

Provincial policy makers in the past have focused on minimizing labour costs by excluding farm workers from most statutory employment rights (Barnetson, 2009; Danysk, 1995). Federally enacted immigration policies ensured farm owners that a succession of ethnic groups (often immigrants), temporary visa workers, and non-status migrants were available to perform agricultural labour and supplement Canadian workers (Basok, 2002; Parr, 1985; Preibisch & Hennebry, 2012; Sharma, 1996; Trumper & Wong, 1997). For example, during the 1920s and 1930s, the federal government facilitated farmers' use of southern European immigrants in Alberta's sugar beet industry. Subsequently, during the Second

World War, the government forced interned Japanese-Canadians, German prisoners of war, and conscientious objectors to labour, sometimes without pay. Tomic and Trumper observe at the end of this volume that food producers in the Okanagan Valley of British Columbia also drew from these labour pools. Farmers hired European immigrants after the war; however, when these sources proved inadequate, the federal government financially coerced Indigenous peoples to migrate from reserves in northern Alberta and Saskatchewan to work in the beet fields (Laliberte, 2006; Laliberte & Satzewich, 1999; Thompson & Seager, 1978). Beginning in the 1980s, farmers replaced Indigenous workers with a predominantly Mexican-Mennonite labour force that comprised migrants with dual Canadian and Mexican citizenship. This change reflected an increased mechanization of farms and a consequent reduction in farmers' need for hand labour; yet, it also reflected the racial discrimination of employers who believed that Mexican-Mennonites would be more reliable and productive than Indigenous workers (Laliberte, 2007).

The federal government encouraged farm mechanization starting in the mid-20th century. Farmers began substituting capital (i.e., machinery) for labour; a resultant reduction in the overall agricultural workforce is a well-established trend in agro-industrialization (Munton, 1992). In Alberta, mechanization spanned more than 30 years and contributed to farm consolidation (MacPherson & Thompson, 1989; Parr, 1985; Skogstad, 2007). Mechanization can initially reduce demand for waged farm workers (Ghorayshi, 1987; Wall, 1994), although farm consolidation that increases farm size beyond that which a single operator can manage may necessitate additional workers (Bowler, 1992). In the late 1960s, to provide an adequate agricultural labour force the federal government negotiated agreements that allowed farmers to access temporary foreign workers from Mexico and the Caribbean (Weston, 2007). While the SAWP was initiated to meet labour needs in Ontario, it now operates across the country. In 2013, Alberta farmers employed approximately 3,000 migrant workers under various federal programs (Employment and Social Development Canada, 2014), but their experiences in Alberta is little studied (Smart, 1997).

The 2011 Census of Agriculture (Statistics Canada, 2012) identified 37,852 paid farm workers, including 15,598 year-round and 22,254 part-year employees, who worked 898,452 weeks in Alberta (73% by year-round workers) (Human Resources and Skills Development Canada, 2013). Paid farm workers do not include farm operators (either owner-operators or co-owner-operators) or unpaid workers, but they include 2,396 international migrant workers (Employment and Social Development Canada, 2014). Between 1991 and 2011, the number of farm operators reporting on paid farm workers decreased from 22,482 to 12,798, although the number of weeks of employment reported per farm climbed from 34.9 to 70.2 (Alberta Agriculture and Rural Development, 2013a). The fact that fewer farmers are reporting hiring paid farm workers—and that those who do report paid workers also report a greater volume of work being performed—suggests that paid agricultural work became concentrated on a subset of farms between 1991 and 2011.

Data limitations preclude a chronological analysis of employment patterns; it is possible, however, to determine the kinds of Alberta farms on which paid farm work occurred in 2011. As farm size increases, so too does the chance that farm operators will have employees. Larger farms are also more likely than smaller farms to have more employees and to have year-round employees (see Table 1.4 in Appendix). Indeed, in 2011, while farms of 1,120 acres or more made up only 26.4% of all farms, these operations employed a disproportionately large percentage (52.9%) of all paid workers and were responsible for a disproportionately large share (59.4%) of all weeks of paid work. In this same period, the largest category of farms (those consisting of at least 2,880 acres) represented only 8.9% of all farms in Alberta; yet, these farms employed 28.9% of paid workers and were responsible for 37.6% of weeks of paid work.

Examining paid employment by farm gross receipts yields a similar pattern: Owners and operators of large farms employ the majority of workers (see Table 1.5 in Appendix). Specifically, the larger the farm gross receipts, the greater the likelihood that the farm owners will hire employees. The number of employees also increases as gross receipts grow, as does the presence of year-round employees. Farms with gross annual receipts above $250,000 make up 20.0% of farms. These farms employed 67.3% of all paid workers and accounted for 81.2% of all weeks of paid work. The largest category of farms (those farms with at least $2 million in annual gross receipts) made up only 1.8% of farms, yet employed 21.5% of paid workers and accounted for 33%

of weeks of paid work. These farms employed an average of 10.4 workers each. As these comparisons reveal, the trend among owner-operators in Alberta is to amalgamate small and moderately sized farms into geographically and financially large farms. While the number of farmers reporting paid work declined between 1991 and 2011, the number of weeks worked per farm increased. It seems likely that farmers with smaller operation have been able to minimize their need for workers, perhaps via mechanization, self-exploitation, and increased use of fertilizer and pesticide (de Allivez, 2011), whereas farmers with larger operations may utilize similar strategies but also require additional workers to maintain production levels. The number of workers on large farms also suggests that farmers with larger operations appear to have adopted practices consistent with capitalist agriculture wherein the role of the farmer becomes that of manager rather than labourer. The wages these farmers pay their hired agricultural workers averaged $18.19 per hour in 2012, which was well below the average Alberta wage of $26.70 per hour (Alberta Agriculture and Rural Development, 2013b). Thus, by paying hired workers low wages, farm owner-operators further minimize their costs of production.

John Shields (1992) asserts that the agro-food complex has a three-tiered class structure: agribusiness, which includes suppliers, processors, and retailers on the top; farmers in the middle class; and waged agricultural workers on the bottom. Within this structure, individual producers compete among themselves as they purchase supplies and sell commodities to quasi-monopolies that set prices and limit the farmers' market power. In turn, farmers often seek to maximize profitability by minimizing labour costs. One factor that enables farmers to minimize labour costs is the exclusion of farm workers from most of the statutory rights available to workers in all other employment sectors.

Regulatory Exclusion of Farm Workers

The state manages antagonisms between capital and labour, such as balancing the conflicting demands of production (i.e., making things, including profit) and social reproduction (i.e., recreating the preconditions for production, including workers), while maintaining the legitimacy of the state and capitalist social formation (Mandel, 1992; Picchio, 1992; Tucker, 1983/84). Among the ways Canadian policy makers maintain the conditions necessary for production is the establishment of workers' rights through legislation. These rights (at least theoretically) protect key worker interests (and thereby dampen class conflict), although, as Leah Vosko (2006) notes, not all workers are entitled to access basic workers' rights. For example, the Alberta government historically excluded farm workers from many employment standards (including child labour laws), and, as well, disallowed farm workers to unionize and collectively bargain under the Labour Relations Code (Barnetson, 2009). Alberta also excluded farm workers from the ambit of its Occupational Health and Safety Act, thereby denying farm workers the right to know about the hazards they face and the right to refuse unsafe work. Significantly, the Alberta government also never required farmers to carry workers' compensation coverage, which is mandatory in most other industries. In 2013, only about 7.5% of farmers took out voluntary coverage for their workers (Workers' Compensation Board, 2013).

These exclusions began in the early 20th century, when farmers lobbied for wage ceilings as well as for the exemption of the agricultural sector from workers' compensation based on the claim that such coverage was unaffordable to them (Thompson, 1978). Alberta policy makers also excluded farm workers from the ambit of its 1917 Factory Act and the 1922 Minimum Wage Board Act (Leadbeater, 1984). Farmers colluded with one another and with provincial labour offices to set wages (Thompson). Moreover, Danysk (1995) notes that the provincial and federal government made significant efforts to disrupt union organizing among farm workers. During the late 1930s and early 1940s, the Social Credit government (1935–1971) excluded farm workers from legislation that addressed male minimum wages, hours of work, collective bargaining rights, and wage security (Finkel, 2012), a pattern that continued during the Progressive Conservative Party's time in power.

Alberta's history of exclusion of farm workers from occupational health and safety (OHS) requirements is particularly troubling, given that the agricultural industry has among the highest fatality rates of any Canadian occupation (Picket, Hartling, Brison, & Guernsey, 1999). Data on non-fatal agricultural injuries in Canada is elusive, but American data suggests farm workers have the highest incidence of workplace fatalities and higher rates of many occupational diseases and injuries (Hovey & Magana, 2002; Sakala, 1987). These injuries stem from well-known agricultural dangers, such as farm workers' exposure to hazardous chemical and biological agents, and their handling of dangerous equipment and livestock. The failure of employers to provide personal protective equipment and training to their employees exacerbates these workplace hazards (Moore, 2004; Quandt, Hernandez-Valero, Grzywacz, Hovey, & Gonzales, 2006; Verduzco and Lozano, 2003). Farm workers also face increased risk of injury due to unsafe transportation, and health risks due to inadequate housing and sanitation. Moreover, working alone and working while fatigued due to performing physically demanding and repetitive tasks over many hours each day is a further contributing factor to a high injury rate (Anthony, Williams, and Avery, 2008; Arcury & Quandt, 2007; Arcury, Quandt, Cravey, Elmore, & Russell, 2001; Hansen & Donahue, 2003; Hennebry, 2010; Otero & Preibisch, 2010).

Most Canadian jurisdictions subject farm workers to OHS regulations (Fairey et al., 2008; Ontario Department of Labour, 2011; Prince Edward Island Department of Agriculture, 2007). Australia and the United States also include farms within the ambit of OHS legislation, but American standards apply to about only half of hired farm workers (Runyan, 2001; Temperley & Fragar, 2010). In addition to providing farm workers with basic safety rights, statutory inclusion empowers the state to monitor occupational hazards and prevent injuries through enforcement of laws and policies. To justify the continued exclusion of Alberta farm workers from the ambit of the OHS Act, the Progressive Conservative (Tory) Members of the Legislative Assembly (MLAS) used three narratives: (1) that education is preferable to regulation, (2) that farms cannot be regulated, and (3) that farmers don't want and can't afford regulation (Barnetson, 2012a). A recurring trope in their political discussions has been the notion that excluding farm workers from statutory rights is necessary to protect the so-called family farm from bankruptcy. These Conservative MLAS provided a similar rationale to justify the exclusion of farms from mandatory workers' compensation, thereby allowing farm owners to externalize approximately $7.6 million in farm injury costs by passing them onto the workers and the public health system (Barnetson, 2012b, 2015; Workers' Compensation Board, 2013).

None of the narratives the Tory MLAs offered stand up to scrutiny. There is no evidence that education reduces agricultural injuries (Beseler & Stallones, 2010; Department of Agriculture and Agri-Food Canada, 2003; Hagel et al., 2008; Lee, Westaby, & Berg, 2004; Rautlainen et al., 2004). Rather, evidence suggests that enforcement could prevent injuries (Finnegan, 2007; Lower, Fragar, & Temperley, 2011; Marlenga, Berg, Linneman, Brison, & Pickett, 2007). The fact that every other province in Canada subjects all farms to OHS regulation, and that Alberta subjected sod farms, nurseries, mushroom farms, and greenhouses to regulation, falsifies the notion that farms cannot be regulated. Similarly, the fact that farmers in other jurisdictions bear the costs of regulation suggests that farms can cope with the (unspecified) costs associated with regulation. The lack of validity of these narratives leaves bald the motivation behind some farmers' desire for limited regulation. Moreover, it brings to mind that the desire of employers is not generally accepted as a valid basis for a public policy. Some farmers, understandably, may wish to minimize their production costs in order to maximize profits; yet, to externalize such costs by denying their workers employment rights is a questionable means to do so. Nonetheless, farmers were remarkably successful at maintaining this exclusion in the past, even in the face of moral and legal challenges. Their success demands explanation.

Politics and Agriculture

So what explanation, then, could reasonably justify the widespread exclusion of Alberta farm workers from basic employment rights? Alberta's historical privileging of farmer interests over farm worker interests reflects the great political power of farmers. A similar dynamic has been found in Ontario, American, and West German agriculture (Johnson & Smit, 1985; Tarrant, 1992). Farmers' political power during the Progressive Conservative administration flowed from their support of the Tories, whose electoral reliance on them as rural voters was rewarded (in part) by electoral overrepresentation via the gerrymandering of electoral boundaries. Indeed, only since 1993 has it been mathematically possible for a political party to form a majority government in Alberta by winning solely "urban" seats, and the

Tories continued to require rural seats to maintain their hold on government thereafter (see Table 1.6 in Appendix). Rural over-representation in terms of seats in the Legislature varies by year and location. In 2006, for example, the urban riding of Edmonton Centre had a population of 41,299 as compared with 30,403 people living in the rural riding of Battle River-Wainwright. At the most extreme, rural Dunvegan-Central Peace had 23,649 residents while urban Calgary-North West had 60,511 (Archer, 1993; Johnscrude, 2010; Thomson, 2008). In effect, the Tories granted voters in rural Alberta a disproportionate number of seats in the Legislature, which, in turn, helped the Tories ensure they remained in power.

Rural electoral support for the Tories was contingent upon (but not guaranteed by) their provision to rural communities of economic support, including the following: the maintenance of government-operated services, such as hospitals, schools, and seniors' care facilities (Alberta Agriculture and Rural Development, 2009); attracting medical personnel (Alberta Agriculture and Rural Development, 2011a); increasing post-secondary access (Alberta Agriculture and Rural Development, n.d.); providing broadband internet (Alberta Agriculture and Rural Development, 2011b); providing informational and financial support to rural businesses (Alberta Agriculture and Rural Development, 2011c); and providing hundreds of millions of dollars to compensate farmers for loss of income as a result of bovine spongiform encephalopathy, an outbreak that was caused, partly, by government deregulation and, partly, by other cost pressures (Roy, Klein, & Klvacek, 2006; Urban Renaissance Institute, 2002). Another way in which the Conservative government supported rural communities was by limiting government regulation (in part by excluding farm workers from the ambit of statutory employment laws). According to Dennis Cooper, president of the Innisfail-Sylvan Lake Progressive Conservative Riding Association, this support would be endangered if a riding were to elect non-Conservative MLAS. As Cooper observed, his "riding always had a member who was a member of the government. We went three years without having [an MLA] who is in the government; therefore, it was tougher for towns and counties to get things" (qtd. in Bachusky, 2014). For its part, the Conservative government also carefully cultivated its rural power base so as to minimize dissension from constituents (Epp, 2001; Larsen, 2005; Neitsch, 2011; Wilson, 1995).

The symbiotic relationship between the Conservative government and rural voters may explain why Conservative MLAs were reluctant to extend basic workplace rights to farm workers. If Tory politicians were to impose additional regulatory burdens on farmers, they risked losing the votes of rural constituents. The consequence of lost rural votes was made obvious during the 2012 election, when, due to rural dissatisfaction with Tory policies on land-owner rights, the Wildrose Party won in traditionally Tory ridings. By maintaining the regulatory exclusion of farm work and proliferating false narratives about the regulation of farm work, Tory MLAs prevented themselves from appearing as craven vote-seeking politicians. These narratives also served politically and, ostensibly, to legitimize farm owners' and managers' moral decisions to trade the health of farm workers for profit. The Tories conflated assertions that farmers cannot afford regulation and that education provides adequate protection, thus allowing policy makers to legitimize employer behaviour in a manner that was ethically acceptable to the public. In effect, the Tories erected a rhetorical shield between agribusiness employers and public wrath over the exploitation of farm workers. Tory MLAs may have maintained the false distinction between "industrial farms" and "family farms" to distract the public from their efforts to legitimize worker injury, yet no clear criteria existed to distinguish these two kinds of farming operations (Barnetson, 2012a).

The 2015 election of the New Democratic government appears to have fundamentally altered the political economy of farm worker regulation. The New Democrats won 39 of 51 urban seats and an additional 15 rural seats (*National Post*, 2015). The rural seats won by the New Democrats were not in ridings where agriculture is the dominant economic activity; those ridings went almost exclusively to the Wildrose Party. The Tories were reduced to third-place status with only 10 seats. This voting pattern destabilized the long-term family compact between farmers and the Tories (which had been eroded in the 2012 election) and has left farmers without much political influence. Not surprisingly, the current government is moving forward on its promise to grant farm workers basic employment rights following consultation with stakeholders in the industry (Canadian Broadcasting Corporation, 2015). In January 2016, employers were required to provide workers' compensation coverage to paid farm workers, and paid farm workers were granted basic workplace health and safety rights. Working groups were then established to develop industry-specific occupational health and safety criteria as well as examine how to apply the Employment Standards Code and the Labour Relations Code to farms. This abrupt policy change demonstrates that the Tory narrative around the inevitability of the farm worker exclusion was, in fact, simply a (craven) political choice dressed up as a policy imperative.

Conclusion

Alberta's Progressive Conservative government long justified its exclusion of farm workers from basic statutory employment rights as necessary to protect the so-called family farm. As this chapter has endeavoured to reveal, the "family farm" is a category that has little utility for policy makers because the vast majority of farms (from 25-acre "hobby farms" to 2,000+ acre "industrial farms") are all family owned. The Conservative government's endeavour to maintain regulatory exclusions for so-called family farms has obscured the real basis upon which farm work ought to be regulated: the employment of workers.

While both owner-operators and capitalistic farmers use waged labour to some degree, the majority of waged farm work occurs on (and the majority of waged farm workers may be employed by) capitalist farms—operations (more or less) approximating the physically and financially largest quarter of all farms. While such operations may be family owned, their sheer size and total revenue suggests they are dissimilar from the traditional cultural and agricultural institutions evoked by images of the mixed-operation type of farm. The managerial and organizational practices of capitalist farms more closely mirror the practices of industrial worksites, for which most employment regulations were initially developed. While this analysis seems to augur in favour of differential regulation of farm work based on farm size or the number of farm workers employed, it is useful to recall that employment rights for non-farm workers extend into even the smallest of "mom-and-pop operations," such as restaurants, convenience stores, and other retail operations. This extension reflects that the power difference (and subsequent worker exploitation) that gave rise to workplace legislation exists because of the nature of the employment relationships, not the size of the workplaces. Such explanation, in turn, suggests that all workplaces where there are waged employees (including owner-operator, capitalistic, and capitalist farms) should fall within the ambit of employment law.

The fact that the "family farm" label is both misleading and irrelevant to the public policy reason for employment regulation raises the question of what dynamic truly motivated the Tories to deny basic employment rights to farm workers. There appear to have been two factors at play. The first was that farmers faced a long-term cost-price squeeze that incentivized them to minimize their labour costs in order to maintain profitability. The second was that farmers were important rural constituents upon whom the Conservative government relied for electoral success. These circumstances, in turn, incentivized Tory MLAS to continue the exclusion of farm workers from employment rights. MLAS politically justified this exclusion via the unsubstantiated (and patently false) assertion that, were they to extend workplace rights to farm workers, such regulations would pose a threat to so-called family farm operations.

The exclusion of farm workers from basic statutory rights not only provided electoral benefits to the Conservative government but, more broadly, it helped MLAS cope with the often conflicting pressures the state faces to maintain both economic production and social reproduction. Within agriculture, owners and shareholders of agro-corporations can increase their profits without bankrupting producers if the government allows farmers to exploit farm workers. Outside of the agricultural sector, inexpensive food increases the profitability of all businesses by reducing wage pressures and increasing consumers' disposable income. The costs of this arrangement have long been borne by farm workers who have received low wages, and who have worked in poor and unsafe conditions that frequently resulted in workplace injuries. The exploitation of farm workers also facilitated social reproduction (for which food is a basic necessity). In this way, the statutory exclusions subsidized the capital accumulation process by transferring the cost of production and reproduction associated with food to farm workers. The degree of instability that develops as the New Democratic government extends workplace rights to farm workers is yet unclear, as is the manner with which the New Democratic government will manage any such instability.

Appendix

Table 1.1 Number of Farms by Size (Acres), 1981–2011

	<560 acres	560–1,119 acres	1,120–1,599 acres	1,600–2,239 acres	2,240–2,879 acres	>2,880 acres	Total farms
1981	32,915	14,004	4,978	2,849	1,222	2,088	58,056
1991	32,143	12,497	5,188	3,232	1,512	2,673	57,245
2001	30,875	10,225	4,382	3,297	1,594	3,279	53,652
2011	24,512	7,255	3,335	2,694	1,575	3,863	43,234
% chg	-25.5%	-48.2%	-33.0%	-5.4%	+28.9%	+85.0	-25.5%

Source: Alberta Agriculture and Rural Development, 2013a.

Table 1.2 Receipts, Expenses, Net Cash Income and Realized Net Income, 1983–2012 (nominal $millions)

	Total Cash Receipts	Operating Expenses After Rebates	Income in Kind	Depreciation	Realized Net Income
1983	3,751	2,734	20	725	311
1984	3,987	2,999	19	709	298
1985	3,837	3,028	18	705	122
1986	3,783	2,981	15	706	111
1987	4,038	3,000	13	686	365
1988	4,467	3,107	13	686	686
1989	4,599	3,421	13	716	475
1990	4,283	3,407	13	745	143
1991	4,234	3,541	12	726	-20
1992	4,956	3,645	12	717	605
1993	5,064	4,013	14	735	330
1994	5,581	4,344	15	785	466
1995	5,969	4,648	15	850	484
1996	6,528	4,875	16	923	745
1997	6,464	5,126	9	988	358
1998	6,418	5,276	8	1,036	114
1999	6,530	5,717	8	1,072	-251
2000	7,583	6,148	9	1,084	358
2001	8,368	6,458	8	1,122	796
2002	8,315	6,321	8	1,111	891
2003	7,101	6,323	8	1,144	-358
2004	8,013	6,235	10	1,140	648
2005	7,876	6,562	14	1,185	143
2006	7,756	6,780	10	1,200	-213
2007	8,673	7,305	8	1,250	126
2008	10,182	8,116	8	1,303	770
2009	9,351	7,830	6	1,366	161
2010	9,006	7,830	7	1,361	-177
2011	10,515	8,592	8	1,441	490
2012	12,001	9,125	8	1,515	1,368

Source: Alberta Agriculture and Rural Development, 2013a.

Table 1.3 Farm Corporate Structure, 1981–2011

	1981	1991	2001	2011
Sole proprietor	50,169	35,875	30,409	24,459
Partnership with agreement	1,446	2,455	2,135	1,239
Partnership without agreement	3,723	14,287	14,012	9,708
Family corporation	2,269	3,663	6,124	6,821
Non-family corporation	190	644	733	771
Other	259	321	239	236
Total	58,056	57,245	53,652	43,234

Source: Alberta Agriculture and Rural Development, 2013a.

Table 1.4 Paid Employment on Alberta Farms by Size, 2011

Acres	% farms	% with paid workers	% of year-round workers	% of seasonal/temp workers	% of weeks paid work	% of weeks year-round work	% of weeks seasonal/temp work	Paid workers per farm
≤559	56.7	17.0	28.6	37.0	28.8	26.6	34.8	0.51
560–1,119	16.8	32.7	12.8	9.6	11.7	12.2	11.2	0.71
1,120–1,599	7.7	42.0	7.4	9.4	6.9	6.8	7.1	0.97
1,600–2,239	6.2	49.7	8.0	8.8	7.7	7.6	7.8	1.19
2,240–2,879	3.6	58.0	6.8	7.1	7.2	6.9	8.0	1.68
≥2,880	8.9	67.2	36.5	23.6	37.6	39.9	31.1	2.84

Source: Statistics Canada, 2012.

Table 1.5 Paid Employment on Alberta Farms by Gross Receipts, 2011

$000s	% farms	% with paid workers	% of year-round workers	% of seasonal/temp workers	% of weeks paid work	% of weeks year-round work	% of weeks seasonal/temp work	Paid workers per farm
<50	50.0	10.6	5.8	12.8	3.8	2.8	5.6	0.08
50–99	13.7	25.6	4.9	8.9	4.0	3.8	4.7	0.46
100–249	16.2	42.4	12.5	17.6	11.0	10.8	11.4	0.84
250–499	9.7	59.9	14.5	17.9	14.0	13.9	14.4	1.48
500–999	5.8	76.1	17.2	15.3	17.7	17.7	17.8	2.44
1,000–1,999	2.7	84.9	16.0	11.2	17.3	17.7	16.2	4.25
≥2,000	1.8	76.6	29.1	16.2	32.2	33.0	29.9	10.4

Source: Statistics Canada, 2012.

Table 1.6 Alberta Electoral Ridings, 1982–2012

	1982	1986	1989	1993	1997	2001	2004	2008	2012
Ridings	79	83	83	83	83	83	83	83	87
Seats needed to form majority	40	42	42	42	42	42	42	42	44
Urban ridings	29	32	32	45	47	47	48	48	51
Rural ridings	50	51	51	38	36	36	35	35	36
Total Tory	61	61	55	51	63	74	62	72	61
Urban Tory	28	25	22	21	28	38	28	37	39
Rural Tory	33	36	33	30	35	36	34	35	22

Source: Elections Alberta, 2012.

Note: The researcher used Elections Alberta data to code ridings in each election as "urban" and "rural" based on the ridings' boundaries. Ridings were coded as "urban" if the majority of the riding's boundaries fell within the corporate limits of a municipality. This approach has methodological limitations, yet it provides a useful way to examine high-level voting patterns over time.

References

Agricuture and Agri-Food Canada. (1981). *Challenge for growth: An agri-food strategy for Canada.* Ottawa, ON: Author.

Agriculture and Agri-Food Canada. (1993). *Multifactor productivity for Canadian agriculture, update to 1990 with analysis.* Ottawa, ON: Author.

Agriculture and Agri-Food Canada. (2009). *An overview of the Canadian Agriculture and Agri-Food System.* Ottawa, ON: Author.

Alberta Agriculture and Rural Development. (n.d.). *Seeing success: Increasing learning opportunities in rural communities.* Edmonton, AB: Author.

Alberta Agriculture and Rural Development. (2009). *Alberta's rural development strategy: 2009 update report.* Edmonton, AB: Author.

Alberta Agriculture and Rural Development. (2011a). *The Alberta rural physician action plan website.* Edmonton, AB: Author. Retrieved Sept. 28, 2011 from http://www.rpap.ab.ca/

Alberta Agriculture and Rural Development. (2011b) *Rural connections: Community broadband infrastructure pilot program approved projects.* Edmonton, AB: Author.

Alberta Agriculture and Rural Development. (2011c). *Programs and services for all audiences.* Edmonton, AB: Author. Retrieved Sept. 28, 2011 from http://www.agric.gov.ab.ca/app52/programsservices

Alberta Agriculture and Rural Development. (2013a). *Agriculture statistics yearbook 2012.* Edmonton, AB: Author.

Alberta Agriculture and Rural Development. (2013b). *Industry profiles: Agricultural industry.* Edmonton, AB: Author. Retrieved Oct. 5, 2013 from http://eae.alberta.ca/documents/profiles/industry-profile-agriculture.pdf

Anthony, M., Williams, J., & Avery, A. (2008). Health needs of migrant and seasonal farm workers. *Journal of Community Health Nursing, 25,* 153–160.

Archer, K. (1993). Conflict and confusion in drawing constituency boundaries: The case of Alberta. *Canadian Public Policy, 19*(2), 177–193.

Arcury, T., & Quandt, S. (2007). Delivery of health services to migrant and seasonal farm workers. *Annual Review of Public Health, 28,* 345–363.

Arcury, T., Quandt, S., Cravey, A., Elmore, R., & Russell, G. (2001). Farm worker reports of pesticide safety and sanitation in the work environment. *American Journal of Industrial Medicine, 39,* 487–498.

Bachusky, J. (2014). Prentice wows Tory faithful in Innisfail. *Innisfail Province.* Retrieved June 10, 2014 from http://m.innisfailprovince.ca/article/20140610/INN0801/306109970/-1/inn0801/prentice-wows-tory-faithful-in-innisfail&template=JQMArticle

Barnetson, B. (2009). The regulatory exclusion of agricultural workers in Alberta. *Just Labour: A Canadian Journal of Work and Society, 14,* 50–74.

Barnetson, B. (2012a). No right to be safe: Justifying the exclusion of Alberta farm workers from occupational health and safety legislations. *Socialist Studies. 16*(1), 3–29.

Barnetson, B. (2012b). Farm safety questioning continues. Labour & Employment in Alberta. Retrieved Nov. 1, 2012 from http://albertalabour.blogspot.ca/2012/11/farm-safety-questioning-continues.html

Barnetson, B. (2015). "Fortis et liber" unless you are a farm worker: Workers' compensation exceptionalism in Alberta, Canada. *Journal of Workplace Rights*, April–May, 1–13.
Basok, T. (2002). *Tortillas and tomatoes: Transmigrant Mexican harvesters in Canada*. Montreal, QC: McGill-Queen's University Press.
Basran, G., & Hay, D. (1988). Crises in agriculture in western Canada: A theoretical explanation. In G. Basran & D. Hay (Eds.), *The political economy of agriculture in western Canada* (pp. 41–54). Toronto, ON: Garamond Press.
Beseler, C., & Stallones, L. (2010). Safety knowledge, safety behaviours, depression and injuries in Colorado farm residents. *American Journal of Industrial Medicine, 53*(1), 47–54.
Bowler, I. (1992). The industrialization of agriculture. In I. Bowler (Ed.), *The geography of agriculture in developed market economies* (pp. 7–31). New York, NY: Longman.
Busch, L. (2010). Can fairy tales come true? The surprising story of neoliberalism and world agriculture. *Sociologia Ruralis, 50*(4), 331–351.
Canadian Broadcasting Corporation. (2015). Alberta labour minister to move on farm worker safety. Edmonton, AB: Author. Retrieved Aug. 21, 2015 from http://www.cbc.ca/news/canada/calgary/alberta-labour-minister-to-move-on-farm-worker-safety-1.3198966
Carton de Grammont, H., & Lara Flores, S. (2010). Productive restructuring and "standardization" in Mexican horticulture: Consequences for labour. *Journal of Aagrarian Change, 10*(2), 228–250.
Danysk, C. (1995). *Hired hands: Labour and the development of prairie agriculture, 1880–1930*. Toronto, ON: University of Toronto Press.
Department of Agriculture and Agri-Food Canada. (2003). *Evaluation of the Canadian agricultural safety program*. Ottawa, ON: Author.
de Avillez, R. (2011). A half-century of productivity growth and structural change in Canadian agriculture: An overview. *International Productivity Monitor, 22* (2011), 82–99.
Du Toit, A., & Ewert, J. (2002). Myths of globalization: Private regulation and farm workers' livelihoods on western Cape farms. *Transformation: Critical Perspectives on Southern Africa, 50*(77), 77–104.
Elections Alberta. (2012). Summary of results by electoral division, 1982–2012. Edmonton, AB: Author.
Employment and Social Development Canada. (2014). Labour market opinion annual statistics. Ottawa, ON: Author. Retrieved Nov. 3, 2014 from http://www.esdc.gc.ca/eng/jobs/foreign_workers/lmo_statistics/annual-agriculture.shtml
Epp, R. (2001). The political de-skilling of rural communities. In R. Epp & D. Whitson (Eds.), *Writing off the rural west: Globalization, governments, and the transformation of rural communities* (pp. 301–324). Edmonton, AB: University of Alberta Press.
Fairey, D., Hanson, C., MacInnes, G., McLaren, A.T., Otero, G., Preibisch, K., & Thompson, M. (2008). Cultivating farm workers' rights: Ending the exploitation of immigrant and migrant farm workers in BC. Vancouver, BC: Canadian Centre for Policy Alternatives.

Federal Task Force on Agriculture. (1969). *Canadian agriculture in the seventies*. Ottawa, ON: Author.

Finkel, A. (Ed.). (2012). *Working people in Alberta: A history*. Edmonton, AB: Athabasca University Press.

Finnegan, A. (2007). *An examination of the status of health and safety in Irish farms* (Doctoral dissertation). National University of Ireland.

Ghorayshi, P. (1986). The identification of capitalist farms: Theoretical and methodological considerations. *Sociologica Ruralis, 26*(2), 146–159.

Ghorayshi, P. (1987). Canadian agriculture: Capitalist or petit bourgeois? *Canadian Review of Sociology and Anthropology, 24*(3), 358–373.

Hagel, L., Pickett, W., Pahwa, P., Day, L., Brison, R.J., Marlenga, B., ... Dosman, J.A. (2008). Prevention of agricultural injuries: An evaluation of an education-based intervention. *Injury Prevention, 14*, 290–295.

Hansen, E., & Donohue, M. (2003). Health issues of migrant and seasonal farm workers. *Journal of Healthcare for the Poor and Underserved, 14*, 153–164.

Haythorne, G. (1933). Harvest labour in western Canada: An episode in economic planning. *Quarterly Journal of Economics, 47*(3), 533–544.

Heather, B., Skillen, L., Young, J., & Vladicka, T. (2005). Women's gendered identities and the restructuring of rural Alberta. *Sociologica Ruralis, 45*(1–2), 86–97.

Hennebry, J. (2010). Not just a few bad apples: Vulnerability, health and temporary migration in Canada. *Canadian Issues/Thèmes canadiens*, Spring, 73–76.

Hovey, J., & Magana, C. (2002). Psychosocial predictors of anxiety among immigrant Mexican migrant farm workers: Implications for prevention and treatment. *Cultural Diversity and Ethnic Minority Psychology, 8*, 274–289.

Human Resources and Skills Development Canada. (2013). Table 10a. Number of temporary foreign worker positions on positive labour market opinions under agricultural occupations, by location of employment. Ottawa, ON: Author. Retrieved Oct. 5, 2013 from http://www.hrsdc.gc.ca/eng/jobs/foreign_workers/lmo_statistics/annual2011.shtml

Johnscrude, L. (2010). The value of your vote: Rural votes are worth up to three times as much as urban votes. *Alberta Views, 13*(2), 26–33.

Johnson, T., & Smit, B. (1985). An evaluation of the rationale for farmland policy in Ontario. *Land Use Policy, 2*, 225–237.

Konefal, J., Maccarenhas, M., & Hatanaka, M. (2005). Governance in the global agro-food system: Backlighting the role of transnational supermarket chains. *Agriculture and Human Values, 22*(3), 291–302.

Kubik, W., & Moore, R. (2002). Women's diverse roles in the farm economy and the consequences for their health, well-being, and quality of life. *Prairie Forum, 27*(1), 115–129.

Laliberte, R. (2006). The "Grab-a-Hoe" Indians: The Canadian state and the procurement of Aboriginal labour for the southern Alberta sugar beet industry. *Prairie Forum, 31*(2), 305–324.

Laliberte, R. (2007). *Why move Aboriginal labour in and then out? The transition of migrant labour from Aboriginal to Mexican workers in southern Alberta's sugar beet industry*. (Unpublished doctoral dissertation). University of Calgary, Calgary, AB.

Laliberte, R., & Satzewich, V. (1999). Native migrant labour in the southern Alberta sugar-beet industry: Coercion and paternalism in the recruitment of labour. *Canadian Review of Sociology and Anthropology, 36*(1), 65–85.

Larsen, K. (2005). Alberta's thirty year war against the family farm. In T. Harrison (Ed.), *The return of the Trojan horse: Alberta and the new world (dis)order* (pp. 190–212). Toronto, ON: Black Rose Books.

Leadbeater, D. (1984). An outline of capitalist development in Alberta. In D. Leadbeater (Ed.), *Essays on the political economy of Alberta* (pp. 1–76). Toronto, ON: New Hogtown Press.

Lee, B., Westaby, J., & Berg, R. (2004). Impact of a national youth health and safety initiative: Results from a randomized controlled trial. *American Journal of Public Health, 94*(1), 1743–1749.

Lopez, R., Azzam, A., & Liron-Espana, C. (2002). Market power and/or efficiency: A structural approach. *Review of Industrial Organization, 20*(2), 115–126.

Lower, T., Fragar, L., & Temperley, J. (2011). Agricultural health and safety performance in Australia. *Journal of Agromedicine, 16*(4), 292–298.

MacLachlan, I. (2005). Feedlot growth in southern Alberta: A neo-Fordist interpretation. In S. Essex, A. Gilg, R. Yarwood, J. Smithers, & R. Wilson (Eds.), *Rural change and sustainability: Agriculture, the environment and communities* (pp. 25–47). Cambridge, UK: CABI.

MacLachlan, I., & Townshend, I. (2010). Regional impacts of BSE in Alberta: Exploring regional and structural dynamics of Alberta's cattle herd using a shift-share model. In D. Winchell, D. Ramsey, R. Koster, & G. Robinson (Eds.), *Geographic Perspectives on Sustainable Rural Change* (pp. 263–283). Altona, MB: Brandon University.

Macpherson, C. (1953). *Democracy in Alberta: The theory and practice of a quasi-party system.* Toronto, ON: University of Toronto Press.

MacPherson, I., & Thompson, J. (1989). The business of agriculture: Prairie farmers and the adoption of "business methods," 1880–1950. In P. Baskerville (Ed.), *Canadian papers in business history* (pp. 245–269). Victoria, BC: Public History Group.

Mandel, E. (1992). *Power and money.* New York, NY: Verso.

Marlenga, B., Berg, R., Linneman, J., Brison, R., & Pickett, W. (2007). Changing the child labor laws for agriculture: Impact on injury. *American Journal of Public Health, 97*(2), 276–282.

McGinnis, D. (1977). Farm labour in transition: Occupational structure and economic dependency in Alberta, 1921–1951. In H. Palmer (Ed.), *The settlement of the West* (pp. 174–186). Calgary, AB: University of Calgary Press.

McMichael, P. (1996). Globalization: Myths and realities. *Rural Sociology, 61*(1), 25–55.

Mitchell, D. (1975). *The politics of food.* Toronto, ON: James Lorimer.

Moore, G. (2004). *Hand-harvesters of Fraser Valley berry crops: New era protection of vulnerable employees.* Vancouver, BC: British Columbia Federation of Labour.

Munton, R. (1992). Factors of production in modern agriculture. In I. Bowler (Ed.), *The geography of agriculture in developed market economies* (pp. 56–84). New York, NY: Longman.

National Post. (2015, May 6). Alberta election results 2015: A riding-by-riding breakdown. Retrieved from http://news.nationalpost.com/news/canada/canadian-politics/alberta-election-results-2015-live

Neitsch, A. (2011). *Political monopoly: A study of the Progressive Conservative Association in rural Alberta 1971-1996* (Doctoral dissertation). University of Ottawa, Ottawa, ON.

Ontario Department of Labour. (2011). *Occupational Health and Safety Act: Application to farming operations: Frequently asked questions*. Toronto, ON: Author.

Otero, G., & Preibisch, K. (2010). *Farm worker health and safety: Challenges for British Columbia*. Burnaby, BC: Simon Fraser University.

Parr, J. (1985). Hired men: Ontario agricultural wage labour in historical perspective. *Labour/Le Travail, 15*, 91–103.

Picchio, A. (1992). *Social reproduction: The political economy of the labour market*. Cambridge, UK: Cambridge University Press.

Pickett, W., Hartling, L., Brison, R., & Guernsey, J. (1999). Fatal work-related farm injuries in Canada, 1991–1995. *Canadian Medical Association Journal, 160*, 1843–1848.

Preibisch, K., & Hennebry, J. (2012). Buy local, hire global: Temporary migration in Canada. In P. Lenard & C. Straehle (Eds.), *Legislated inequality: Temporary labour migration in Canada* (pp. 48–72). Montreal, QC: McGill-Queen's University Press.

Prince Edward Island Department of Agriculture. (2007). *Farm safety week March 14–27*. Charlottetown, PE: Author.

Qualman, D. (2001). Corporate hog farming: The view from the family farm. In R. Epp & D. Whitson (Eds.), *Writing off the rural west: Globalization, governments, and the transformation of rural communities* (pp. 21–38). Edmonton, AB: University of Alberta Press.

Qualman, D., & Wiebe, N. (2002). *The structural adjustment of Canadian agriculture*. Ottawa, ON: Canadian Centre for Policy Alternatives.

Qualman, D., & Tait, F. (2004). *The farm crisis, bigger farms and the myths of "competition" and "efficiency."* Ottawa, ON: Canadian Centre for Policy Alternatives.

Quandt, S., Hernandez-Valero, M., Grzywacz, J., Hovey, J., & Gonzales, M. (2006). Workplace, household and personal predictors of pesticide exposure for farm workers. *Environmental Health Perspectives, 14*, 943–952.

Rautlainen, R., Lange, J., Hodne, C., Schneiders, S., & Dinham, K. (2004). Injuries in the Iowa certified safe farm study. *Journal of Agricultural Safety, 10*(1), 51–63.

Reardon, T., & Barrett, C. (2000). Agroindustrialization, globalization, and international development: An overview of issues, patterns, and determinants. *Agricultural Economics, 23*(3), 195–205.

Roy, D., Klein, K., & Klvacek, T. (2006). *The losses in the beef sector in Canada from BSE*. Guelph, ON: Canadian Agricultural Trade Policy Research Network.

Runyan, J. (2001). Federal laws and regulations affecting farm safety. Washington, DC: National Agricultural Safety Database. Retrieved June 27, 2012 from http://nasdonline.org/document/1842/d001777/federal-laws-and-regulations-affecting-farm-safety.html

Sakala, C. (1987). Migrant and seasonal farm workers in the United States: A review of health hazards, status and policy. *International Migration Review, 21*, 659–687.

Sharma, N. (1996). *Home economics: Nationalism and the making of "migrant workers" in Canada*. Toronto, ON: University of Toronto Press.

Shields, J. (1992). The capitalist state and farm labour policy. In D. Hay & G. Basran (Eds). *Rural Sociology in Canada* (pp. 246–266). Toronto, ON: Oxford University Press.

Skogstad, G. (1979). Farmers and farm union in the society and politics of Alberta. In C. Caldarola (Ed.), *Society and politics in Alberta* (pp. 223–255). Toronto, ON: Taylor and Francis.

Skogstad, G. (2007). The two faces of Canadian agriculture in a post-staples economy. *Canadian Review of Political Science, 1*(1), 26–41.

Smart, J. (1997). Borrowed men on borrowed time: Globalization, labour migration and local economies in Alberta. *Canadian Journal of Regional Science, 20*(1–2), 141–160.

Smithers, P., & Johnson, P. (2004). The dynamics of family farming in North Huron County, Ontario, Part 1: Development trajectories. *The Canadian Geographer/Le Géographe canadien, 48*(2), 191–208.

Sommerville, M., & Magnan, A. (2015). Pinstripes on the prairies: Examining the financialization of farming systems in the Canadian prairie provinces. *Journal of Peasant Studies, 42*(1), 119–144.

Statistics Canada. (2007). Selected historical data from the Census of Agriculture, 95-632-XWE. Ottawa, ON: Author.

Statistics Canada. (2012). *2011 Census of Agriculture.* Ottawa, ON: Author.

Stirling, B. (2001). Work, knowledge and the direction of farm life. In R. Epp & D. Whitson (Eds.), *Writing off the rural west: Globalization, governments, and the transformation of rural communities* (pp. 247–262). Edmonton, AB: University of Alberta Press.

Tarrant, J. (1992). Agriculture and the state. In I. Bowler (Ed.), *The geography of agriculture in developed market economies* (pp. 239–274). New York, NY: Longman.

Taylor, D. (2013). [Former supervisor, Farm Training, Green Certificate, Alberta Agriculture and Rural Development]. Personal communication. April 12, 2013. Edmonton, AB.

Temperley, J., & Fragar, L. (2010). *Rural worker safety induction: A practical guide for employers.* Moree, NSW: Australian Centre for Agricultural Health and Safety.

Thomson, G. (2008, March 22). First shot fired in battle of electoral boundaries. *Edmonton Journal.* Retrieved Sept. 28, 2001 from http://www2.canada.com/edmontonjournal/columnists/story.html?id=01d897fe-bea5-4f48-9813-aa2e7669ce6d&p=2

Thompson, J. (1978). Bringing in the sheaves: The harvest excursionists, 1890–1928. *Canadian Historical Review, 58*(4), 467–498.

Thompson, J., & Seager, A. (1978). Workers, growers and monopolists: The "labour problem" in the Alberta beet sugar industry during the 1930s. *Labour/Le Travail, 3*, 153–174.

Troughton, M. (2005). Fordism rampant: The model and reality, as applied to production, processing and distribution of food in the North American agro-food system. In S. Essex, A. Gilg, R. Yarwood, J. Smithers, & R. Wilson (Eds.), *Rural change and sustainability: Agriculture, the environment and communities* (pp. 13–27). Cambridge, UK: CABI.

Trumper, R., & Wong, L. (1997). Racialization and genderization: The Canadian state, immigration, and temporary workers. In B. Bolaria & R. Bolaria (Eds.), *International labour migrations* (pp. 153–191). Delhi, India: Oxford University Press.

Tucker, E. (1983/84). The determination of occupational health and safety standards in Ontario, 1860–1982. *McGill Law Journal, 29*, 260–311.

Urban Renaissance Institute. (2002). *Agricultural subsidies in Canada, 1991–2001.* Retrieved Oct. 15, 2011 from http://urbanrenaissance.probeinternational.org/2002/06/13/agricultural-subsidies-canada-1992-2001/
Verduzco, G., & Lozano, M. (2003). *Mexican workers' participation in CSAWP and development consequences in the workers' rural home communities.* Ottawa, ON: North-South Institute.
Vosko, L. (2006). Precarious employment: Towards an improved understanding of labour market insecurity. In L. Vosko (Ed.), *Precarious employment: Understanding labour market insecurity in Canada* (pp. 3–42). Montreal, QC: McGill-Queen's University Press.
Wall, E. (1994). Farm labour markets and the structure of agriculture. *Canadian Review of Sociology and Anthropology, 31*(1), 65–81.
Workers' Compensation Board. (2013). Industry Synopsis, Farming Operations. Edmonton, AB: Author. Retrieved Oct. 5, 2013 from https://my.wcb.ab.ca/lcr/Public/GetReport/867606. Author's calculations.
Weis, T. (2010). Breadbasket contradictions: The unstable bounty of industrial agriculture in the United States and Canada. In G. Lawrence, K. Lyons, & T. Wallington (Eds.), *Food security, nutrition and sustainability* (pp. 41–60). New York, NY: Earthscan.
Weston, A. (2007). *The changing economic context for Canada's seasonal agricultural workers program.* Ottawa, ON: North-South Institute.
Weston, A., & Scarpa de Masellis, L. (2003). Hemispheric integration and trade relations: Implications for Canada's seasonal agricultural workers program. In North-South Institute, *Findings, conclusions & recommendations of the first comprehensive study on Canada's seasonal agricultural workers program* (pp. 31–37). Ottawa, ON: North-South Institute.
Wilson, B. (1995). Cultivating the Tory electoral base: Rural politics in Ralph Klein's Alberta. In T. Harrison & G. Laxer (Eds.), *The Trojan horse: Alberta and the future of Canada* (pp. 61–69). Montreal, QC: Black Rose Books.
Winson, A. (1993). *The intimate commodity: Food and the development of the agro-industrial complex in Canada.* Toronto, ON: University of Toronto Press.
Winson, A. (1996). In search of the part-time capitalist farmer: Labour use and farm structure in central Canada. *Canadian Review of Sociology/Revue canadienne de sociologie, 33*(1), 89–110.

TWO

THE PERSONAL EXPERIENCES OF AN ALBERTA FARM WORKER AND ACTIVIST

Darlene A. Dunlop with Shirley A. McDonald

This chapter outlines Darlene Dunlop and Eric Musekamp's experiences since the 1980s as farm workers, as advocates for farm workers, and as activists who seek changes in government policies in Alberta that exclude farm workers from virtually all of the employment rights enjoyed by other Alberta workers. The information, provided by Ms. Dunlop and submitted to the editors as a testimonial, has been edited and shaped into the form of an interview for readability.

Shirley McDonald: Why did you and Eric Musekamp decide to work in the farm sector?

Darlene Dunlop: We chose farm work as our vocation. We weren't born into it, nor were we forced into it. When we heard of a land where you could bale hay all day long, we wanted to be a part of it. Living in the country had always been our number one priority, and working with the seasons made us happy. We worked for large corporate farms, historic family farms, small farms, for farm owners, and for farmers who rented a couple of sections. Big and small, we worked them all. Eric and I were a husband and wife team. We were sought after and shared by farmers and recognized as skilled, hardworking, and caring.

SM: Where did you work for the most part?

DD: In southern Alberta, but we also travelled the prairies and British Columbia, hauling hay to farms, ranches, and feedlots. Our experience, formed over 25 years, put us in touch with many farm workers.

SM: Where did you get most of your farming experience?

DD: This we got working on the largest hay farm in North America. The main reason Eric and I went there was because we desperately wanted to learn how to drive semi-trucks and, in those days, you had to practically be born into the job. It was no easy task for outsiders like us to get the opportunity to learn to drive them. So there we were. We were told we could fulfill our dream, but we would have to do a little farm work, too.

SM: Historically, farm workers have been expected to have many diverse skills. What kind of skills did you and Eric have before you took on your first jobs as farm workers?

DD: Eric is a trained and certified welder. His years of work in the steel industry proved invaluable. Other than that, we had almost no experience and we received no training beyond instructions like "this lever does this" and "don't break anything." But we brought with us an attitude of safety, which was the effect of Eric's work. We also brought with us the ability to say no to things we knew to be dangerous—some of them, anyway. Other people weren't as lucky. They had mortgages, children, no English skills, or confidence—just the need to please the boss at any cost.

SM: Was this where you experienced the real Wild West?

DD: Yes, and it was an eye opener. Everything huge, everything fast, this place really knew how to give 'er. This combination of farm, ranch, and feedlot was a little country unto itself and the farmer was its dictator. He owned everything you could see and then some. His favourite expression was "I'm a farmer in Alberta so I can do whatever the fuck I want." And he usually did. The farmer had a workforce of men, women, and children, Canadians, Mennonites, and temporary foreign workers. Some lived on the farm all year long; some came just for the season. But, we all had one thing in common: We were at the mercy of our employer. This farmer was a real screamer, I mean a real screamer. His temper put us all on edge and placed an extra burden on our daily tasks. The best you could hope for was that he would take his wrath out on someone else. It is difficult to listen to a fellow worker being verbally abused, but better him than me.

I found myself bullied by this farmer. I was operating a payloader on the roads between fields. He wanted everything done as fast as possible. He would drive behind you honking his horn and waving his arm out the window pushing you to go faster. The problem was that you would lose steering control if you went past a certain speed. I refused to accelerate. One of my co-workers was pressured to go faster when he found himself in this situation. He lost control and the payloader flipped over and crushed him to death. Eight farm fatalities were attributed to this farming operation over a 20-year period. That is what comes of no standards, no template for safety.

SM: Why did you stay on this farm if the situation was difficult?

DD: Working there gave me my first opportunity to drive one of those big rigs. It came when the farmer held the keys out. He didn't care who drove it, me or a 9-year-old boy. This was the first time I had to work with a very young child on a farm. The lad was the son of the new housekeeper. They had moved from the city, so farm work was new to this young fellow. It was common practice to let him drive the big rig on the roads to the fields. He was also tasked with operating large farm equipment, but he could often be seen playing around with it, which was dangerous when there is no roll bar. I wasn't about to be chauffeured by a 9-year-old, so away I drove. No licence, no knowledge, just the keys and the lad as my passenger.

SM: Were you ever asked to do work you felt was dangerous and even life threatening?

DD: Yes, I had a bad experience with Malathion, a nerve agent to kill bugs. It's commonly added to grain when transferring it by auger from the truck to a grain bin. This pesticide is relatively cheap so it is used freely during harvest. "I want to see it white," one farmer told me—"it" being the grain. He thought that if a little is good, a lot is much better. Another time, I expressed my concerns to a farmer about using a tuna can and my bare hands to scoop the Malathion out of the bag. He scowled. I asked him if he had ever read the label and told him it says: "Do Not Get on Clothes." He squatted, scanned the label and its warnings, then left. Upon his return, he presented me with a tuna can attached to a short stick so I wouldn't have to reach so far into the bag. Alberta agriculture is exempt from regulations around the use of pesticides, so it is not uncommon for untrained workers to deal with chemicals without the benefit of personal protective equipment. Alberta does not track or record farm-related diseases or cancer. Later, in a meeting Eric and I had with Employment Minister Dave Hancock and his senior staff, I learned that cancers and industrial diseases represent roughly one-third of farm-related fatalities.

SM: What about Eric? Has his job put him in danger?

DD: Yes, he had an experience that got us thinking about the lack of rights of farm workers in Alberta. The owner of the large hay farm expected his workers to do exactly what they were told no matter what. He told Eric to do some welding on a fuel tank; Eric would do it only by the book and was fired. The next worker did not refuse. Why he didn't, I don't know. Didn't he know how dangerous it was? What I do know is that he started the welding job and blew up himself, the shop, and all that was in there. The farmer got a new shop and new tools. The farm worker's wife got a funeral and years in court. The last we heard, this young widow and her children were still in court. The hay farmer had lots of money and lawyers and felt no obligation to do right by his employee's family. After that happened, we realized that protecting ourselves by refusing to do a dangerous job meant that someone else, someone who, perhaps, was more timid or inexperienced than us, could get injured or even killed.

SM: Was that the experience that turned you into activists?

DD: No, it wasn't until August 20, 1999, when Terry Carl Rash was killed that we awakened. He was a fellow farm worker. Terry was slashed to death on the side of Highway 36 near Taber by his farm boss simply for making a mistake at work. Terry's mistake: he had tipped an old water truck in the ditch. Forty-five minutes after the accident, the farmer showed up, an argument ensued, and the farmer pulled out the knife he carried and slashed Terry while a fellow farm worker looked on. Terry, 52 years old, father and grandfather, bled to death in that roadside ditch for making a mistake at work—a victim of farmer rage. His killing was sobering, but not surprising to many of us who call ourselves farm workers. We have all made mistakes at work and, yes, many of us have seen that look of rage in the eyes of a farm boss. Farm work has a multitude of dangers; death by farmer is but one of them. In fact, when we began our research, the Alberta government listed violence as the fifth most common way that farm workers got injured. They have since removed that statistic.

SM: What was the outcome of Terry Rash's murder?

DD: The harvest of 1999 had a very different feel from the many harvests before. Let's just say it was tense. In 2001, Terry's boss, Charles Henry Beauchamp, was given 14 months with a recommendation for early release. His sentence was revised to 34 months, but it was the original sentence that was remembered by the local workers and even the temporary foreign workers who came into our area the following years. It was the Court's decision that first made Eric put pen to paper. He sent a letter to the editor of the *Taber Times* insisting on a longer sentence and wrote: "We can only hope that the Crown's review of the killer's sentence is mindful of the message this inadequate two-year jail term provides farm employers and their subordinates. Surely Alberta's farm workers deserve, at least, equal protection of Canada's Criminal Code." Eric also wrote an open letter to Employment Minister Clint Dunford asking for inclusion of Alberta farm workers in legislation. When it was published, Minister Dunford announced that the government would work on legislation, but nothing came of it.

SM: Was that when you realized you had become activists?

DD: Not yet. Terry's slaying got our attention, but it did not get us off the couch. Twenty years of griping about our farm employers and the lawlessness in our workplace continued.

SM: What were the circumstances that finally "got you off the couch"?

DD: Following Terry's slaying, we experienced having an employer, Farmer John, withhold all monies owing to us at the end of the season. We had worked for this farmer several times over the years. That year, Eric was his full-time hired man and I worked as an equipment operator. When Eric made a mistake at work, this farmer showed him little mercy. Eric had accidentally damaged the farm truck. He was hauling a load of hay when the wide load caught on a cross beam of a bridge and the extremely rusted out farm trailer gave way. At the time of Eric's mistake, the farmer owed him $5,000. There was no set payday on this farm; it was whenever the farmer got around to it. Farmer John called us up to the big house to settle accounts with Eric. He slid a $120 cheque across the table along with a statement of deductions for the mistake Eric made. The $5,000 was whittled down to $120. There were deductions for parts, labour, and down time for the old farm truck. All this after Eric had offered to work off the costs.

Farmer John told us we should accept the cheque or we would be blackballed and never work around here again. And, he said, if Eric had a problem with that, "Look out, you could end up like Terry," and nodded to the rifle leaning against the wall. Eric did have a problem. Here we were, going into winter, no wages, no Employment Insurance (EI), and a threat of being blackballed in this very small community. This shocked us. Eric had been known as the Happy Hired Man, and we both had gone out of our way for this farm family. They were gone 18 days of harvest that year and that meant more responsibility for us to bring in their harvest. We even tended their flower garden and made sure the farm dogs weren't ignored.

SM: Had you faced challenges in getting paid fairly by other employers as well?

DD: Yes! I worked for a farmer for three months before he thought to pay me. Another time, halfway through harvest, a farm boss reduced my pay rate by 50 per cent. One farmer told me at the end of harvest that he couldn't pay up until spring, because "things were tight." Some farmers would pay us as contractors not employees, and some would issue receipts to Eric and me for the purchase of straw or eggs to avoid dealing with deductions. Others would deduct for EI, but fail to remit payments to the government. And then there were the surprise deductions: "You broke the machinery and I'm not going to pay you for standing there." Most farm workers on the receiving end of these injustices would just leave. Most don't have the English skills or the wherewithal to use the system to get justice.

SM: What was the result of your conflict with Farmer John?

DD: Eric did the unthinkable; he took the farmer to court and won. The judge chastised the farmer and his wife for taking advantage of the lowest man in society. Unfortunately, he used some big words and his message was lost on them. It was this event that caused Eric to decide not to get even with this farmer, that it was the system that was the problem. Historically, Alberta's farmers were allowed to withhold wages. If their hired man did not work the whole harvest, they could legally keep all his earnings. The result of this was that some farmers would pick a fight with their hired help just before the end of harvest. If it worked out, the worker would leave the farm empty handed and the farmer got a wonderful bonus. Perhaps this explains why some Alberta farmers have such an attitude of entitlement.

SM: What did you and Eric do for income after that?

DD: There isn't a lot of work in the country if you aren't near the oil patch and you are prevented from doing farm work, so we secured employment with a produce hauler and hit the road, driving a weekly run to California and Arizona. We did that for two years. Our experiences attending farms and produce houses educated us. We had the opportunity to visit with farm owners, foremen, and workers who had been around before the unions. We also met a berry farmer who had tried to keep the unions out. Eric got the inside scoop from him on the difficulties these farmers had had in planning the season's labour needs before the unions. Since the unions, this farmer and others have been able to plan ahead, knowing they have the workforce. Some of his workers have been with him for many years. The system isn't perfect, but it is working better than it ever has. The farmer told all this to Eric while standing in his state-of-the-art, multi-million dollar produce house, which, he admitted, he clearly wouldn't have been able to afford if things had remained the way they were before. The farmer's son told Eric of his father's struggles, how he took up arms and shot his gun at some workers. The gun misfired, this sobered him up. He asked himself: "What am I doing?" This led to a dialogue with the workers and ended with an overall improvement. We got a look at farming on a really grand scale and we learned about the struggles and the benefits that came with the union effect.

SM: How did you apply this knowledge in Alberta?

DD: While on our California turnarounds in 2002, the Alberta government called for stakeholder submissions on the question: Should farm workers be included in the Labour Relations Code? This was the Marz Committee, 2002, which gave us an opportunity to make our opinions known. We made our submission on behalf of Alberta's farm workers. In our naïveté, we believed the situation of our farm workers was one of oversight by our provincial government and that once we pointed out this egregious violation of Canada's Charter of Rights and Freedoms, it would bring about the needed changes in Alberta's agriculture policy. After all, we, as Canadians, were entitled to equality at law and this was a clear violation of our Charter rights. Our confidence with our stakeholder submission was supported then by a fairly recent Supreme Court decision: *Dunmore v. Ontario* (2001)[1] on the rights of Canada's farm workers. We put our submission and our trust in the hands of the Marz Committee.

SM: Was that the beginning of your activism on the farm workers' issue?

DD: Not quite. What came next put us on our current path. After California, we had secured local non-farm jobs, driving trucks to haul corn. It was a great job. Good pay, pretty good equipment. Then we switched to hauling potatoes. It didn't take us long to realize this was a whole different type of farming. What we noticed first were the different entitlements among employees. We worked with Canadian farm workers without rights, Canadian truck drivers with rights, foreign exchange students, temporary foreign workers, First Nations people, non-status Indians, and children, lots of children. Four of the five farms we hauled potatoes from used child labour. We had worked with children before. Then, it seemed normal, but now, after being exposed to the US system, we were seeing this situation in a whole different light. California had slapped us upside the head.

SM: How old were the children and what were their jobs?

DD: I worked with children as young as 8, 9, and 10 years old, grading potatoes in dangerous worksites. No personal protective equipment. No rest breaks unless the equipment broke down. Worksites without Occupational Health and Safety (OHS) standards. There was a 15-year-old working as an electrician as best he could. These children were working 16 hours a day and being paid less than minimum wage. They were working in the fall when they should have been in school. They worked alongside their parents like you would expect to see in third-world countries. First Nations families from Saskatchewan came for the potato harvest; other children were Mennonites working with their parents. We were troubled by what we saw.

What made us take action was when we went to Brown's Farm. These children were working in the loudest worksite I'd experienced in my 30 years of employment. There was plenty of room on this farm to set up receiving equipment in a much quieter place. Independently and unaware of each other's initiatives, Eric and I went to a safety supply store and purchased earplugs for these wee labourers. Farmer Brown was very unimpressed by our actions. He called our employer at the trucking company and we were called in off the road and fired. A trip home and a look into our filing cabinet showed us we had already been advocating for Alberta's farm workers. It was the total disregard for the well-being of the child labourers at this potato farm near Taber that motivated us to take the drastic action and become advocates for Alberta's men, women, and children who toil as our farm workers. I say drastic action because, as anyone who knew us would tell you, we were hermits, avoiding crowds of more than three or four people.

SM: What did you do to draw attention to the cause?

DD: On September 24, 2004, the day we were fired, we set up an information picket on Highway 36 in Taber, in front of our trucking company. Picketing was therapeutic for us and we knew we had to put a face to this issue, so Eric's face would be it. A few supporters came to help with the picketing and others made donations that helped us pay for the Farmworkers Union of Alberta (FUA) signs and business cards. The FUA business cards gave us respectability among the RCMP. One of the biggest benefits from this action was the FUA got the ear of the press and they have been a constant for 10 years now. We knew we couldn't picket for long (we were now unemployed), so when we got a request to drive truck for the sugar beet harvest, we jumped at it. We have driven for this farm on and off since 1983. A few days into the job, our boss called to say three local farmers asked him to fire us because we were the ones picketing in Taber. We had always done a good job for this farm so were able to work this, our last, sugar beet harvest.

SM: What were your first actions as advocates for farm workers?

DD: First, we set about to satisfy ourselves that this exclusion from basic standards was not the act of an unconscious government, but a deliberate act of an unconscionable government. We had learned about the experiences of farm workers' organizations in California and BC. Both groups started by organizing the workers from the ground up and it took 20 and 30 years to achieve their goals. They both experienced violence and many farm workers were crushed in the process. We decided to leave the farm workers out of it. It is, after all, against the law for them to join a union. We were already damaged, so we may as well be the scapegoats, too. We decided to start at the top with those who wiggle the levers, the lawmakers. Up to this point, we didn't even own a typewriter, so we bought a computer and began working 16 hours a day, 7 days a week for months on dial-up internet. I experienced a very steep learning curve.

SM: Whom did you contact to get the ball rolling?

DD: We wrote to premiers, government ministers, MLAS, the Alberta Workers' Compensation Board, and Human Resources and Employment. We went to the labour unions and the Alberta NDP, and then to Alberta's Official Opposition. This was a necessary, lengthy process, but we discovered this exclusion from basic standards was a deliberate act to appease the farm lobby by an unconscionable government. Our perception had been that the farms where we worked just did not follow rules. It wasn't until the fall of 2004 that we realized there were no rules. This was, indeed, Canada's last lawless frontier.

SM: What were your first events?

DD: We began with a whirlwind of interviews, meetings, and media events. We met with Alberta NDP leader Brian Mason, Alberta Liberal leader Kevin Taft, and agricultural producer groups. We engaged with Alberta Federation of Labour (AFL) president Kerry Barrett and were invited to make a presentation at the AFL biennial convention in May 2005. We saw this as a way to bring the plight of Alberta's farm workers to the attention of the labour movement.

Eric's first speech of his life started with these humble words: "I am more comfortable on a John Deere tractor than most anywhere else." He ended with an adlib about how this was the perfect opportunity for the labour unions to show solidarity by all pulling on the same rope and helping a real underdog in Alberta society, to show the people that unions were about more than just making demands for better pay and pensions, to show the Alberta government that there was true solidarity and a willingness to stand up for basic human rights in Alberta's workplaces. Eric got a standing ovation; grown men with tattoos cried. After Eric's speech, I was approached by a fellow who had worked for Stats Canada. He was tasked with calling farmers across Canada and was puzzled by the fact that while farmers in every other Canadian province hired farm workers, when he spoke with Alberta farmers, only a couple admitted to having hired help. We viewed our participation at the convention as a success. The AFL voted to recognize August 20 as Farm Workers Day in honour of fallen farm worker Terry Rash and voted unanimously to endorse a Farm Worker Action Plan for Alberta.

Eric and I—the FUA—made numerous contacts at the AFL convention. Many of the brothers and sisters pledged their support, and the NDP's David Eggen agreed to introduce Eric and the FUA in the Legislature, which he did on May 16, 2005. Two days later, he tabled the FUA's petition to the Alberta government: "Whereas the Canadian Charter of Rights and Freedoms does proclaim all persons are equal under and before the Law...We do hereby demand and require that Alberta forthwith grant equal status to farm workers."[2] Eric's understanding was that, if a law was revealed to conflict with Alberta's Bill of Rights, the government was obliged to rectify things or use the Notwithstanding Clause.

SM: Did the petition have any results?

DD: None at all. But we persisted. During 2005, we attended the spring/summer legislative session every day for seven weeks. We were able to get questions onto the floor through Alberta's Official Opposition. We spoke to everyone we could, quite literally. If you were standing still or walking slow, we were on you. One of the more notable interactions was with Minister Dave Hancock just outside the Legislature Annex. (I say notable because he served as Alberta's interim premier.) We got him to pause for a moment. "I want to speak with you," said Eric. "What about?" asked the minister. "The emancipation of Alberta farm workers," was Eric's reply. "Oh that," said the minister. Later, as labour minister and in front of cameras at a Medicine Hat Chamber of Commerce event, Minister Hancock had a dust up with Eric. The Canadian Press headline on September 13, 2012, read: "Alberta cabinet minister grilled about child farm workers."

While we were at the Legislature, Eric did a number of media interviews. We spent hours in the building's stunning library doing research and using its computers and printers. It was invaluable. We were living without electricity in truck stop parking lots, which meant that these simple tasks took on a whole new level of difficulty. We got to know most everyone at the Legislature including the janitors, cafeteria workers, commissionaires, gardeners, librarians, reporters, MLAS, and the premier. We grew very comfortable in Alberta's most important edifice. This is where they wiggle the levers.

We had corresponded with several Alberta ministers by this time, and done phone interviews and meetings with Human Resources and Employment managers. We were contacted by Workplace Health and Safety Policy and Legislation's Yan Lau for reports, requested by Employment Minister Cardinal and Children's Minister Heather Forsyth, but we were anxious for face-to-face meetings.

Our first meeting was with Health Minister Iris Evans. Minister Evans slid into the boardroom saying, "Your MLA Leonard Mitzel has turned almost the entire caucus against you. Now, let's get on with our meeting." We had arrived full of hope with e-mails of support from over 3.4 million Canadians—e-mails from Canadian Labour Congress, Alberta Federation of Labour, United Nurses of Alberta, Health Sciences Association of Alberta, United Food and Commercial Workers Canada (UFCW), and many others. "These are worth a dime a dozen," scoffed Minister Evans. This meeting was not the FUA's finest hour.

In early 2005, Eric had travelled to British Columbia to meet with the Canadian Farmworkers Union president Charan Gill. Mr. Gill and the CFU assisted the FUA with its first mass faxing. On that trip, we reached out to the principals of BC's Farm and Ranch Safety and Health Association (FARSHA). Eric always said that if you are going to point to a situation that needs addressing, you had best have a solution in your back pocket. We brought back the FARSHA plan and a pledge from the architects of the plan to work with the Alberta government to improve the health and wellness of Alberta's farm workers. This was what we wanted to share with Minister Evans. We have now presented the plan to the new Notley government. With the FARSHA model, British Columbia had managed to reduce its farm injuries significantly (40% after 10 years at a cost of $30 a year per worker). In 1993, BC brought in FARSHA to protect its farm workers; in 1993, Alberta brought in the toughest farm animal care legislation in North America to protect its livestock.

SM: Are you saying that Alberta's farm animals are protected by laws that farm workers are denied?

DD: Absolutely.

SM: Did you get union help to rectify that injustice?

DD: Yes, and things looked promising at that point. On August 20, 2005, the Alberta Federation of Labour arranged a press conference in Calgary for the announcement of Farm Workers Day, and to launch the "End the Drought" campaign for farm workers' rights. They clearly laid out the exemptions and the remedy to the exemptions. UFCW's Stan Raper flew in from Toronto and signed a protocol with Eric stating that when the FUA secured the right for Alberta farm workers to unionize, UFCW Canada would be the organizing body. We were joined by other union members, the press, and interested individuals. It was uplifting to have the issue taken seriously. Our relationship with the AFL started out with such hope. That was then.

Funds became increasingly short for Eric and me. Nearly two years of steady activism had left us homeless and broke. We had been encouraged by labour to keep going. They told us they would be there, but they weren't. We were on our own. Thirteen months after Eric's speech at the Alberta Federation of Labour convention, they got back to us with a Farm Worker Action Plan. It did not include any funding, just a long list of obligations and expenses to be incurred by us.

We received the Farm Worker Action Plan the same day we were leaving our home for good.

We were in no position to fulfill the demands set forth by the labour union. This was the beginning of the downfall of our relationship with the AFL and the union movement. They were upset that we could not act on their plan and indifferent to our situation. We had explained to them at the 2005 convention that, as soon as we went public in a big way, we would be in serious trouble in our community and would be unlikely to get employment. That is exactly what happened. In the 13 months we waited for the unions to get back to us, we were able to secure only 46 days of employment. It was now time to save ourselves. The farm worker issue would have to take a back seat.

The last thing we did as we were leaving our beloved community for good was pick up a newspaper. There, on the front page, was a photograph of a farm worker's widow holding her wedding portrait. We looked at each other. Not a word was spoken, but we both knew that we couldn't quit. We had lost only our home, money, community, and our careers. This widow and her young children had lost everything. They needed us. We couldn't stop now!

The widow was Lorna Chandler, whose husband Kevan John Chandler was killed in a silo at Tongue Creek Feeders in 2006 on Father's Day. He was doing a job he was told to do, but that he was afraid to do because it was unsafe. This feedlot had approximately 40 employees, but no WCB coverage. Kevan was not the first worker killed at this worksite and, without WCB, there was no safety net for Lorna and her family. We met Lorna and her beautiful young children about six weeks after Kevan's tragic death. We told her that we weren't sure what we could do for her and her family, but we would do our best.

SM: What did you do to help Mrs. Chandler and her children?

DD: We made the second annual Farm Workers Day barbecue in Turner Valley into a fundraiser. We hosted MLAs Dr. David Swann, Harry Chase, and Ted Morton (Lorna's MLA), who read greetings from Agriculture Minister Doug Horner. Members of Alberta's unions and media were in attendance along with many Albertans who were moved by Lorna's sad tale. We raised $12,000 for Lorna that day. If Kevan had worked in an industry covered by WCB and OHS, he would not have been allowed to enter the silo that took his life. The lack of mandatory WCB insurance caused Lorna and her young children additional hardship at a time of great sorrow.

SM: The fundraising was obviously successful. Were other gains made that day?

DD: Lorna Chandler received a lot of press because of the event and, combined with our years of correspondence with government, the years of newspaper editorials, front-page stories, and pressure by the AFL, Justice Minister Alison Redford granted Lorna a public fatality inquiry into her husband's death and appointed Judge Peter Barley to conduct the inquiry. Here was the opportunity we had been waiting for, a chance to take this issue out of the hands of the Alberta government and the farm and ranch lobby and put it into the hands of a learned judge.

SM: Is it uncommon to get a review of farm workers' deaths or standard procedure?

DD: It is rare to get a public fatality inquiry for a fallen farm worker. There are no workplace investigations into farm workers' fatalities or serious injuries, because of our exemptions from OHS legislation, so they get only a look by RCMP for criminal wrongdoing. We learned from Lorna's lawyer, Clint Docken, that there was a chance for Eric to be involved in the case. Eric made an appeal to the judge to have an opportunity to argue to be included, which was granted. Then he researched the law material provided by Crown counsel and, during the *voir dire*,[3] put forth his assertion, the FUA was the voice for Alberta farm workers seeking equality at law. The feedlot owners' lawyer argued vigorously against this inclusion, saying that farm workers are not an analogous group. Lorna's lawyer pointed out that the reason Eric's group is not a formal group is because they cannot form a union. They are legally barred. Judge Barley returned with his decision. He stated that farm workers have such an identity to the deceased. They have a substantial and direct interest to the case and that the interest of farm workers is so unique that Eric was permitted to make a written submission to the Court. I recall this from the notes of the trial on October 22 and 23, 2008.

Legal standing allowed the FUA to present the judge with an argument and an opportunity to counter-argue. In January 2009, we got everything we wanted from the investigation: Judge Barley's recommendation to include farm workers in the Occupational Health and

Safety Act, and a quote from him that "no logical explanation was given as to why paid employees on a farm are not covered by the same."[4] By 2014, only one of Judge Barley's four recommendations had been acted on: education through the Agriculture Ministry. No employment or labour ministers had acted on the most important recommendation: OHS inclusion.

SM: Your advocacy for farm workers and activism to have the legislation changed has been long and time consuming. What successes and what disappointments have you faced and continue to face?

DD: Eric and I (the FUA) have attended every legislative session for 11 years and have managed to build a firm understanding of the issues with many questions on the floor of the Legislature. Still, Alberta government ministers and premiers attempt to divert the public's attention from the plight of farm workers by repeating: "We must protect the family farm." *Hansard* is full of governmental support for the family farm and dismissals of farm workers' legal rights. We attempted with a private members' motion to keep the farm worker issue alive. On June 1, 2009, Official Opposition leader Dr. David Swann introduced Private Members' Motion 510, which aims to increase paid farm worker safety. It reads, "Be it resolved that the Legislative Assembly urge the Government to introduce amendments to the Occupational Health and Safety Act to protect paid farm workers while continuing to exempt family members and other unpaid labourers."[5]

The Honourable Members refused to debate the issue. I witnessed government ministers watching soap operas or playing solitaire on their computers, and my own MLA, Leonard Mitzel, who was sitting in the Speaker's chair, was texting all the while. We had waited years for this chance to get the issue on the Floor of the House and to see elected officials completely disregard the solemnity of this exercise riled me. I corresponded with Speaker Kowalski, and we parried back and forth by mail, but I received no satisfaction from him. He told me that he couldn't make the members behave honourably and declined my request for the motion to be brought forward again.

SM: That must have been disappointing. What has been your biggest step forward?

DD: One of our greatest highlights was also one of our greatest disappointments. It has to do with Alison Redford, who, while campaigning to become the leader of the Progressive Conservatives and premier, came out boldly on the farm worker issue. Ms. Redford recognized the family farm clause as a loophole and she promised to close it if elected premier. The FUA publicly endorsed her. We were walking on air. Here was a Conservative, vying for the premier's chair, who recognized the rights of farm workers. We'd been waiting 10 years for this. Ms. Redford promised to extend the protection of occupational health and safety laws to farm workers of commercial operations. Then she got elected premier and was told to back off. In spite of her campaign promise, she did what she was told. The farm and ranch lobby is opposed to reforms in agriculture, and represents only 3% of Alberta's gross domestic product. Here was a clear example of a small tail wagging a really huge dog.

SM: Nonetheless, you have made ground as a result of your activism.

DD: Yes, definitely. The upshot of our work at the Legislative Assembly—the questions, the tabling of petitions and Members' Bills, and Statements—is that no Alberta politician can say they are unaware of the farm worker issues. We have proven that the exclusion of farm workers from the labour legislation was a deliberate act on the part of Alberta's Conservative government.

SM: What are your goals now?

DD: Our goals are the same as they have always been. We want Alberta farm workers to have equality at law. Now we are armed with arguments for a Charter challenge to farm workers' exclusion from four pieces of legislation. The *Calgary Herald* published an editorial on June 11, 2014, titled "Fairness for Farm Workers," stating "it should never have come to this," referring to Charter-challenge arguments that are the work of professor Jennifer Koshan and her students at the University of Calgary's Faculty of Law. The group determined that farm workers' exemptions from OHS laws are a "government-created violation of [a farm worker's] right to security of the person under section 7 of the Charter." The *Calgary Herald* has been an agent for change throughout Alberta's history. Alberta's farm workers definitely have a powerful ally. We have disseminated this information to unions, clergy, retailers, producer groups, civil rights groups, and to those who wiggle the levers federally and provincially. We have four compelling arguments and that leaves us more hopeful than ever.

SM: Did the legal arguments have the desired effect on the government?

DD: Alberta's Conservative government wasn't the least bit moved by the Charter arguments. It seemed it would take nothing short of a Supreme Court challenge to secure equality for these workers and that would take someone with deep pockets. In the meantime, Alberta's Progressive Conservative government and the Wildrose Official Opposition were comfortable using these workers' rights as bargaining chips. These exclusions were purely political.

SM: Can you describe the political climate that you faced at that point?

DD: We experienced a tumultuous political scene in Alberta having three different premiers in as many years. Jim Prentice stepped into the fray and kept it going when he won the leadership election of the Progressive Conservative Association of Alberta in September 2014 and took over from interim Premier Dave Hancock, who became premier when Alison Redford resigned. The FUA engaged with Premier Prentice and immediately realized he was no different than the other premiers. He even used the same security force to have Eric muscled aside. Premier Prentice perpetuated the chaos when he encouraged the floor crossing of nine Official Opposition MLAs to the Progressive Conservative caucus that effectively silenced and crippled the Official Opposition. But that all changed when, even though he held 70 of 83 seats in the Legislature, Premier Prentice called an early election in the spring of 2015.

SM: What was your first reaction to the election?

DD: When Premier Prentice called the snap election in the spring, Eric and I contemplated yet another Conservative government and were in despair. The daunting task of launching appeals with the International Labour Organization (ILO) and North American Free Trade Agreement (NAFTA) and a Supreme Court challenge left us weak. Then, in our tradition of barking up every tree in the forest, FUA president Eric Musekamp saw the provincial election as an opportunity and threw his hat into the ring. He ran as the Liberal candidate in the Cypress-Medicine Hat riding. He didn't win though, but election day did prove to be a good one.

SM: Were you surprised by the outcome?

DD: Not just surprised, but encouraged. On 5 May 2015, after a 44-year dynasty in Alberta, the Progressive Conservative government went down to a stunning defeat (10/83 seats). Some people have called this upset a genuine miracle. It may just be a coincidence, but in a Hail Mary pass prior to Easter, I wrote Pope Francis once again. This time I asked him to say a prayer for farm workers. The early election call came the day after Easter Monday.

As I write this, Alberta has a progressive government, an NDP government. Our new premier, the Honourable Rachel Notley, follows the FUA on Twitter, and Eric and she are on a first-name basis. Brian (Mason) and David (Eggen) are now government ministers. We have friends in the big house. While once we stalked the halls of Alberta's Legislature seeking a sympathetic ear, we are now greeted with open arms, open hearts, and sometimes hugs. Most importantly, we now have the government's understanding of the farm worker issue.

Since May 5, 2015, the FUA has been working with our new government to ensure the farm worker issue does not get hidden behind political agendas. The newspapers have given us plenty of ink. The unions are involved again. The naysayers are still out there and Alberta's Official Opposition the Wildrose remain opposed.

SM: You and Eric have held an annual Farm Workers Day for a number of years now. Did the election of the new government shape this year's event?

DD: Yes. This was the 11th annual Farm Workers Day, on August 20, 2015. It started with a barbecue hosted by MLA Dr. David Swann. Farm worker widow Lorna Chandler did us the honour of attending. What was unusual is that the Calgary & District Labour Council hosted a second event by observing Farm Workers Day in the Marquis Room at the Palliser Hotel in Calgary. There, we were joined by nine Alberta MLAS, eight of whom were NDP and one Liberal MLA, Dr. David Swann; professor Jennifer Koshan; agriculture writer Will Verboven;

and other concerned Albertans. I was moved when the hosts called for a moment of silence to honour fallen farm worker Terry Carl Rash.

The event at the Palliser Hotel was much different than any previous Farm Workers Day. The FUA had asked our new government to send greetings on August 20 to the men, women, and children who toil in Alberta's agricultural industry. Ricardo Miranda (MLA for Calgary-Cross) did just that: He brought "Greetings" from Premier Notley and said, "We're working on it." That same day, as we were heading home, CBC reporter Tim Devlin phoned to ask if we had heard the news. He told us that Jobs Skills Training & Labour Minister Lori Sigurdson had called a media scrum to announce that she was bringing forward workplace safety changes for farm workers in the fall. Mr. Devlin said there were no details yet, but it was a formal announcement. This is what we had been waiting for, the word from our labour minister.

SM: Do you feel that your work is now over, that you have met your goals?

DD: Not yet. We won't stop even now that the legislation is changed. We will still take every opportunity to push the issue. One must always be prepared for unexpected setbacks and for opportunities. You, yourself, seized the opportunity when the Honourable Minister Lori Sigurdson was in the Okanagan Valley, a mere four days after her farm worker announcement in September 2015. Speaking to the minister about her position on Alberta's farm worker issue and giving her two chapters of our book a year ahead of publication helped to further the arguments. Maybe, now, we can get down to the nuts and bolts of making these important changes happen.

Notes

1. See Medeiros and McIntyre (2014), "The Constitutionality of the Exclusion of Farm Industries under the Alberta Workers' Compensation Act."
2. Dated 18 May 2005 (*Hansard* p. 1608).
3. Canada: A *voir dire* is in-trial hearing that is considered a separate hearing from the trial itself. It is known as a "trial within a trial" and designed to determine an issue separate from the procedure or admissibility of evidence. Wikibooks.org
4. See Barley (2008) "Report to the Minister of Justice and Attorney General, Public Fatality Inquiry by the Honorable Judge Peter Barley."
5. Alberta. (2009). *Hansard*, David Swann (Liberal), June 1, p. 1439.

References

Barley, P. (2008). Report to the Minister of Justice and Attorney General, Public Fatality Inquiry by the Honourable Judge Peter Barley. Okotoks, AB: Author. Retrieved June 28, 2013 from http://www.ufcw.ca/Theme/UFCW/images/en/harvestofdeath/Dir-Fatality%20Attachment-Jan%202009.pdf

Calgary Herald. Editorial: Fairness for Farm Workers. 10 June 2014. Retrieved Jan. 17, 2015 from http://calgaryherald.com/opinion/editorials/editorial-fairness-for-farm-workers

Dunmore v. Ontario (Attorney General), SCC 94 (2001).

Eggen, D. (2005, May 18). *Alberta Hansard*, p. 1608. Edmonton. Retrieved from http://www.assembly.ab.ca/Documents/isysquery/3a7401fe-a6f6-49fc-82f2-6cc003ec5fd8/3/doc/20050518_1330_01_han.pdf#xml=http://www.assembly.ab.ca/Documents/isysquery/3a7401fe-a6f6-49fc-82f2-6cc003ec5fd8/3/hilite/

Swann, D. (2009, June 1). *Alberta Hansard*, p. 1439. Edmonton. Retrieved from http://www.assembly.ab.ca/ISYS/LADDAR/docs/hansards/han/legislature_27/session_2/20090601_1330_01_han.pdf

Voir dire. (2014, April 26). Canadian Criminal Procedure and Practice/Pre-Trial Matters/Applications and Motions Procedure. Wikibooks.org. Retrieved Sept. 7, 2015 from https://en.wikibooks.org/wiki/Canadian_Criminal_Procedure_and_Practice/Pre-Trial_Matters/Applications_and_Motions_Procedure

THREE

GEORGIC THEMES AND MYTHS OF ENTITLEMENT IN THE LIFE WRITING OF PRAIRIE SETTLERS

Shirley A. McDonald

An important issue in this book is the class and racial discrimination that is reflected in the relationships between farmer owners and farm workers in western Canada. Class structures in labour and in all social realms are determined by ideologies that many people accept without question. Ideologies, however, are dynamic and open to revision. In medieval times, the social hierarchy in the western world—reflected in St. Thomas Aquinas's *Great Chain of Being*—privileged the aristocracy and determined that the role of peasants was, ostensibly, to serve as menial labourers. This chapter proposes that the class system of rural Alberta can fruitfully be examined in terms of deeply rooted ideologies. It explores the history of class structures and ideological justifications that have given landowners a sense of entitlement to rights that are denied to farm workers. John Locke first introduced the concept of land entitlement at the end of the 17th century when he asserted that labour was "the ultimate basis for legitimate property rights" (qtd. in Greer 2012, p. 366). Such criterion served to determine title in the early 1900s under the Dominion Lands Act (Alberta Genealogical Society, 2010). This proposition closely parallels a "yeoman" ethic that was popular among prairie settlers. The belief that landowners are privileged both in social and moral status has an extensive and even ancient history.

Farmers and farm labour have long been represented, historically, in terms of an idealization of rural life. W.J. Tregillus, president of the United Farmers of Alberta from 1912 to 1914, promoted the myth that farm life "was a wellspring of happiness and virtue, [...] 'the most natural and healthful life we can live'" (qtd. in Rennie, 2007, p. 246). To Tregillus, the farmer was "the Jeffersonian ideal of the honest, contented yeoman—the moral fabric of the nation" (p. 246). Agrarian myths have also valorized aristocratic rural figures such as capitalist investors A.E. Cross, A.J. McLean, Pat Burns, and George Lane, who, since the first Calgary Stampede in 1912, have been presented as men that "tower larger than life over the oral and written record" (Evans, 2004, p. xv). Decades later—near the time of Canada's centennial celebrations—rural communities valorized prairie settlers in selective histories like *Leaves from the Medicine Tree* (1960) and *Our Foothills* (1975). Today, regional museums guarantee pioneer farmers hallowed places in history.

This chapter explores the lives of some of these pioneers by analyzing their diaries, letters, and memoirs. In a comprehensive study of life writing in Canada, Julie Rak (2005) maintains that scholars in a variety of fields, including post-colonial theory, historiography, women's studies, and Aboriginal studies, are now analyzing life narratives "to 'trouble' the idea of Canada as a nation with an unproblematic history" (p. 3). The history that I propose to "trouble" is one that depicts pioneer farmers as powerfully autonomous individuals who, with courage, vigour, and tenacity, faced the challenges of prairie settlement. I examine the diaries or journals of Henry Norman Sheppard Sr. (1907–1934) and those of his sons, Henry Fleetwood Sheppard Jr. (1919, 1929–1952) and Herbert (Bert) Sheppard (1938–1942, 1947). The Sheppards settled in High River, Alberta, where their journals are housed at the Museum of the Highwood. I also examine the letters of Claude Gardiner (1894–1896), published as *Letters from an English Rancher* (1988), and four memoirs written many decades after settlement: Bert Sheppard's *Spitzee Days* (1971) and *Just About Nothing* (1977), Georgina Thomson's *Crocus and Meadowlark Country* (1963), and Monica Hopkins's *Letters from a Lady Rancher* (1981). The Sheppards, Gardiner, and Hopkins emigrated from England to southern Alberta seeking property, while Thomson's family migrated from Ontario.

A feature that drew my attention to these texts is the authors' patterning of their lives in the agrarian cycle that Virgil represents in *The Georgics*, four books of poems (written circa 39 BCE) that valorized farmers and encouraged "a revival of farming" following civil war in Italy (Wilkinson,

1982, pp. 20–23). Simply defined, "*Georgica* derives from Greek words for farmer, agriculture, working in the earth (*geo*, earth, and *ergon*, work)" (Ferry, 2005, p. 189). Anthony Low (1985) attests to Virgil's influence in England, which began in the 17th century, when "the scientific-technological movement" instigated in The New Science of Francis Bacon "harnessed the old Virgilian vision" (p. 118). By the 18th century, "when Dryden established the georgic as a popular mode and genre...[the] long transformation in English agriculture finally reached its culmination in what was called the New Husbandry and, later, the Agricultural Revolution" (Low, 1985, pp. 118–119, p. 129). Low asserts that "this combination of pragmatic experience with literary insight proved remarkably fertile" (p. 118), for Virgilian precepts were foundational to the science of agriculture. Georgic traditions are preserved in the poems of Shakespeare, Wordsworth, Walt Whitman, and Robert Frost (Ferry, 2005, pp. xvii–iii), and in fiction, such as the novels of Jane Austen, which foreground and celebrate estate owners and their country houses and obscure the presence of menial labourers by placing them in the background as props or parts of the scenery. Arguably, Virgil's *Georgics* did ideological service for two different classes of agriculturalists in Britain. The text supported the idyllic visions of aristocratic landowners while also justifying their efforts to improve the landscapes they contemplated and implement the agricultural reforms they sought (McRae, 2002). *The Georgics* also resonated with a different set of ideals held by the more prosperous of their tenants, ideals associated with the "yeomanry" and its associated ethic.

Yeoman ideals trace back at least to the early Tudor era, and the yeomanry, as a distinct group in the medieval rural hierarchy, even further. In England, by the late 12th century, the yeomanry constituted a class of agricultural tenants who farmed, but also rendered skilled military service (for example, capability with the longbow) to their landlords. This rendered them desirable to their superiors and also gave them the social basis to take a relatively prominent role in local affairs and to develop a keen sense of their own rights and virtues (Rollison, 2010, pp. 241–246). The yeoman emerged contiguously with property consolidation as a result of the enclosure of the commons, which fostered capitalist relationships between landowners and workers. "By the end of the eighteenth century," Raymond

Williams (1973) asserts, "nearly half of the cultivated land" in England was owned by 5,000 families (p. 60). At that time, Williams goes on to explain, 400 families in a population of "seven or eight million people, owned nearly a quarter of the cultivated land" (p. 60). Thus, the peasantry, "in any classical sense," disappeared, and what emerged was "an increasingly regular structure of tenant-farmers and waged labourers: the social relationships that we can properly call those of agrarian capitalism" (p. 60). The yeomen had evolved into a favoured tenant class, whose members were often literate and were increasingly engaged in commercial rather than subsistence farming. They were the vanguard of reforming landlords' initiatives and were bound to them by interests in commercial gain and by status association. They were also, typically, employers of hired agricultural labour and in some instances had subtenants of their own. At the same time, they were sharply distinguished from their superiors by their tenant status, and by the fact that, unlike landowners, they worked alongside their families and hired help, and saw little virtue in idleness. As an "in between" class, they also suffered status and economic anxieties and resentments, especially over rent. Williams critically analyzes georgic literary representations of agriculture, Alastair Fowler argues, in a manner that "rehearse[s] a Marxist scenario of oppression by landlords—enclosure, rack-renting, 'the household economy put on a business footing'" as a consequence of the new gentry's focus on capital gain (Williams qtd. in Fowler, 1994, p. 9). Yeomen were eager consumers and disseminators of georgic literature, which valued hard work and practical intelligence over aristocratic leisure. With the development of settlement opportunities in the Americas and elsewhere, they were eager to translate these virtues into a setting in which they imagined themselves as landholders (Chambers, 2008, pp. 107–132). Rarely did yeomen aspire to be a kind of landed gentry, however. Their georgic visions had an economic basis; they sought to settle and make prosperous the so-called *terra nullius* of the United States and British North America.

How pioneer farmers in Alberta came under Virgil's influence is a matter of speculation. Some British settlers were educated at Oxford and Cambridge; among the classics studied at these universities were those by Horace and Virgil, who attested to "the benefits of retirement and return to the land" and exacerbated a growing "antagonism between town and country" (Rothblatt, 1976, p. 37). Such antagonism may have motivated British subjects to immigrate to Canada, for many came in pursuit of the idyllic life represented in Virgil's pastorals. "*The Georgics* was present in every educated man's mind" in England throughout the past few centuries, "and in the last decade of the eighteenth century," L.P. Wilkinson (1982) claims, "it was among the specified American college texts" (pp. 48–49). A distinctly aristocratic version of Virgilian ideals was well established in the plantation culture of the American South by the early 19th century, and was later joined by a distinct smallholder agrarianism (Hahn, 2010). That century also brought the extension of educational opportunities and the publication of cheaper editions of classic and modern texts, along with a lively and surprisingly literary culture of agrarian journalism. This material spread Virgilian and yeoman ideas to literate farmers who appropriated them into a mythology of virtuous labour and wise stewardship, and, increasingly, to a defence of the virtues of smallholder property rights (Hagenstein, Gregg, & Donahue, 2011). The perpetuation of georgic practices in Alberta was, perhaps, due to their modelling by settlers from Britain and eastern Canada, by American cattlemen who brought the first herds into the province, and later by prosperous American farmers who moved north during and after the Civil War period. Historian Terry Jordan (1993) asserts that the dominant practices in the cattle industry in North America are based on traditions that were culturally transmitted by "the Midwesterners [with] their preference for British cattle breeds, obsession with haying and its paraphernalia, desire to build pasture fences and sizeable barns, tendency to irrigate meadows," and techniques of instilling "herd docility" (p. 313). Virgil recommends similar practices in *The Georgics*.

Virgil also strongly promoted "the moral value of hard work," Wilkinson (1982, p. 20) asserts, which is an ethos that "is now long rooted in western, especially puritan, mentality" (p. 18). Yet, georgic literature, Michael Genovese (2013) reveals, also serves to "reinforce the power of a dominant class," for it recreates and promotes "beliefs and practices that ensured the dominance of estate-owning gentlemen," such as "cheap labor, forced enclosure, [and] intellectual and cultural distance from agricultural work" (p. 198). Georgic literature often features estate-owning gentlemen governing from cities or country houses while menial workers do the labour. In England, the establishment of the institution of the country estate coincided with enclosure of the commons (Landry, 2001, p. 2). In North America, a similar process occurred during colonization. As Allan Greer (2012) notes, colonizing powers dispossessed Indigenous peoples of their land through forced enclosure or imperial encroachment—a conflict in which colonists emerged as the victors (p. 380). The result was the creation of "a class of low-wage agricultural workers" (p. 380), along with landholding opportunities for both cattlemen with aristocratic pretensions and for yeoman settlers who, as in the case of the Sheppards, were complicit in and at times agents of the removal of Indigenous peoples to reserves. Henry Sheppard Sr. was licensed as a magistrate in 1898 (*Leaves*, 1960, p. 98) and recorded his cases and civic duties in his journals. On May 17, 1913, he wrote: "Issued warrant for Willie Dickson Stony Indian for horse stealing" (Sheppard, 1907–1934). Such journal accounts reveal his role as an agent of colonization. Expressing colonial attitudes in his memoir *Spitzee Days*, Bert Sheppard (1971) maintains that the Siksika and Stoney Nakoda surrendered the land to the British government. Reiterating governmental discourse, he commends "Chiniquai, head chief of the Stony Tribe of Indians," for deciding to situate his "Reservation along the Bow River at Morley" when the tribe turned over their country "to the Great White Mother" during the signing of Treaty 7 in 1877, for had he chosen the "upper reaches of the Spitzee country," it would not have been "possible for many fine ranches to be established in the upper High River country" (p. 12). Settlers like the Sheppards functioned as reinforcers of new systems of property based on private, freehold land title. Thus, the history of colonial settlement offers insight into the ideological basis of the class structure governing farm labour today.

The primary texts in my study constitute colonial discourses, for they record or re-enact settlement experiences and support the authors' claims of land title. Georgina Thomson's memoir, for example, re-enacts her family's fulfillment of the requirements of the Dominion Lands Act, which states that after improving a "homestead claim [which entailed] (occupying the land for at least three years and performing certain improvements, including building a house and barn, fencing, breaking and cropping a portion of the land), the homesteader could apply for patent (title) to the land"

(Alberta Genealogical Society, 2010). Like other pioneer writers in my study, Thomson (1963) foregrounds her family's labour and occludes the labour of hired hands on whom the Thomsons depended to ensure their success. Literary representations of agriculture have, for centuries, mystified labour by "a simple extraction of the existence of labourers" (Williams, 1973, p. 32). By occluding the labour of hired hands, the authors of my primary texts betray a class distinction that privileges landowners, whether of the ranching aristocracy or agrarian smallholders.

The Sheppards accounted for labour in their journals as calculative empirical data, such as when Henry Sr. wrote: "Hot day Branded 70 head of steers and found it hard work" (Sheppard, 1907–1934). They recorded such experiences without assigning further meaning, which imparts both an enterprising and an existential quality to the entries and to their lives. In contrast, the memoirists give meaning to their experiences. For example, Thomson (1963), feeling a sense of pride from having participated in her family's farming enterprise, proclaims that she, "too, had a hand in [the first] harvest. Hadn't I picked stones and poisoned gophers?" (p. 163). Transforming these tasks into symbols of labour and emphasizing her contribution to their completion amounted to a claim that she possessed the vitality that enabled settlers to succeed in their farming ventures. To some extent, the differences in these accounts reflect the different purposes of journals and memoirs, and likely also gendered differences in what was thought worthy of recording. However, Thomson's exclamation above also indicates a class sense of entitlement as well as a gendered one, an attitude that is still evident in the way contemporary farmers treat farm workers in today's agricultural labour sector.

Before discussing the historical and ideological foundations of the relations between farm owners and farm workers in Alberta, I will briefly introduce the authors. They were the kind of settlers that historian Lewis G. Thomas (1986) calls "privileged"; that is, they had "access to financial resources" to enable them to establish themselves as landowners (p. 177). They sought to create styles of living "modelled," Thomas contends, "on that of the worlds from which they came, or to which they aspired" (p. 161). They can, nonetheless, be subdivided into two broad groups. In *Gentlemen Emigrants*, Patrick A. Dunae (1981) identifies a genteel group of "British public school boys, retired military officers, university graduates, and aristocrats" who attempted to replicate their cultural traditions and social values as they "fanned out across the prairies, and poured into the valleys of British Columbia" (p. 1). With the exception of Thomson (1963), who migrated from Ontario, these more aristocratically oriented writers were members of families for whom the decision to immigrate was motivated by the promise of cultivating a "way of life of which the light horse was at once the symbol and the centre" (Thomas, 1986, p. 88). Often, though not exclusively, these were ranching families, or families with the capital to purchase larger tracts of land. Settlers of more modest means sometimes participated in equestrian sports, but were often suspicious of the need for the leisure time they required. Agrarian progressives among them later developed a cynical view of the gambling that accompanied horse racing (Morton, 2003, pp. 11–12), which conflicted with the virtues of wealth earned by work. However, agricultural settlers who managed to do well economically did pride themselves on the possession of purebred heavy draft horses rather than common stock or oxen. For example, John Turner, "for whom Turner Valley was named," was a breeder of purebred Clydesdales (*Leaves*, 1960, p. 362). Likewise, Frank Bedingfeld bred prize-winning Clydesdales and polo ponies (Sheppard, 1971, p. 217). Lifelong friends of the Sheppards, the Shakerleys raised purebred Shires to which the Sheppards bred their mares to produce horses they could use for hauling wagons, for plowing the fields in preparation for planting, and for cutting, raking, and stacking hay. Evidence of equestrian sports and farm labour done with horses is abundant in my primary texts.

Claude Gardiner (1988) was an equestrian who trained in the military before emigrating from England in 1894. His social connections guaranteed him work when he arrived in Alberta. Letters written by Gardiner's father to "Clarence C. Chipman, Chief Commissioner of the Hudson's Bay Company," secured him a position on the Belleview Ranch owned by pioneer rancher James W. Bell of Fort Macleod (Dempsey, 1988, pp. vi–vii). Initially, Gardiner presented himself in his letters as subordinate to Bell, but later, contrary to myths of cowboys stoically bearing the discomforts of their jobs, he complained about Bell's mistreatment. Gardiner's goals were first to become a cowboy and, then, a ranch owner so he could enjoy a quality of life to which he sensed he was entitled according to his social status.

After working as a hired hand for a couple of years, Gardiner purchased the Wineglass Ranch near Pincher Creek. His social affiliations then guaranteed him a place in the elite society of Anglo-Canadian ranchers.

Monica Hopkins, born Monica Maggs "in Dorset, England in 1884" (Jameson, 1981, p. viii), also self-identified as a member of an elite. She uses her memoir to reassert claims of her social standing in spite of the loss of status incurred by her immigration to Alberta in 1909 when she married Francis (Billie) Hopkins, a horse rancher, who homesteaded "nine miles southwest of Priddis" (p. viii). Hopkins's memoir is a reminiscence of her first two years on the ranch. At times, Hopkins (1981) emphasizes her social rank in playful yet lofty comments on the ill-mannered hired hands who drop her linen napkins on the floor under the dining table (p. 20). At other times, she demonstrates her status in her ownership of horses, boasting that she has five of her own, including a pleasure horse (p. 61). Hopkins learned to ride immediately upon her arrival in Alberta, for, she observes, women "who do not ride and are dependent on their men folk to take them about evidently do not get taken out very much"; thus, she reasons, "I'm not going to be dependent on anyone so I ride nearly every day" (p. 17). Yet her claim of independence is ironic, for to generate time for equestrian activities, she relied on her husband and hired hands to do the ranch chores. Moreover, in relating anecdotes about her riding experiences, Hopkins promotes both her personal and her social aspirations, for she was no doubt cognizant of the financial means necessary to sustain the luxury of keeping a pleasure horse.

Georgina Thomson (1963) also claims that her riding skills afforded her independence, but her memoir indicates a more yeomanlike perspective on settlement. Thomson and her family migrated from Ontario to Nanton, Alberta, in 1904 and kept several horses for pleasure and utility. Their goal was to grow grain and raise a few cows, chickens, and pigs to satisfy their nutritional needs; this subsistence pattern recreated their farming practices in Ontario. Thomson's purpose in writing her memoir, she professes, is to assure "future generations" that while "there were hardships we wouldn't want to go back to, and there was hard work for everyone in the family, [...] there was fun and happiness too" (p. 5). Yet, more often than not, Thomson's memoir stresses work. She foregrounds her family's labour by naming its members in conjunction with the chores they did. Thomson's father and her brother Jim cultivated grain and hay, and, because her mother preferred outdoor farm chores to housework, Thomson's eldest sister, Bee, cooked the meals. Thomson and a younger sister, Chaddy, learned to milk cows when they were still young and became quite good at it (p. 69). Indeed, Thomson boasts that her skills in the dairy were developed to such a degree that when she came home from university for summer holidays, she was still able to "assemble the separator parts in the summer twilight without bothering with a lamp" (p. 71). At other times, however, Thomson depicts farm chores as dirty and tiresome duties that she performed reluctantly. This attitude, perhaps, anticipates a later agrarian-feminist condemnation of household and agricultural "drudgery" (Halpern, 2001) that, despite its aspirations to democratic "uplift," also harboured a class connotation.

Thomson (1963) dedicates a chapter to descriptions of chores, such as the "perennial job" of picking stones, the drudgery of digging wells and hauling water, the work of putting up hay for the winter and feeding livestock, and the intense labour of breaking new land and plowing (pp. 69–76). The degree of adversity presented by each chore equals the measure of praise she bestows on the labourers, such as her father and brother, for whom plowing all day in the heat, the dust, and the flies "was really a tough job" (p. 161). Thomson's memoir is an example of a settler narrative that fosters yeoman myths of farming as a noble occupation, a myth centred "on the belief that farming is a virtuous activity that often entails personal sacrifice" (Barnetson, 2009, p. 65). Thomson emphasizes her own and her family's sacrifices in the service of maintaining their propertied independence while reminiscing about her youth, but she comments little on the fact that the Thomsons depended on the men they hired seasonally and year-round to help complete the work involved in farming.

During the settlement of southern Alberta, yeoman and aristocratic ethics coexisted and even converged. Henry Sheppard Sr. also emphasizes work in his journals. He was born in Sheffield, England, in 1861, "the son of a rector." He was educated at Oxford, but chose to give up that gentle life for the labour-intensive life of a rancher when he immigrated to Alberta in 1887 to raise and train horses to sell to the military (*Leaves*, 1960, p. 98). He was an expert equestrian who competed in gymkhanas and larger horse shows. His journals begin in 1907, when he and his wife Bee (née Beatrice

Godden) resided at the Cottonwood Ranch near High River and were members of a society that spent its leisure time on tea parties, dinners and dances, and polo matches. Like Gardiner, Bee and Henry Sr. had connections and arrived with guarantees of employment. Henry initially worked as a hired hand on the Grieg family's Paleface Ranche near Pekisko, and Bee worked "as governess to the Greig children" (p. 98). They homesteaded "on Hay Creek" (now called Sheppard Creek), where Henry Jr. was born on April 6, 1889 (p. 99).

Henry Sheppard Jr. was also an expert equestrian, but his experience with horses occurred mostly in the context of farm work, for he plowed, seeded, and harvested hay and grain with horses. His journals, which span the years from 1919 to 1951, are exemplary models of the cyclical pattern of an agrarian life, for they served as a kind of farmers' almanac in which he recorded the weather, the amounts of hay and grain handled, the names of his dairy cows and his work horses, and the nature of the labour performed each day. Henry Jr. also used his journals to keep track of crop rotation, a practice Virgil had recommended 2,000 years previously and that 18th-century improvers had revived on a more scientific basis (Wilkinson, 1982, p. 48). His 1938 volume includes an article clipped from the *High River Times*, dated March 3, 1938, that identifies summer fallowing and livestock pasturing as two components of a weed control and soil revitalization plan, which offers evidence that High River community members were aware of "improved" sustainable farming practices. Henry Jr. ran a mixed farming operation, which integrated the raising of grains and cattle with the keeping of small dairy and poultry operations, and the growing of gardens for the family's nutritional needs (Elofson, 1996, pp. 207–209). Henry Jr. produced marketable crops including many varieties of potatoes—Ohio, reds, kidneys, netted gems, and McGregors—which he graded, sorted, bagged, and sold to local customers. His livelihood also depended partly on the sale of cream, which he collected, kept cold in metal containers in a "spring box" (a wooden crate in the creek), and sold to the creamery in High River. Henry Jr. fed not only his family, but also many neighbours. He used his journals as account books to record his production and sales, and to note, by first name, the various men he hired, the number of hours they worked each day, and the payment they received.

Bert Sheppard self-identified as a cattle rancher, not a farmer. He was born on the Cottonwood Ranch on February 26, 1901. Bert's first job, as a cowboy on the Bar U Ranch, was, he claims, the realization of a "boyhood dream" (Sheppard, 1977, p. 83). He eventually became a successful breeder of pedigreed Hereford cattle on the TL and Riverbend ranches. Like his father and brother, he kept a journal in which he wrote the names of the men who worked for him and the labour they performed. His mother also kept a journal, although its whereabouts is currently unknown. In a few entries featured in *Leaves from the Medicine Tree*, Bee demonstrates wit and resourcefulness. She wrote on April 3, 1893: "'Clematis' calved (heifer calf). Hal made me seed boxes for my garden. He and Guy bored post holes in the morning. Guy went for a load of rails in afternoon. [...] Seven eggs. Had to kill dark yellow hen for eating eggs on Thursday, thirtieth. Ate her yesterday'" (qtd. in *Leaves* 1960, p. 101). "Guy" is Guy Pallister, who also arrived from Sheffield, England, and lived and worked with the Sheppards for two years (p. 402). Cecilia Danysk (1995) asserts that the nature of labour relationships in the days of settlement was one of relative equality based on the understanding that hired hands would acquire their own land and become neighbours with the families who sponsored them (pp. 14–15). At that time, hired hands were household members who ate with their employers, worked with them, and took part in family life as they developed the skills to operate their own farms and ranches.

"Co-operation rather than competition was necessary for survival in the early years," Danysk states (1995, p. 75). Yet, according to William C. Pratt (1975), scholars constructed a myth of "frontier individualism" that conflicts "with imperatives of mutual aid that rural people observed" (p. xii). The Sheppard journals discredit that myth with evidence of mutual aid in the High River and Longview communities—the locations of their properties. In an entry for June 18, 1918, Henry Sr. wrote that, returning home, he "saw smoke at Ranch and found stables had [?], impossible to say how fire started [...] All the neighbours turned out to help [...] Rooney & his man. Palton. Brown. Hanson. A H Grant. Johnston & Palton sat up all night" (Sheppard, 1907–1934). Henry Jr. also referred to co-operative labour in an entry for December 16, 1931, when he wrote that he "killed two pigs with Sams help. got done about 4" (Sheppard, 1919, 1929–1951). "Sam" is Jonas Sam Rider, a lifelong family friend. The Sheppards belonged to a social group of ranchers whose members concerned themselves with each other's well-being and, initially, with those they employed. Eventually, however, growing class divisions alienated landowners from their employees. Escalating land prices in the 1920s prevented hired hands from establishing farms and ranches and becoming invested members of the community; thus, they were subjected to lives of endless menial labour without the pending reward of land ownership (Danysk 1995, p. 173).

Land acquisition was a primary goal for settlers. British yeoman immigrants came in search of freehold land on which they could establish their independence, while more aristocratic or moneyed arrivals imagined they could develop the land they acquired into estates. Interestingly, both groups gave names to their properties. In Britain, both landed estates and the larger tenant farms had typically been named. The Thomsons called their homestead "'Parkhouse' after a farm in Ontario where [they] had lived" (Thomson, 1963, p. 121), while Hopkins (1981) referred to her ranch as Enmore, named after her husband "Billie's father's ship" (p. 5). Gardiner purchased the Wineglass Ranch, a patented homestead. Likewise, the Sheppards purchased established ranches: the Cottonwood, the Riverbend, and the TL, founded by Tom Lynch, who brought one of the first herds of cattle to Alberta. The Sheppards also sought to add to their land holdings. On June 28, 1907, Henry Sr. noted that he "drove onto Sections 29, 19, 23 West of 4 which I have applied for. Saw some good land south of Blackfoot reserve" (Sheppard, 1907–1934). Like English country estates and yeoman leaseholds, ranches and farms were different manifestations of their owners' utopian desires for plenitude and prosperity. Such visions came, Raymond Williams (1973) observes, "not only from the Christian idea of the Garden of Eden," but also from Virgil's *Georgics* (p. 54, p. 57). Lewis Mumford (1962) cautioned that utopianism of the more aristocratic sort yields notions of exclusivity, for country houses are "concerned not with the happiness of the whole community but with the felicity of the governors," whose entitlement "is based upon privilege and not upon work" (p. 202). Mumford points out that running a country house requires the help of menial labourers. Some of the job titles changed when estate living was adapted to the foothills or (less often) the prairies, yet the roles were similar and they were performed without much note.

Julian Yates (2007) suggests that aristocratic-utopian models "produce a hybridized feudal model of the manor" (p. 195). Thomas (1986) detects utopianism in the aspirations of civil servants like William Pearce, who imagined "elaborate schemes for southern Alberta's development that combined large land holdings and peasant villages complementing one another in an ordered society that might have done credit to Sir Thomas More or even St. Augustine" (p. 194). The yeoman ethic generated its own utopian myths of prairie settlement, which had both humanist and religious foundations. These myths emphasized ideals of democratic equality as in Edward Bellamy's implicitly socialist utopian novel, *Looking Backward, 2000–1887* (2009), which was wildly popular in the agrarian progressive movement of the early 20th century. Middle-class farmers, however, championed co-operativist philosophies that left private ownership of land intact, and saw private landownership as guaranteeing political and economic independence (Badgley, 2000; Chambers, 2008; Rennie, 2000). Thus, they tended to see agricultural workers either as future farmers or as a lesser class. Yeoman ideals are reflected in the words of United Farmers of Alberta presidents and "idealistic leaders" who, Bradford J. Rennie (2007) claims, led farmers to believe they were building "an Arcadian paradise, but also the kingdom of God on earth, a truly Christian society" (p. 256). Withstanding the uncertainty of success and the disappointments of failure in farming required a kind of faith that is not unlike religious faith. The Social Gospel championed by the agrarian progressives who eventually formed the United Farmers of Alberta also proclaimed a faith in a new sort of pioneering—the establishment of a future New Jerusalem of co-operative democracy and equality (Allen, 1971, 1976). Utopian ideologies are implied, as well, in neophyte settlers' anticipation of regular bumper crops. The promise of wealth was the rhetorical content of pamphlets the Canadian government distributed in Europe to entice immigrants to settle on the prairies.

The Foundations of Racialized Labour

In early 20th-century agrarian progressivism, georgic and religious ideologies combined with a yeoman ethic of the virtuous primacy of the agricultural producer to provide images of an ideal society called the co-operative commonwealth. "Commonwealth" ideals, identified closely with the English yeomanry, dated back to the Tudor and Elizabethan ages (McRae, 2002; Rollison, 2010) and foregrounded lateral social relations and democratic mutual aid over hierarchy and subservience. With the rise of industrial society, this emphasis took on an added edge of opposition to combines and trusts, to domination of city over country, to negatively competitive individualism and exploitation, and to political patronage and party machines (Badgley, 2000; Chambers, 2008; Thompson, 1985). This was combined in the latter 19th century with ideas from English and Danish co-operativism and the Social Gospel (Knuttila & Stirling, 2007). In this mix there was some pro-labour sentiment, and the United Farmers of Alberta government in Alberta first came to power as a farmer-labour coalition. But the alliance with urban labour was fragile, and the rights of hired farm workers had little place in the co-operativist political universe. Further, the common tropes of early 20th-century racism found their way into the speech of agrarian progressives; these were deployed to achieve stratification of those "races" judged educable or enterprising and those judged to be a potential drag on agricultural prosperity or the public purse. In 1909, the social reformer and Social Gospel exponent James S. Woodsworth described the prairies as a "land of milk and honey" (Francis, 2007, pp. 225–227). Imagining the variety of settlers and urban immigrants who would populate this new Eden, Woodsworth wrote, in *Strangers within Our Gates* (1972) about which immigrants he had determined would lead and which would labour (p. 154). He reasoned that the "most intelligent and progressive of the Slavic races are the Czechs," for they are "chiefly engaged in manufacturing," and, thus, "constitute no peculiar 'problem'" (p. 108). Woodsworth wrote unfavourably of the Galicians, however, whose "unpronounceable names appear so often in police court news, [and] figure so frequently in crimes of violence that they have created anything but a favorable impression" (p. 110). His intention, editor Marilyn Barber asserts, had been to make the attributes of European and Asian immigrants familiar "to other Canadians," but he "defeated much of his own purpose when he presented the immigrants by nationality divisions" (p. ix), thereby fostering racism.

Clifford Sifton also promoted racism along with a rather patronizing variant of yeoman ideals in his promotion of the settlement of the Canadian West. He believed that "the agricultural immigrant was the ideal settler" and sought them in "the peasant heartland of central Europe" (Koroscil, 2008, p. 3). Sifton's ideal farming family comprised a "stalwart peasant in a sheepskin's coat, born of the soil, whose forefathers have been farmers for ten generations, with a stout wife and half a dozen children" (qtd. in Koroscil, p. 3). Frank Oliver's preference "was for the 'right class of British immigrants from the Old Land, [the] Englishman, Irishman, Scotsman [...for they are] of the same race [and speak] the same language as Canadians'" (qtd. in Koroscil, p. 3). The British justified their "claims to power throughout their empire" historian Sarah Carter (2006) asserts, by imagining themselves at the "top of the hierarchy of races [...] with other peoples occupying various degrees of inferiority beneath them" (p. 79). The authors in my study betray such attitudes. Their vision of the prairies was that of a propertied utopia that existed mainly for white Anglo-Canadian settlers like them.

Henry Sheppard Sr., a magistrate who recorded his cases in his journals, reveals common attitudes about race in the early days of Alberta. For example, on April 29, 1909, he tried "a chinaman [?] for selling liquor" (Sheppard, 1907–1934). On January 11, 1912, he had "Charles Starkey and George Marcus (colours) up for fighting—fined $5 costs $2." In *Spitzee Days*, Bert Sheppard (1971) reveals the community's attitude of racial superiority in an article, "An Impudent Jap," originally published in the *High River Times* in May 1911 (p. 149). Sheppard relates another story, as well, about a "Chinaman" named Jim Ting, a cook at the Alberta Hotel in 1908, who, having angrily "poured some hot grease" on a waitress, had his queue (or braid) forcefully severed as punishment (p. 152). Sheppard states that the cook was taken outside and, "in about the same manner that a calf is wrestled down and marked, he was stretched out over the chopping block and trimmed up with the woodpile axe" (p. 152). By recounting and humourizing the actions of these cowboy vigilantes enacting their own brand of justice, Sheppard implies that racial violence was an unquestioned part of High River society.

The only references to Asian immigrants in Henry Jr.'s journal are to a Chinese man who resided on the edge of the Sheppard farm near High

River. Other than identifying his neighbour as "Chink," Henry Jr. did not make deprecating comments about him. Indeed, he seems to be one of the neighbours with whom the Sheppards regularly conducted business. For example, they rented 30 acres to him for growing potatoes and sold old laying hens to him to make soup. Henry Jr. wrote on January 24, 1938, that "Chink came bought 10 old hens @ 10 5.10" (Sheppard, 1919, 1929–1951). At times, he helped the man with certain chores. On June 23, 1943, he noted that he "thinned turnips & Sugar Beets a.m. [...] went over to Chinks to alter pigs." The Sheppards did not employ Chinese household staff, but other families in their social circle did.

Agnes Skrine wrote in 1898 of the benefits of employing "'one servant in the house, an able-bodied cook'" to whom she refers as "'the Chinaman,'" whose labour allowed her time for equestrian activities (qtd. in *Leaves*, 1960, pp. 504–505). She also mentions the hired hands on the ranch, referring to them as "the 'boys'" (p. 504). In 1884, Mary Ella Inderwick (1997) wrote of the benefits of keeping a Chinese cook, which provided her time to engage in her favourite pastime: horseback riding (pp. 75–79). "When John, my cook, breaks my best cut glass dish," she states, "I fly to the stables and have my Joy saddled and ride till I know that cut glass is nothing to make or mar one's lovely day" (p. 76). Tones of sarcasm, intolerance, and anger toward hired domestic help are evident in various examples of life writing—diaries and memoirs alike—when these individuals fail to do their assigned work, for its lack of completion threatened the disruption of the quality of life to which the authors felt they were entitled. Skrine's and Inderwick's memoirs seem to reflect their society's reluctance and even annoyance in having to manage Asians, who were a source of cheap labour. At the same time, Anglo-Canadians saw immigrant others as threats to cultural hegemony. Reflecting on the prejudices that were exacerbated by increasing immigration of Asians and Indians in the early 20th century, Woodsworth (1972) reasoned: "As long as immigration from the Orient was confined to a few odd Chinamen a year, who were quite content to do work distasteful to a white man, no particular objections were raised" (p. 142). In contrast to hiring Asians, some British settlers preferred to employ their countrymen as farm labourers and domestic workers, a practice that maintained a hierarchical social structure in Alberta.

Despite the racialized nature of Canadian society in the settlement era, Carter (2006) observes that "being white and British did not guarantee privilege, power or even acceptance in Western Canada" (p. 48). "Just as whiteness had its own hierarchies," she explains, "so too did Britishness" (p. 48). Prejudice against remittance men was prevalent, for example. Imagining that these "greenhorns" were incompetent and lazy, employers posted signs stating "No Englishmen need apply" (Danysk, 1995, p. 79). However, regardless of disparaging rumours, the Hopkinses hired only young Englishmen and English women. "Many lads, fresh from England, got their start" on the Enmore Ranche, *Our Foothills* contributor E.J. Park (1975) revealed; Billie had hired hands to help with the ranch chores and "Mrs. Hopkins had several English girls to help her" in the house (pp. 304–305). Park identifies the domestic workers as "Denise Sampson, Kathleen McConnell (Mulder) and Memmie Scott, who stayed the longest before returning to England" (p. 304). Hopkins neglects to mention them in her memoir. Settler memoirists tended toward self-flattery; here, it appears that Hopkins downplayed or obscured the fact that she and Billie were *not* robust enough pioneers to do without hired help to complete both ranch and household chores.

Hopkins's memoir is often a reflection of daydreams about a life beyond her financial means. Reality thwarts her desires when she finds that if she is to feed herself it must be at the expense of her own labour. In that respect, her memoir is truly georgic for, as Wilkinson (1982) proclaims, "work is a dominant theme" in *The Georgics* (p. 52). "Gardening is quite new to me," Hopkins observes, and admits that she "never did any at home, never even had the slightest inclination to do so, though I enjoyed the results of someone else's efforts. Now I am learning that it is quite hard work and I still fail to see where there is much pleasure in it" (1981, p. 52). Cognizant of the fact that her attitude will probably offend "enthusiastic gardeners"—advocates of georgic practices—she moves on quickly to pastoral descriptions of the surrounding landscape (p. 52). She remarks that "the Rockies" towering behind the foothills, "all white and glistening with the sun on them," were "so lovely that it was hard to return to the prosaic work of planting potatoes" (p. 53). Often, pastoral and georgic visions mix in settler narratives as the authors reflect on the natural beauty of their land while imagining the future aesthetic pleasures wrought from their labour.

Hopkins obviously does continue with the task of planting potatoes, though, since she writes that she and Billie often ride on horseback in the evening to work together on the garden, but she does not offer as much detail about the work as she does about the aesthetics of the environment. For the most part, Hopkins assigned menial tasks to hired hands and lived in relative comfort at their expense. Nonetheless, she complains about them in her memoir. For example, when a man she calls "Crazy Jenks" is given the task of hoeing the weeds, she later discovers that he has "dug up all the mint [she] had so carefully planted in a corner of the garden" (pp. 61–62). "Darn the idiot!" she exclaims; "we have a lamb [...] and I had been so looking forward to lamb and mint sauce" (p. 62). Such language, while adding humour to Hopkins's narrative, discloses the power of discourse to harm the recipients of such social ridicule, Charles Taylor (1992) asserts, by reflecting "back to them a confining or demeaning or contemptible picture of themselves" (p. 25). Indeed, Hopkins also depicts Jenks as lacking in self-confidence. Thus, he serves as a foil for her self-portrait, for, by depicting Jenks as a ne'er-do-well who depended on her good will for work, food, and shelter, Hopkins supports her sense of superiority over him and entitlement to his labour.

A Settler's Personal Experiences as a Hired Hand

Claude Gardiner (1988) worked for two years as a ranch hand and reveals bitterness toward his employer, James W. Bell. In a letter written in 1894, he condemned Bell as "being very mean with his food" and described the "grub" he provided him and another worker as hardly edible: "All we have to eat now is potatoes, some green bacon and stewed dried apples. The apples are the best thing but we can hardly eat the bacon" (p. 17). Gardiner debunked mythical images of cowboys in a letter written on October 13, 1895, reflecting on his experiences riding night herd: "People write all sorts of rot about it but I fail to see the beauty of riding round and round a herd of cattle in the moonlight with the thermometer nearly at zero" (p. 48). Instead, he disclosed the reality of the job. "You cannot wonder at my wanting to start in business for myself," he wrote in another undated letter, "as there is no necessity to live like a pig or to work on Sunday" (p. 16). In spite of his dissatisfaction with his employment, he told his parents in a letter dated October 5, 1894, that he expected to remain with Bell for the winter, for his "chances of getting another job are very small as there is nothing doing in the winter in this country. The cold is so intense that work out of doors (except feeding cattle) is impossible and as that only requires a few men, one is lucky to get a job" (p. 25). Elofson (2000) explains that in the summer, the major ranches employed a few men to round up the cattle and treat them for diseases, but in the "winter when the animals were expected to survive on their own and unattended, a number of the ranch hands were laid off and the manager, one or two foremen, and a few others looked after the entire operation" (p. 6). Elofson points out that A.E. Cross and Matthew Cochrane "have been viewed as shrewd businessmen with foresight and vision," but their success was temporary and depended partly on keeping "the numbers of cowboys they hired to drive and tend the cattle on their spreads" as low as possible (p. 6). Gardiner's letters illustrate how the agricultural economy in place in Alberta's early days depended on cheap labour.

Gardiner's relief from his exploitation came by way of financial assistance from his family. He wrote in a letter, dated March 4, 1895: "My dear Father, I have just got your letter telling me about Grandfather giving me a £1000 for a start" (1988, p. 34). Then, in a letter to his mother, dated June 6, 1895, he wrote: "I have been to look at a ranch in the Porcupine Hills that is for sale. [...] It is very good land and grows a good crop so that one has something to help besides the cattle" (p. 40). Two weeks later, Gardiner announced that he had "bought a ranch" and was "now the owner of 160 acres of land, 80 acres of which is under crop. The rest is good grass ground" (p. 41). When Gardiner purchased the Wineglass Ranch, he realized his romantic notion of becoming a gentleman rancher, who looked very much like a cowboy. The settlement accounts in my study, whether constructed as frontier or utopian myths, reflect georgic and yeoman traditions that promote the moral value of labour; yet, to justify their sense of deserving the privilege of landed property, the authors foreground their labour and obscure the labour of their hired hands.

Once Gardiner made the transition from the role of hired hand to that of ranch owner, he appeared to assume the same kind of viewpoint as the employer who had once fed him substandard food. He seemed to forget the bitterness he felt when, as a hired hand, an employer disregarded his rights. Having hired menial labourers to bring in the harvest in the fall of 1895, Gardiner wrote on October 13, 1895: "I am getting my potatoes in now. I have a lot of Indians working on the job. They take their wages out in potatoes. [...] I cannot afford to pay cash as one gets so little for the potatoes" (p. 50). (Whether he could really not afford to pay them or merely felt their work was worth little remuneration is indeterminable.) Gardiner's reference to these seasonal labourers as faceless "Indians" indicates a racial bias. He referred to other hands by name, such as Jim Ferguson, "a young fellow" who came to rope for him, but not to the "Indians," not even the man who herded his cattle, in spite of the fact that Gardiner acknowledged his superior capabilities (1988, pp. 50–51). Hopkins betrays a similar sentiment, but identified her "Indian" hands by name. For example, she relates a story about a Stoney Nakoda elder, "Ben Big Woman," who was left by his family to cut brush on the Hopkinses' ranch in August 1911 (1981, p. 142). When the elder, while cutting brush one day, sustained a wasp sting on his face, and came to Billie for relief, Billie offered him a bag of blueing that Hopkins used for whitening her laundry, explaining "by pantomime how to rub it on the sting." Later, Hopkins asked the old man what he had done with the bag, and he "opened his mouth wide. He had *eaten* it" (p. 142; original emphasis). By portraying the man as a buffoon, Hopkins reveals her sense of intellectual superiority. She concludes her tale with the hope that his family "won't forget" to come back for him, or she and Billie "will have to adopt Ben" (p. 144), implying a reluctance to provide the man with his basic needs as well as menial employment.

Thomson (1963) presents the farm workers her family employed as faceless figures: "We had so many hired men over the years," she writes, "that I cannot remember even the names" (p. 249). She does recall Harry Wakeman, who "lived as one of the family" and slept in a "small bedroom partitioned off at the end of the back kitchen" until a "bunk-house" was built for hired hands (p. 247). He left her family's employ, Thomson explains, when he "took up land of his own" (247). Danysk (1995) contends that, especially in the early years of settlement, hired hands were ambitious "to move quickly beyond the stage of waged labour" (p. 67). Wakeman was one of the farm workers who became a farm owner and began to work for his own benefit.

Henry Sheppard Jr. and Bert Sheppard, members of a family with financial means, acquired their own land in their adult years. Because of the amount of labour required to operate ranches, they depended, at times, on itinerant workers. They mention the names of hired hands, however, only to record the work they performed each day. For example, Henry Jr. wrote on April 17, 1929, that he "Went to Montcrieffs for wheat. 40 bushels @ 1.50 cold winds. Jack plowed all day" (Sheppard, 1919, 1929–1951). Yet, frequently, Henry Jr. worked alongside his hired help, as did Bert, in spite of a professed aversion to farm labour. Bert indicates that, according to the season, the men on his ranches plowed and manured gardens to grow potatoes and other vegetables, grew grain, cut and stored hay, cleaned chicken coops, fixed cars, poured cement, did laundry, and milked cows. Recording the labour done on the TL Ranch, Bert presents himself as an employer whose employees' compliance with a hegemonic work ethic enables him to realize his vision of progress. In 1939, the fences on the TL needed repair and he hired a large crew of "Indians" under the leadership of Jonas Sam Rider to complete the job (Sheppard, 1951). Like Gardiner, Bert identifies his employees merely as "the Indians" who take the "grub" he brings them. The exception is Jonas Sam Rider, who he may have named because he organized the crew and perhaps also negotiated and received wages on their behalf. Otherwise, they remain anonymous.

In his memoirs, Bert pays tribute to Sam Rider, an "outstanding and expert Stony Indian cowhand and roper," in a story about branding on the Bar U in the 1920s (Sheppard, 1977, p. 141). Depicting the scene as though it had occurred just prior to his writing, Bert relates that

> [t]he calves were fairly thick around the fire and [Rider] just had to swing his horse to get one. Before the first calf was up [after being branded] a second one was down and a third in the hands of the wrestlers. There were three sets of husky Indian wrestlers and one or two younger bucks ready to spell them off. Jonas harangued them

> constantly in Stony, telling them to fly at it and get the rope off. Each day before we were through I heard them complaining, "Too hard work," "Too fast." (p. 141)

Bert's valorization of Rider and other highly skilled cowboys transforms them into powerfully autonomous individuals, like the mythical cowboys who exist only in Western film and fiction. Bert's selective portraits of ranchers and cowboys serve to shape his self-identity, for, by emphasizing their accomplishments, Bert promotes their reputations and, by association, his own. In contrast to these stereotypical characters, which are more typical of the memoirist's genre, the people to whom his father and brother refer in their journals are actual individuals who shared their lives and labour. Henry Sr. mentions Rider by name on April 2, 1934, when he noted: "Sam Rider came to supper." Likewise, Henry Jr. wrote on July 13, 1940, that "Sam Rider [...] landed up about 9.30 to stay the night & have supper." The Sheppard journals thus foster the reader's awareness of settlers and farm workers as actual individuals while hinting at a hierarchy of farm workers in terms of their skills and their relation to their employer.

A reading of Bert's memoirs reveals that they serve certain purposes while also reproducing latent hierarchies. One purpose is to portray the men hard at work, as cowboys always are in Western films, for work is the ethos of the genre. While Bert uses his memoirs as a means to articulate such values, he also inadvertently displays his racial prejudices in, for example, disparaging remarks about the young hired hands who had not yet developed a proper work ethic. His use of the phrase "two younger bucks" to refer to the workers and his mimicry of their language, omitting parts of speech to imply they lacked fluency in English, aligns his memoir with a kind of colonial discourse that "construe[s] the colonized as a population of degenerate types on the basis of racial origin, in order to justify conquest and to establish systems of administration and instruction" (Bhabha, 1994, p. 70). Bert's affiliation with Rider indicates a preference for assimilated "Indians." He ridicules the young Stoney Nakoda men for being slow and lazy and suggests that they ought to aspire to adopt the work ethic Rider models. As Darlene Dunlop explains in the previous chapter, employers can use ridicule in the workplace as a means to assert dominance over employees. Ridicule serves to imply that hired workers are undeserving of the privileges enjoyed by those who employ them.

Conclusion

My goal in examining the life writing of the Sheppards, Gardiner, Hopkins, and Thomson through a lens shaped by a post-colonial reading of georgic and yeoman traditions is to shed light on the history of employment relationships that exist in Albertan agriculture today and the myths upon which they are founded. At work in utopian and frontier myths of settlement are ideas used to perpetuate notions of deserved property rights and privilege for some—but not all—people living in Canada. Taylor (2004) contends that myths can shape our worldviews and motivate our actions, yet, like "social imaginaries," they can also conceal "certain crucial realities" (p. 183). We may have a sense of ourselves as living in a democratic state in principle, but in imagining it as "integrally realized," Taylor argues, we are "engaging in a cover-up, averting our gaze from various excluded and disempowered groups or imagining that their exclusion is their own doing" (p. 183). The long history of exclusion and marginalization of farm workers continues, partly, due to neoliberal ideologies, and partly to ideologies embodied and brought forward in time by re-appropriations of georgic literature and yeoman mythologies that valorize the labour of farmers and obscure that of farm workers. Further, as Genovese (2013) observes, the georgic tradition also models "traditional social relations associated with benevolent paternalism—a presumably more mutual relationship between workers or tenants and estate owners [that] might be adapted to a modern world of expanding commerce and large farms" (p. 198). Virgil is an advocate of benevolent social relationships. In Book Four of *The Georgics*, he lectures on the responsibilities of landowners and farmers to the welfare of the community as a whole. Such attitudes have yet to be adopted by contemporary farmers and agribusiness employers in Alberta.

References

Alberta Genealogical Society. (2010). Index to Alberta Homestead Records 1870 to 1930. Retrieved Feb. 17, 2010 from http://abgensoc.ca/homestead/

Allen, R. (1971). *The social passion: Religion and social reform in Canada, 1914–1918*. Toronto, ON: University of Toronto Press.

Allen, R. (1976). The Social Gospel as the religion of agrarian revolt. In C. Berger & R. Cook, (Eds.), *The West and the nation: Essays in honour of W.L. Morton*. Toronto, ON: McClelland & Stewart.

Badgley, K. (2000). *Ringing in the common love of good: The United Farmers of Ontario, 1914–1926*. Montreal, QC: McGill-Queen's University Press.

Barnetson, R. (2009). The regulatory exclusion of agricultural workers in Alberta. *Just Labour: A Canadian Journal of Work and Society, 14*, 50–74.

Bellamy, E. (2009). *Looking backward, 2000–1887*. New York, NY: Signet.

Bhabha, H. (1994). *The location of culture*. London, UK: Routledge.

Carter, S. (2006). Britishness, "Foreignness," Women and Land in Western Canada: 1890s–1920s. *Humanities Research, 13*, 43–60.

Chambers, M.A. (2008). *Traditional values and progressive desires: Tensions of identity in the rhetoric of the Granger movement in Illinois, 1870–1875*. (Doctoral dissertation, University of Maryland, College Park). UMI Microform 3343460.

Danysk, C. (1995). *Hired hands: Labour and the development of prairie agriculture, 1880–1930*. Toronto, ON: McClelland & Stewart.

Dempsey, H.A. (2008). Introduction. In *Letters from an English Rancher* (pp. v–xii). By Claude Gardiner. Calgary, AB: Glenbow Museum.

Dunae, P.A. (1981). *Gentlemen emigrants: From the British public schools to the Canadian frontier*. Vancouver, BC: Douglas & McIntyre.

Elofson, W. (1996). Not just a cowboy: The practice of ranching in Southern Alberta, 1881–1914. *Canadian Papers in Rural History, 10*, 205–216.

Elofson, W. (2000). *Cowboys, gentlemen and cattle thieves*. Montreal, QC: McGill-Queen's University Press. Print.

Evans, S. (2004). *The Bar U and Canadian ranching history*. Calgary, AB: University of Calgary Press.

Ferry, D. (2005). Introduction. In *The Georgics of Virgil* (pp. xi–xx). Trans. David Ferry. New York, NY: Farrar, Straus and Giroux.

Fowler, A. (1994). Introduction. In *The country house poem: A cabinet of seventeenth-century estate poems and related items* (pp. 1–29). Edinburgh, UK: Edinburgh University Press.

Francis, R.D. (2007). The kingdom of God on the prairies: J.S. Woodworth's vision of the prairie as promised land. In R.D. Francis & C. Kitzan (Eds.), *The prairie west as promised land* (pp. 225–242). Calgary, AB: University of Calgary Press.

Gardiner, C. (1988). *Letters from an English rancher*. Ed. H. Dempsey. Calgary, AB: Glenbow Museum.

Genovese, M. (2013). An organic commerce: Sociable selfhood in eighteenth-century georgic. *Eighteenth-Century Studies, 46*(2), 197–221.

Greer, A. (2012). Commons and enclosure in the colonization of North America. *American Historical Review, 117*(2), 365–386.

Hagenstein, E.C., Gregg, S.M., & Donahue, B. (2011). *American georgics: Writings on farming, culture, and the land.* New Haven, CT: Yale University Press.

Hahn, S. (2010). *The roots of Southern populism: Yeoman farmers and the transformation of the Georgia upcountry, 1850–1890.* Oxford, UK: Oxford University Press.

Halpern, M. (2001). *And on that farm he had a wife: Ontario farm women and feminism, 1900–1970.* Montreal, QC: McGill-Queen's University Press.

Hopkins, M. (1981). *Letters from a lady rancher.* Ed. S. Jameson. Calgary, AB: Glenbow Museum.

Inderwick, M.E. (1997). A lady and her ranch. In T. Poirier (Ed.), *Cowgirls: 100 Years of writing the range* (pp. 75–79). Red Deer, AB: Red Deer College.

Jameson, S. (1981). Introduction. In M. Hopkins, *Letters from a lady rancher* (pp. vii–xvii). Calgary, AB: Glenbow Museum.

Jordan, T.G. (1993). *North American cattle-ranching frontiers: Origins, diffusion, and differentiation.* Albuquerque, NM: University of New Mexico Press.

Knuttila, M., & Stirling, B. (2007). *The prairie agrarian movement revisited.* Regina, SK: Canadian Plains Research Center.

Koroscil, P.M. (2008). *The British Garden of Eden: Settlement history of the Okanagan Valley, British Columbia.* Naramata, BC: Milverton.

Landry, D. (2001). *The invention of the countryside: Hunting, walking and ecology in English literature, 1671–1831.* Hampshire, UK: Palgrave.

Leaves from the Medicine Tree: A History of the Area Influenced by the Tree, and Biographies of Pioneers and Old Timers Who Came Under Its Spell Prior to 1900. (1960). Lethbridge, AB: High River Pioneers' and Old Timers' Association.

Low, A. (1985). *The Georgic revolution.* Princeton, NJ: Princeton University Press.

McRae, A. (2002). *God speed the plough: The representation of agrarian England, 1500–1660.* Cambridge, UK: Cambridge University Press.

Morton, S. (2003). *At odds: Gambling and Canadians, 1919–1969.* Toronto, ON: University of Toronto Press.

Mumford, L. (1962). *The story of utopias.* New York, NY: Viking.

Our foothills. (1975). Calgary, AB: Millarville, Kew, Priddis, and Bragg Creek Historical Society.

Park, E.J. (1975). Francis William R. Hopkins. *Our foothills.* Calgary, AB: Millarville, Kew, Priddis, and Bragg Creek Historical Society. 304–305.

Pratt, W.C. (1997). Introduction: An American Perspective. *The agrarian revolt in Western Canada: A survey showing American parallels* (pp. ix–xvi). By P.F. Sharp. Regina, SK: Canadian Plains Research Center.

Rak, J. (2005). Introduction. In J. Rak (Ed.), *Auto/biography in Canada: Critical directions* (pp. 1–29). Waterloo, ON: Wilfrid Laurier University Press.

Rennie, B.J. (2000). *The rise of agrarian democracy: The United Farmers and Farm Women of Alberta, 1909–1921.* Toronto, ON: University of Toronto Press.

Rennie, B.J. (2007). "A Far Green Country unto a Swift Sunrise": The utopianism of the Alberta Farm Movement, 1909–1923. In R.D. Francis & C. Kitzan (Eds.), *The prairie west as promised land* (pp. 243–258). Calgary, AB: University of Calgary Press.

Rollison, D. (2010). *A commonwealth of the people: Popular politics and England's long social revolution, 1066–1649.* Cambridge, UK: Cambridge University Press.

Rothblatt, S. (1976). *Tradition and change in English liberal education: An essay in history and culture*. London, UK: Faber and Faber.

Sheppard, Henry Fleetwood. Journals: 1919, 1929–1952. Unpublished. Housed at the Museum of the Highwood, High River, AB. Archival ref: 999.039.023-999.039.034.

Sheppard, Henry Norman. Journals: 1907–1934. Unpublished. Housed at the Museum of the Highwood, High River, AB. Archival ref: 999.039.001 to 999.999.018.

Sheppard, Herbert (Bert). Journals: 1938 to 1942 and 1947. Unpublished. Housed at the Museum of the Highwood, High River, AB. Archival ref: 000.038.003, 000.038.004, 000.038.005.

Sheppard, Herbert (Bert). (1951). The TL Ranch 1887. Unpublished. Housed at the Bert Sheppard Stockman's Foundation Library and Archives, Cochrane, AB.

Sheppard, Herbert (Bert). (1971). *Spitzee Days*. Calgary, AB: Author.

Sheppard, Herbert (Bert). (1977). *Just about nothing: The hardest part of doing nothing is knowing when to quit*. Calgary, AB: Author.

Taylor, C. (1992). The politics of recognition. In A. Gutmann (Ed.), *Multiculturalism and "The Politics of Recognition": An essay by Charles Taylor* (pp. 25–73). Princeton, NJ: Princeton University Press.

Taylor, C. (2004). *Modern social imaginaries*. Durham, NC: Duke University Press.

Thomas, L.G. (1986). *Ranchers' legacy: Alberta essays by Lewis G. Thomas*. Ed. P.A. Dunae. Edmonton, AB: University of Alberta Press.

Thomson, G. (1963). *Crocus and meadowlark country: Recollections of a happy childhood and youth on a homestead in Southern Alberta*. Edmonton, AB: Institute of Applied Art.

Thompson, J.H. (1985). "The Beginning of Our Regeneration": The Great War and Western Canadian reform movements. In R.D. Francis & H. Palmer (Eds.), *The prairie west: Historical readings* (pp. 450–465, 661–662). Edmonton, AB: University of Alberta Press.

Virgil. (1982). *The Georgics*. Trans. L.P. Wilkinson. Markham, ON: Penguin.

Virgil. (2005). *The Georgics of Virgil*. Trans. and intro. by D. Ferry. New York, NY: Farrar, Straus and Giroux.

Wilkinson, L.P. (Ed.). (1982). General introduction. *The Georgics* (pp. 11–54). By Virgil. Markham, ON: Penguin.

Williams, R. (1973). *The country and the city*. New York, NY: Oxford University Press.

Woodsworth, J.S. (1972). *Strangers within Our Gates*. 1909. Intro. by M. Barber. Toronto, ON: University of Toronto Press.

Yates, J. (2007). Humanist habits; Or, "Eating Well" with Thomas More's *Utopia*. In M. Floyd-Wilson & G.A. Sullivan, Jr. (Eds.), *Environment and embodiment in early modern England* (pp. 187–209). Hampshire, UK: Palgrave Macmillan.

FOUR

COWS, MEAT, PEOPLE

The Social Effects of Migrant Meat Processors in Brooks, Alberta

Michael J. Broadway

The City of Brooks in southeast Alberta, a small city of about 14,000 people, is an unlikely magnet for immigrants and refugees from around the world. It has the familiar prairie townscape of automobile dealerships, motels, and fast food restaurants, yet a drive through town reveals African, Asian, and Latino stores catering to the city's newest arrivals. Their presence can be attributed to a single event: the expansion in the late 1990s of Lakeside Farm Industries, a meat-processing plant located five kilometres northwest of Brooks (Broadway, 2013). Lakeside started in 1966 as a feedlot operation. Over the years, the company's owners expanded their operations to include feed grains processing, fertilizer distribution, and hog and poultry production. In 1974, with an investment of capital from the Japanese firm Mitsubishi, Lakeside executives constructed a small beef slaughter plant, Lakeside Packers, across the Trans-Canada Highway from its feedlot. Over the years, Lakeside's owners increased their plant's slaughter capacity until the company was acquired in 1994 by the American meat-processing company IBP, which later became Tyson Foods Inc. (MacLachlan, 2001). The plant's acquisition and subsequent expansion became a catalyst for international immigration that so altered Brooks's demographic composition that it is now known as the "City of 100 Hellos" (Yanchyk, 2010).

The sudden population growth that accompanies the opening of a meat-processing plant in a rural area means that towns are confronted with an array of boomtown issues, including shortages of housing and inadequate social infrastructure to meet newcomers' needs (Broadway, 2000; Stull & Broadway, 2012). For Brooks, the result of Lakeside's expansion was an increase in demands for health care, education, policing, and other social services (Broadway, 2001, 2007). Behind Brooks's metamorphosis lies the "invisible hand" of various provincial and federal policies that have facilitated the meat-processing industry's relocation from large urban centres to small prairie towns and cities including Brandon and Neepawa in Manitoba, and High River in Alberta. At the same time, the meat processors and other industry officials utilized immigration and temporary foreign worker (TFW) regulations to meet an unrelenting demand for labourers. The purpose of this chapter is threefold: to describe how changes in the labour force transform towns with meat-processing plants into multicultural communities; to explain the roles transnational capital and government have played in transforming Brooks; and to illustrate how Lakeside administrators transferred production costs to the town's citizens, who pay for social programs, and to their employees, particularly foreign migrant workers, by exposing them to poor housing and working conditions.

This chapter presents material based mostly on informal interviews I conducted with town officials, residents, Lakeside employees, and local social service providers between July 1995 and November 2013. It is also based on my personal observations during a tour of the plant with its former owner who became plant manager after Tyson took over the company. On my first visit to Lakeside in 1995, the plant employed about 500 workers and the kill floor consisted of mostly Canadian citizens, who appeared to be on a first-name basis with the plant manager. Such familiarity would cease over the next few years with the addition of 2,000 workers and an increase in employee turnover.

Alberta's Cattle Industry

Although cattle accompanied European settlers to the Hudson's Bay Company's Edmonton House in 1833, 50 years passed before cattle grazing became common on the western prairies. In 1881, the Canadian government began leasing land close to the Montana border and, within three years, there were 47 ranches raising cattle in the vicinity of Fort Macleod, Alberta (Horner, 1981). The completion of the Canadian Pacific Railway a few years later enabled ranchers to ship cattle east and west to be slaughtered in urban markets. The era of open-range grazing ended when homesteaders arrived around 1900 and, over the next decade, established 55,000 farms in the province. To lessen farmers' dependency on the grain market during the Great Depression, the Alberta government promoted livestock farming and so began the province's rise to dominance in Canada's cattle industry (Barr & Lehr, 1987). From the 1950s to 2000, the number of cattle in Alberta increased from approximately 2 million to over 5.5 million. At the same time, Alberta's share of Canadian cattle production doubled from 20 per cent to 40 per cent (Alberta Agriculture, Food and Rural Development, 2000).

Until the 1980s, ranchers in the province shipped a portion of their cattle east to be finished and slaughtered in Ontario's meat-processing plants; however, increased competition from lower cost American meat processors led to the closure of these eastern plants. In response, Alberta's ranchers increased their cattle shipments to the United States, taking advantage of a decline in the value of the Canadian dollar, low tariffs, and the Canada–US Free Trade Agreement (Marsh & Young, 1998). Throughout the 1990s, Alberta ranchers exported about 600,000 cattle a year to their southern neighbours (Alberta Agriculture and Rural Development, 2012). From a public policy perspective, these exports represented a lost economic opportunity for the province, since meat processors—had they slaughtered and processed cattle in modern plants—would have created thousands of jobs in Alberta. Thus, provincial policies came to favour the development of large slaughter-capacity plants in Brooks and High River (60 kilometres south of Calgary). By 2010, Alberta meat processors handled about two-thirds of all the cattle slaughtered in Canada, a 43 per cent increase from 20 years earlier (Alberta Agriculture, Food and Rural Development, 2000, 2012).

Transnational Capital and Canadian Meat Processing

During the 1960s and 1970s, American meat processors transformed the industry from one that offered high-wages in a unionized urban environment into one that offered low wages, was non-unionized, and was located in rural areas. Alberta meat processors would eventually replicate such changes. The company most closely associated with the American transformation was IBP (Broadway, 1995). Company owners located their first plant in a cattle-raising area of northwest Iowa. IBP's close proximity to market-ready cattle meant the owners were able to lower their transportation costs and reduce the shrinkage and bruising that occurs when cattle are shipped long distances. IBP managers realized further cost savings by purchasing cattle directly from producers and adopting the Can-Pak system for on-the-rail dressing of carcasses (MacLachlan, 2001, p. 172), which they argued required less skill from their workers and so they paid them lower wages. At the same time, company officials strongly resisted their employees' efforts to unionize. IBP officials also reduced shipping costs when they replaced the practice of shipping whole carcasses to customers to shipping boxed beef, which is meat that is cut into retail-ready portions that are vacuum-packed and shipped in boxes. Lower transport costs meant that IBP's owners could construct large slaughter-capacity plants close to supplies of finished cattle in western Kansas and the Texas Panhandle to maximize economies of scale. Cargill, an American transnational agribusiness firm, entered the beef industry when its owners acquired Missouri Beef Packers in 1979 (renaming it Excel) and replicated IBP's business plan by constructing what was then the world's second largest meat-processing plant in southwest Kansas.

The Canadian meat-processing industry in the mid-1970s was a mirror image of what its American counterpart had been a decade earlier. The industry was urban-based and unionized. In Alberta, slaughterhouses were located in Edmonton, Calgary, and Lethbridge (MacLachlan, 2001). Industry stability had been maintained since the late 1940s when administrators of the major meat-processing companies negotiated a nationwide collective bargaining agreement—the so-called master contract—with union representatives. The union contract yielded standardized wages among meat-processing companies and helped maintain the industry's relatively high standards of pay in comparison with other manufacturing jobs (Forrest, 1989). The master contract remained in place until 1984 when declining domestic meat consumption and increased meat imports from the United States culminated in an industry-wide problem of overcapacity. Meat-processing company owners responded by closing plants and demanding wage concessions. In Calgary, Burns Meat laid off 600 meat-processing workers when they went on strike and refused management's demand for a 40 per cent reduction in the $11.99 hourly base rate. Members of the United

Food and Commercial Workers (UFCW) initiated a strike at Lakeside and company administrators responded by hiring local replacement workers to take the place of striking workers at wages 30 per cent below the union rate, a cut of $3–$3.80 an hour, forcing the de-unionization of the plant. At Gainers meat-packing plant in Edmonton, company executives made a similar effort to replace unionized labourers with cheaper non-unionized workers but were unsuccessful (Noël & Gardner, 1990). Instead, Gainers workers accepted a two-tier pay scale with lower rates for new hires (Forrest, 1989; Noël & Gardner, 1990). To stay competitive, Canadian meat processors, in addition to eliminating the master union agreement and lowering wages, adopted boxed beef, which meant lower shipping costs and also enabled supermarkets to eliminate butchering costs.

In 1987, Cargill owners announced plans to construct Canada's first fully integrated beef slaughter facility at High River. Cargill's location was ideal; it allowed company managers to draw from a large labour pool in nearby Calgary, Alberta's largest city, and supply 80 per cent of the cattle from within a 150-mile radius of the plant (MacLachlan, 2001; Zielinski, 1990). The technologically advanced plant, which opened in 1989, had an initial slaughter capacity of 6,000 cattle a week, making it twice as productive as older plants (Novek, 1992). The absence of a union allowed Cargill owners to pay their 410 production workers $2–$3 an hour less than the industry's union rates (Climenhaga, 1990).

To help defer some of the costs associated with the construction of a waste-water treatment plant, Cargill's owners secured a $4 million provincial government grant. In announcing the grant, Alberta's Minister of Agriculture stated that he hoped that it would lead to the "modernization of the province's most important manufacturing industry" (Cybulski, 1989). Critics warned that adding to the industry's slaughter capacity would only exacerbate the province's overcapacity and lead to more plant closures (Zielinski, 1988), while others charged Cargill's owners with selling beef below its market value as a strategy to force their competitors out of business (Stevenson, 1991). Cargill's High River plant administrators did lower the plant's production costs, which led to the closure of most of the old unionized plants in Edmonton, Calgary, and Lethbridge, leaving Cargill and Lakeside to process most of the province's cattle.

Cargill's owners were not the sole recipients of provincial largesse. In the 1970s, Lakeside owners had received nearly $13 million from Vencap Equities Alberta, a provincial Crown corporation (Sheremata, 1994). The Alberta provincial government later provided a $10 million loan and $6 million grant to help Lakeside owners modernize their plant (Campbell, 1994). In 2003, the Alberta government gave Cargill's owners $9 million and IBP's owners $33 million as compensation for the fall in cattle prices that accompanied an outbreak of bovine spongiform encephalopathy (BSE or "mad cow disease") in the Canadian cattle herd (Alberta Agriculture, Food and Rural Development, n.d.). Between 2009 and 2012, Lakeside owners received an additional $2.2 million in provincial grants to improve productivity, product quality, and the food safety environment (Wingrove, 2012).

Meat Processing, Labour Recruitment, and a Strike

For labourers, working on a meat-processing line is physically intensive. They first stun and kill the 1,200-pound cow on the kill floor, and then hang it from an overhead conveyor system that steadily moves the animal "past stationary workers who stick, bleed, skin, gut and split the steer into a carcass, from stations positioned to maximize their specific task" (Stull & Broadway, 2012, p. 92). After the carcass is refrigerated for 24 hours, the workers then process it. Meat processing requires workers to stand along the production line wielding razor-sharp knives with which they cut the meat into ribs, loins, and rounds. Once the meat is cut, they vacuum-pack the portions to prepare them for shipment to retail stores. Company managers expect workers to quickly master their tasks and repeatedly perform them for sustained periods at high speed. Workers who are unable to do so are typically terminated. Others quit or, suffering injury, are forced to leave.

Workplace injuries are common in meat-processing plants, especially carpal tunnel syndrome, caused by the repetitive motions workers are required to perform while skinning, sawing, gutting, trimming, bagging, boxing, and loading beef products (Gorsche et al., 1999; Personick & Taylor-Shirley, 1989; Stull & Broadway, 2012). In Alberta during the early 2000s, the probability of a meat-processing worker developing a disabling injury or disease was more than double the rate for manufacturing as a whole (Alberta Human Resources and Employment, 2005). A disabling injury is one that prevents the worker from performing some or all of their duties the day after sustaining it. By 2010, there were 12.42 disabling injuries for each 100 person-years worked at a meat-processing plant, which at the time was the highest rate among the manufacturing and processing sectors in the province (Alberta Human Services, 2011). Plant managers organize workers to perform repetitive tasks on quick-moving production lines. Workers must either become "hardened" to this type of work or quit. In a new processing plant, employee turnover often exceeds 200 per cent *per year*. Over time, turnover typically declines to 6 to 8 per cent *per month*, which reflects the development of a workforce comprising workers who are willing and able to withstand the rigors of production (Stull & Broadway, 2012).

In 1996, as Lakeside owners expanded their company's capacity with a boxed beef plant and additional fabrication and rendering facility, plant managers struggled to meet their ongoing need for new workers. Company officials openly wondered where they would obtain the 600 employees necessary to staff the facility and where these employees would live. Lakeside's official policy was to increase its recruitment of men and women from the Brooks area (Burgess, 1996). Expecting outside recruits to live in Brooks proved unrealistic since rental vacancies were almost non-existent and lots sold at prices comparable to Calgary (Sillars, 1995). As a result, by 1999 nearly half the plant's employees lived in Medicine Hat, an hour's drive southeast of Brooks on the Trans-Canada Highway. Others found housing in surrounding villages and hamlets. As a temporary solution, Lakeside executives erected several dormitory-style trailers at the plant and surrounded the area with a chain link and barbed wire fence. They did not provide kitchen facilities; rather, they assumed that the 162 single workers who lived there would eat in the plant's cafeteria. To discourage long-term residency in the dorms, they charged workers for meals and increased the dormitory's rental fees the longer an employee resided there. These costs, plus charges for required equipment such as rubber- or steel-toed boots, made it difficult for Lakeside employees to save money to place a rental deposit on other accommodations. After a decade, Lakeside managers demolished the trailers due to mould problems. Brooks developers built an additional 410 single-family homes between 2004 and 2006, which helped solve the city's housing shortage; nonetheless, in 2012, 200 workers continued to live in Medicine Hat (Pye-Matheson, 2013).

High employee turnover and low pay undermined Lakeside owners' ability to fulfill their staffing needs with locally available labour and so company officials adopted a strategy perfected by American meat processors: they began targeting immigrants. Unlike American meat processors, who brought workers from Mexico and Central America, Lakeside administrators recruited recent African immigrants. According to several informants, the possibility of employment at Lakeside was well-known among refugees in Kakuma, a northeast Kenyan refugee camp that is home for over 100,000 persons fleeing civil unrest in the horn of Africa. Recruiters showed videos translated into Arabic and other languages to potential recruits at Calgary's Catholic Immigration Society. Lakeside officials paid employees $1,000 bonuses for encouraging friends and family members to join the company, provided that they stayed beyond a minimum period (Lakeside, n.d.). In the fall of 1998, Lakeside officials provided on-site space for Medicine Hat's Saamis Immigration Service to provide employees with assistance in filling out immigration forms and to help deal with family reunification. By 2002, due to increased demand to address newcomer needs, Brooks sought assistance from the non-profit Global Friendship Immigration Centre. Funding for the centre's immigrant and refugee services was provided through contracts with the federal government. The effect of Lakeside's recruitment strategy was dramatic. By 2006, immigrants and refugees made up 60 per cent of Lakeside's workforce and an even higher percentage among its line workers (Altwasser, 2006).

Lakeside's managers were able to meet their labour supply challenge; however, they could not have predicted the pivotal role that their immigrant workers would play in a strike. In 2004, the UFCW regained its certification to represent Lakeside's workers. A year later, the union attempted to negotiate their first contract. Workers struck the plant on October 12, 2005, after company officials rejected a provincially appointed mediator's proposed settlement. The strike revealed deep divisions within the plant's workforce. Most union members who supported the strike were immigrant and refugee line workers. Those who opposed the strike formed a group called Concerned Lakeside Employees for Everyone's Rights, which submitted an ultimately unsuccessful petition signed by 877 workers to have the union decertified by the provincial Labour Relations Board (Crnogorac, 2005). For three weeks, plant managers attempted to continue operations, albeit at a reduced capacity, while picketers did everything they could to prevent workers from entering the plant. Despite the presence of police officers, several violent confrontations occurred between workers who wanted to cross the picket line and strikers. In response Lakeside owners filed an injunction to restrict picketing.

The strike at Lakeside was eventually settled, but relations were strained between workers who struck the plant and those who crossed the picket line. In an interview, Frank McDoul, a worker who crossed the picket line, remarked:

> We've taken abuse, physical, verbal. People have had property damage, lives threatened. And what? They expect [us] to walk in there and... shake their hands and work alongside them? Not a chance. [If the strikers] want a war, they can come into the factory, they'll get a war. (qtd. in Canadian Broadcasting Corporation, 2005)

In a news release published less than a year after the strike's conclusion, Lakeside officials announced that in order to staff the plant, they intended to bring in 250 temporary foreign workers from China, the Philippines, El Salvador, and Ukraine, because such workers, they reasoned, were "'accustomed to physical labour'" (qtd. in *National Post*, 2006, p. WK5). Local community members interpreted this change in recruitment strategy as retaliation against the African workers who had supported the strike. Within two years, Lakeside recruited and hired more than 700 new employees with the newest hires arriving from Mexico, Colombia, and the Philippines. Whether meat processors were able to resolve their endemic labour supply problem by hiring temporary foreign workers remained to be seen.

Meat Processing and Temporary Foreign Workers

Temporary foreign workers are integral to Lakeside's operations and are part of a broader structural change in Alberta's labour market. In 2006, the number of TFWs arriving in the province began to eclipse the number of permanent immigrants (Cundal & Seaman, 2012). By 2011, there were 58,228 temporary foreign workers in Alberta (Barnetson & Foster, 2014). This trend in employment reflects a broader shift in Canadian immigration policy away from granting permanent status to immigrants and toward bringing in guest workers as members of a temporary workforce (Hennebry, 2010). Much of Alberta's demand for temporary foreign workers comes from its energy sector. Elsewhere, employers claim that increased job opportunities have resulted in labour shortages throughout the province, including the service industry. This claim is, however, contested (Barnetson & Foster, 2014; Gross, 2014).

In light of high employee turnover in the meat-processing industry, a principal concern regarding the hiring of temporary foreign workers is the lack of job mobility associated with the work permit. If meat-processing workers wish to change jobs, they must apply for a change of conditions on their permits and, at the same time, find an employer who has or is willing to apply for a labour market opinion from the federal government permitting the employer to hire a TFW. To obtain a favourable labour market opinion, the federal government requires employers to verify that the foreign worker fills a labour shortage. Employers must also provide proof that they have advertised the job for a minimum of 14 days on the national Job Bank and that the wages for such jobs are commensurate with what Canadians or permanent immigrants are earning for similar work. Such requirements pose obstacles for temporary foreign workers who wish to leave their jobs, no matter how unpleasant or unsafe those jobs might be. Indeed, Preibisch and Hennebry (2011) indicate that migrant workers are more likely than local workers to work when ill or injured, because they fear they may lose their job if they are absent. Moreover, temporary foreign workers' future employment is dependent upon their relationship with their current employer, which might deter them from lodging complaints about working conditions. Thus, Foster and Taylor (2013) maintain that the rules governing TFWs place workers in potentially vulnerable positions with their employers, which makes "it more difficult for them to access their statutory employment rights" (p. 170). Fudge (2012) provides evidence that foreign workers are more likely to experience violations of those rights. By hiring temporary foreign workers, employers reduce recruiting costs, obtain a docile workforce, and decrease worker attrition.

United Food and Commercial Workers officials argue that Lakeside administrators' preference for hiring TFWs is demonstrated in company policies. Among these policies is a mandatory three-month waiting period for local residents to reapply for positions if they fail their interviews or if they leave jobs at the plant. In fall 2013, social service providers noticed an increase in the number of local workers dismissed by company managers prior to the completion of their 12-week probationary period. Company policies thus deter Canadian residents from working at Lakeside, which, in turn, provides company officials with evidence of labour shortages, evidence they need to secure favourable labour market opinions from the federal government. In fall 2013, Lakeside owners notified social service providers that they should expect to see an increase in the numbers of Filipino and Mexican temporary foreign workers at the plant in early 2014.

Some temporary foreign workers are eligible to apply for permanent residency through the employer-sponsored Provincial Nominee Program (PNP), which is designed to attract immigrants to smaller cities and rural areas where labour shortages exist. Each province can determine its application criteria. The Manitoba government has various recruitment "streams" under its PNP. In Brandon, Maple Leaf Foods managers use the "employer direct" stream to recruit workers for its meat-processing facility. Company administrators encourage worker integration by allowing those admitted under the program to apply for permanent residency within six months of their arrival (Carter, 2012). In contrast, temporary foreign workers in Alberta meat-processing plants have to wait two years to become eligible to apply for permanent residency. The UFCW union has successfully negotiated contracts in Manitoba and Alberta that require meat-processing firms to assist workers in their permanent residency application. If workers fail to meet residency eligibility requirements, such as a certain level of fluency in English, the company must then help them meet the requirements (Carter, 2012; Hildebrandt, 2014).

Once former temporary foreign workers achieve permanent residency, they can sponsor other family members to come to Canada. Family reunification brings its own set of practical and emotional challenges. Couples who have been apart for several years may find themselves confronted with different behavioural expectations, which can sometimes erupt into domestic violence. The RCMP detachment in Brooks formed a special task force to deal with this problem, while local agencies like Support Prevent Educate Counsel (SPEC) provide support services to young parents and their children. SPEC newcomer family liaisons are contracted to serve 200 families a year, but most liaisons serve twice as many due to the continued process of family reunification. Housing, child-care, and schooling needs for temporary foreign workers also change, which impacts the local community. For example, in autumn 2012, the number of students attending Catholic schools in Brooks increased 30 per cent from the previous year, while the comparable figure for the public schools was 7 per cent. Many immigrant students require instruction in English as a second language, which creates a staffing challenge for local schools. Much of the student growth has been in the lower grades, and although the school board approved the construction of a new public elementary school in 2011, members feared a continuing space crunch (Stanway, 2011).

Governments Working Together

In 2008, Tyson's owners announced that the Lakeside plant no longer fit into their long-term international business plan and sold the company to XL Foods, a subsidiary of Edmonton-based Nilsson Brothers, a privately held cattle-trading and auction house. Tyson executives attributed the decision to sell to a steady rise in the value of the Canadian dollar against the US currency, which made American exports less profitable than in the past, and to Lakeside's higher operating costs in comparison with other plants (Tait, 2008). Nilsson had little experience in managing a large beef-processing plant, so some industry observers were not surprised when the Canadian Food Inspection Agency shut Lakeside down in the fall of 2012 following an outbreak of *E. coli* bacteria (Warnica, 2012).

On September 27, 2012, with the American border closed to Lakeside's exports, the company laid off 200 probationary workers and released the remaining 2,000 workers two weeks later. The plant closure produced an immediate crisis for Brooks as Lakeside workers, who often lived from paycheque to paycheque, faced a sudden income loss. During the shutdown, JBS USA, a subsidiary of the Brazilian-based world's largest beef processor, agreed to take over Lakeside's operations and purchased it along with several of Nilsson's small plants (Klinkenburg, 2013). Estimating the loss of income arising from the shutdown at about $250,000 a day, Brooks city officials feared that the impact would reverberate throughout the community as people left to seek work elsewhere (Gerson, 2012). When the plant reopened on November 1, 2012, Lakeside management estimated that about 10 per cent of employees failed to return (Dumont, 2012).

Federal, provincial, and local service providers responded to Lakeside's shutdown by expediting the Employment Insurance (EI) application process and providing applicants with support services in English, Swahili, Spanish, Dinka, Arabic, Amharic, and the May and Mahateri dialects of Somali (Pye-Matheson, 2013). Brooks city officials formed a Community Response Committee to identify the needs of Lakeside workers and distributed flyers throughout the community in eight different languages to provide laid-off workers with information about where they could go for assistance. About 200 temporary foreign workers who had not completed their 3-month probationary period with Lakeside were ineligible for EI payments; thus, city officials focused attention on them and provided rent, clothing, and food assistance. Together JBS USA, the UFCW Local 401, the City of Brooks, the Community Foundation of Southeastern Alberta, the Canadian Red Cross, and the United Way donated almost $200,000 in cash. Most donations went to the Food Bank. Yet, even after the plant reopened, workers needed housing and utility assistance because the plant's reduced operating hours meant a continued loss of income. Normal production at the plant resumed in mid-December 2012 after the US Food Inspection Agency re-authorized Lakeside's beef exports to the United States. One of the outcomes of the crisis was that local residents acquired a greater appreciation of the meat-processing plant's importance to the community's economic well-being; another outcome was that residents became aware of the "willingness of government and all sectors to work together for the greater good" (Anon. Brooks resident qtd. in Pye-Matheson, 2013, p. 4).

Conclusions

The terms *cattle* and *meatpacking* have been synonymous in Alberta for over a hundred years. Part of this heritage has been celebrated annually at the Calgary Stampede since 1912, an event to which visitors flock to watch cowboys race chuck wagons and participate in rodeos. Yet, behind the mythical image of lone cowboys riding the range is significant government intervention. The provincial government supports the beef industry in the form of direct investment, grants, loans, and special one-time payments, reasoning that if cattle were to be shipped from Alberta to be slaughtered in the United States, the province would lose an opportunity to add value to the resource and create jobs.

At the federal level, low tariffs and free trade agreements with the United States have led to the closure of older urban plants and the opening of new plants in rural Alberta. These agreements have resulted in the adoption of American-style meat-processing models designed to maximize profit. The federal government's Temporary Foreign Worker Program allows owners of meat-processing plants to solve the industry problem of high employee turnover. Having workers tied to a work permit that restricts them to an employer provides company administrators with a measure of labour force stability and docility because temporary foreign workers are less likely than Canadian citizens to quit or complain about unpleasant or unsafe working conditions. In this way, meat processors externalize production costs by shifting them onto workers in the form of poor working conditions and high risk of workplace injuries.

While temporary foreign workers can apply for permanent residency through the Provincial Nominee Program, as Jill Bucklaschuk reveals in Chapter 5, the requirement for employer support means a two-step immigration process, which, while eventually allowing temporary foreign workers full labour mobility rights, gives employers in the interim yet another form of leverage over them. Employers' incentive to participate in the Provincial Nominee Program may be limited in the meat-processing industry because, once workers have attained permanent residency, they are free to leave their employment. This incentive has not stopped the United Food and Commercial Workers union, however, from successfully negotiating a clause that requires meat-processing company officials to help their temporary foreign workers apply for permanent residency. Through such actions, the union has been able to secure residency rights and a path to citizenship for migrants in programs designed precisely to avoid permanent immigration.

The City of Brooks and its social service providers are left to deal with the human consequences of the meat-processing industry's insatiable demand for labour. While heightened local employment increases tax revenue and reverses rural decline, Lakeside's reliance on immigrant and refugee workers in the past and on temporary foreign workers in the present has created significant social challenges around housing, schooling, and settlement issues. If Alberta were to adopt Manitoba's 6-month eligibility requirement for TFWs to apply for permanent residency, it might help assuage some family reunification issues in Brooks. Instead, provincial grants by the Alberta government and Canadian immigration policies have been significant contributors to the cause and maintenance of the social problems incurred as a result of meat processors' hiring of temporary foreign workers. As this chapter has sought to reveal, Lakeside's owners externalize the social costs of operating their plant onto the community and will continue to do so until such time as the company managers change their business model to one that reduces the rate of employee turnover.

Whether Lakeside owners are willing to change their business and operating procedures is doubtful, because their goal is profit, and in the highly competitive North American beef-processing sector, the most profit goes to those with the lowest production costs. The only reason company owners and administrators in the meat-processing industry will change is if the Alberta government increases the stringency of worker health and safety regulations, or if consumers demand changes in the ways industry employers treat their workers. Neither scenario seems likely at this time. Indeed, evidence suggests that competitive pressures are increasing. Overall Canadian per-capita beef consumption has dropped by nearly a third, from 39.86 kg in 1981 to 27.06 kg in 2013 (Agriculture and Agri-Food Canada, n.d.). Falling domestic demand and limited growth in beef exports in the aftermath of the 2003 BSE crisis means that keeping production costs as low as possible will remain an industry imperative.

In 2000 I published an article, "Planning for change in small towns or trying to avoid the slaughterhouse blues," which discusses the City of Brooks's early efforts to deal with Lakeside's expansion. In my conclusion, I note that "the reality is the Blues cannot be avoided. They can, however, be ameliorated to some degree by a combination of enlightened institutional and individual responses to social change" (Broadway, 2000, p. 45). Over a decade and a half later, that conclusion is still valid; problems in the meat-processing industry continue to impact its workforce and the community. The City of Brooks has formally embraced its new-found diversity with the adoption of its unofficial motto, "City of 100 Hellos," while government funded social service providers and the non-profit sector continue to adapt to the changing demands of Lakeside's workforce and their family members. Amelioration remains the watchword until the plant closes and a new set of challenges arises.

References

Agriculture and Agri-Food Canada. (n.d.). Per-Capita consumption. Retrieved July 2, 2015 from http://www.agr.gc.ca/eng/industry-markets-and-trade/statistics-and-market-information/by-product-sector/poultry-and-eggs/poultry-and-egg-market-information-canadian-industry/industry-indicators/per-capita-consumption/?id=1384971854413

Alberta Agriculture and Rural Development. (2012). *Agriculture statistics yearbook 2011.* Edmonton, AB: Author.

Alberta Agriculture, Food and Rural Development. (2000). *Agriculture statistics yearbook.* Edmonton, AB: Author.

Alberta Agriculture, Food and Rural Development. (n.d.). BSE compensation program payments from June 25, 2003 to June 04, 2004. Edmonton, AB: Author.

Alberta Human Resources and Employment. (2005). *Occupational injuries and diseases in Alberta: Manufacturing, processing and packaging industries 2000 to 2004.* Edmonton, AB: Author.

Alberta Human Services. (2011). *Occupational injuries and diseases in Alberta: Manufacturing, processing and packaging sector 2006 to 2010.* Edmonton, AB: Author.

Altwasser, B. (2006, Jan. 19). *Tyson's crystal ball.* Paper presented at the Tiffin Conference, Canada's Evolving Red Meat Market, Lethbridge, AB.

Barnetson, B., & Foster, J. (2014). The political justification of employment-related geographic mobility in Alberta, Canada. *Journal of International Migration and Integration, 15,* 349–370.

Barr, B.M., & Lehr, J. (1987). The western interior: The transformation of a hinterland region. In L.D. McCann (Ed.), *Heartland and hinterland: A geography of Canada* (2nd ed.; pp. 286–349). Scarborough, ON: Prentice Hall.

Broadway, M. (1995). From city to countryside: Recent changes in the structure and location of the meat and fish-processing industry. In D. Stull, M. Broadway, & D. Griffith (Eds.), *Any way you cut it: Meat processing and small-town America* (pp. 17–40). Lawrence, KS: University Press of Kansas.

Broadway, M. (2000). Planning for change in small towns or trying to avoid the slaughterhouse blues. *Journal of Rural Studies, 16*(1), 37–46.

Broadway, M. (2001). Bad to the bone: Beef processing and social change in rural Alberta. In R. Epp and D. Whitson (Eds.), *Writing off the rural west: Globalization, governments, and the transformation of rural communities* (pp. 39–52). Edmonton, AB: University of Alberta Press.

Broadway, M. (2007). Meatpacking and the transformation of rural communities: A comparison of Brooks, Alberta and Garden City, Kansas. *Rural Sociology, 72*(4), 560–582.

Broadway, M. (2013). The world "meats" Canada: Meatpacking's role in the cultural transformation of Brooks, Alberta. *Focus on geography, 56*(2), 47–53.

Burgess, K. (1996, April 10). Construction at packing plant nearly complete. *Brooks Bulletin*, p. 1.

Canadian Broadcasting Corporation (2005). Lakeside employees start returning to work. Retrieved Oct. 29, 2013 from http://www.cbc.ca/news/canada/edmonton/lakeside-employees-start-returning-to-work-1.520705

Campbell, D. (1994, Sept. 16). US giant to swallow beef firm. *Calgary Herald*, p. A1.

Carter, T. (2012). Provincial nominee programs and temporary worker programs: A comparative assessment of advantages and disadvantages in addressing labour shortages. In P. Lenard & C. Straehle (Eds.), *Legislated inequality: Temporary labour migration in Canada* (pp. 178–201). Montreal, QC: McGilll-Queen's University Press.

Climenhaga, D. (1990, Jan. 9). Cargill dismisses claims of low pay. *Calgary Herald*, p. C1.

Crnogorac, P. (2005, Oct. 14). The new laws. *Medicine Hat News*, p. A1.

Cundal, K., & Seaman, B. (2012). Canada's temporary foreign worker programme: A discussion of human rights issues. *Migration Letters, 9*(3), 201–214.

Cybulski, H. (1989, Mar. 26). Alberta's goal to keep beef business here. *Calgary Herald*, p. F1.

Dumont, M. (2012, Nov. 4). Possibly 200 workers lost. *Brooks and County Chronicle*, p. A7.

Foster, J., & Taylor, A. (2013). In the shadows: Exploring the notion of "community" for temporary foreign workers in a boomtown. *Canadian Journal of Sociology, 38*(2), 167–190.

Forrest, A. (1989). The rise and fall of national bargaining in the Canadian meat-packing industry. *Relations industrielles, 44*(2), 393–408.

Fudge, J. (2012). Precarious migrant status and precarious employment: The paradox of international rights for migrant workers. *Comparative Labor Law & Policy Journal, 34*(1), 95–132.

Gerson, J. (2012, Oct. 20). "I don't have any place to go"; The plant shutdown that closed a prairie town. *National Post*, n.p.

Gorsche, R.G., Wiley, J.P., Renger, R.F., Brant, R.F., Gemer, T.Y., & Sasyniuk, T.M. (1999). Prevalence and incidence of carpal tunnel syndrome in a meat packing plant. *Occupational & Environmental Medicine, 56*(6), 417–422.

Gross, D. (2014). Temporary foreign workers in Canada: Are they really filling labour shortages? Commentary No. 407. Toronto, ON: C.D. Howe Institute.

Hennebry, J. (2010). Who has their eye on the ball? "Jurisdictional fútbol" and Canada's Temporary Foreign Worker Program. *Policy Options*, July/August, 62–67.

Hildebrandt, A. (2014). How a little Alberta union helps temporary foreign workers become Canadian. Retrieved Oct. 18, 2014 from http://www.cbc.ca/news/canada/how-a-little-alberta-union-helps-temporary-foreign-workers-become-canadian-1.2629710

Horner, H. (1981). *A review of the meat industry in Alberta*. Edmonton, AB: Alberta Economic Development.

Klinkenburg, M. (2013, Jan. 10). JBS set to take over XL's Lakeside plant. *Edmonton Journal*, p. D3.

Lakeside. (n.d.). *100 Jobs*. Brooks, AB: Lakeside Packers.

MacLachlan, I. (2001). *Kill and chill: Restructuring Canada's beef commodity chain.* Toronto, ON: University of Toronto Press.

Marsh, J., & Young, L. (1998). Integration and interdependence in the US and Canadian live cattle and beef sectors. *American Review of Canadian Studies, 28*(3), 335–354.

National Post. (2006, Aug. 30). Slaughterhouse's search for workers goes global after shortage hits production, wk 5.

Noël, A., & Gardner, K. (1990). The Gainers strike: Capitalist offensive, militancy, and the politics of industrial relations in Canada. *Studies in Political Economy, 31*(Spring), 31–72.

Novek, J. (1992). The labour process and workplace injuries in the Canadian meat packing industry. *Canadian Review of Sociology and Anthropology, 29*(1), 17–37.

Personick, M.E., & Taylor-Shirley, K. (1989). Profiles in safety and health: Occupational hazards of meatpacking. *Monthly Labor Review, 112*(1), 3–9.

Preibisch, K., & Hennebry, J. (2011). Temporary migration, chronic effects: The health of international migrant workers in Canada. *Canadian Medical Association Journal, 183*(9), 1033–1038.

Pye-Matheson, L. (2013). *XL Foods Community Response Committee Final Report*. Brooks, AB: Grasslands Regional Family and Community Support Services.

Sheremata, D. (1994, Oct. 24). A beef packing giant looks north. *Western Report*, p. 20.

Sillars, L. (1995, Aug. 21). Oil, water and cash flowing in Brooks. *Alberta Report*, p. 17.

Stanway, S. (2011, Oct. 18). Brooks will have three K-6 grades by 2014. *Brooks Bulletin*, p. A3.

Stevenson, M. (1991, May 13). Playing rough in a tough business. *Alberta Report*, p. 21.

Stull, D., & Broadway, M. (2012). *Slaughterhouse blues: The meat and poultry industry in North America* (2nd ed.). Belmont, CA: Cengage.

Tait, C. (2008, April 29). Tyson blames Alberta for woes; US$5M loss in Q2; Labour shortage hits earnings, beef giant says. *National Post*, p. F5.

Warnica, R. (2012). What little we knew. *Canadian Business, 85*(18), 19–20.

Wingrove, J. (2012, Oct. 6). Life on the kill floor is fraught with peril. *Globe and Mail*, p. A4.

Yanchyk, B. (2010). *Brooks—the city of 100 hellos*. Edmonton, AB: Brandy Y.
Zielinski, A. (1988). Alta packers to compete with Cargill. *Food in Canada, 48*(4), 29–33.
Zielinski, A. (1990). Cargill turns meat packing into a science. *Food in Canada, 50*(3), 14–15.

FIVE

A TEMPORARY PROGRAM FOR PERMANENT GAINS?

Considering the Workplace Experiences of Temporary Foreign Workers in Manitoba's Hog-Processing Industry

Jill Bucklaschuk

In Canada, agricultural labour is often dangerous, physically intensive, and seasonal work and, because many labourers lack union representation, the wages are low. For these reasons, most Canadian citizens avoid these jobs. Consequently, employers have turned to immigrant and migrant workers to staff their operations. Indeed, for decades, foreign workers have been the main source of seasonal labour in agriculture (Basok, 1999, 2002; Hennebry, 2009; Preibisch, 2007, 2010; Satzewich, 1991). Since 1966, employers in Canada's primary agriculture sector have accessed migrant workers through the Seasonal Agricultural Worker Program (Government of Canada, Employment, 2013). Similarly, since 2002, employers in Canada's meat-processing industry have utilized the Temporary Foreign Worker Program (TFWP) through a stream that facilitates their employment of low-skilled labourers. The Stream for Lower Skilled Occupations (SLSO) grew exponentially and became one of the largest sources of migrant labour in Canada, with 20,636 individual entries in 2012.[1] Today, temporary migration has outpaced permanent immigration and has become an integral component of economic development and labour market growth in Canada (Government of Canada, Citizenship, 2013).

While there is significant research about employment practices in the meat-processing industry (Champlin & Hake, 2006; Charlebois & Summan, 2014; Stanley, 1992; Stull & Broadway, 2004), there is little written about the experiences of temporary foreign workers. Such individuals migrate to Canada from countries of the Global South and take up temporary jobs that are demanding and often dangerous. They do so, in large part, to support their families, who remain behind for the duration of the 2-year work permits. This chapter, which expands on research on seasonal agriculture workers and live-in caregivers (Basok, 2002; Hennebry, 2009; Pratt, 2012; Preibisch & Hennebry, 2011; Preibisch & Otero, 2014; Stasiulis & Bakan, 2005;), examines the daily physical, mental, and emotional challenges that temporary foreign workers experience in the meat-processing industry and brings attention to their vulnerability as non-citizen labourers.

Temporary foreign workers' experiences in Canada are characterized by unequal access to material and non-material resources and limited power (Basok, 2004; Goldring & Landolt, 2011; Preibisch & Otero, 2014). Such workers are restricted from accessing social supports extended to permanent immigrants and are unable to freely change their employment situations even if their workplace experiences become unbearable or overly burdensome. Nandita Sharma (2006, 2012) argues that temporary foreign workers constitute an "unfree" labour force, because they "*cannot*, for the most part, leave their employment and seek alternative employment without the written permission of the Canadian state as represented by an immigration officer" (2012, p. 36; original emphasis). Nor can workers who arrive through the Stream for Lower Skilled Occupations program become permanent residents in Canada unless they are eligible to apply to a Provincial Nominee Program (PNP). This two-step immigration hinges on sponsorship from an employer and requires a probationary "trial" period during which employers assess whether temporary foreign workers are worthy of continued employment and permanent residency (Hawthorne, 2010; Hennebry, 2012). Thus, workers' dependence on employers to mediate much of their current and future existence in Canada contributes to their vulnerability, exacerbates inequalities, and decreases their autonomy (Preibisch & Otero, 2014; Torres, Spitzer, Hughes, Oxman-Martinez, & Hanley, 2012).

This chapter also examines the factors that motivate temporary foreign workers to migrate to Canada and expounds on their community and workplace experiences. It is based on qualitative interviews conducted between January and June 2013 with current and former temporary foreign workers (18 men, 8 women) in two rural Manitoba hog-processing facilities. Participants were identified by key informants in the immigrant service sector and, subsequently, by snowball sampling (interviewee referrals). Interview transcripts were coded for recurring themes and subthemes with the intention of grouping stories into a nuanced and rich account of migration experiences. All data not otherwise cited comes from these interviews. Twenty-five of the participants arrived in Manitoba through the Stream for Lower Skilled Occupations program to work in the hog-processing industry. Fifteen participants held temporary work permits at the time of the interview, 10 participants were permanent residents, and one had received Canadian citizenship. Most interviewees came from Latin American countries or the Philippines, which reflects the concentration of source countries from which employers in the meat-processing industry recruit. Some of the interviewees had been in Manitoba for only three months, while others had resided for 11 years. Only six of the 26 participants had prior experience in meat processing before arriving in Canada.

An important focus of this study is how temporary foreign workers' option to seek permanent residency through the Provincial Nominee Program in Manitoba affects their workplace experiences, including their manner of coping with workplace injuries and pain in a context in which employment mobility is restricted and employers decide whether they stay or leave. Helly, Depatie-Pelletier, and Gibson (2014), Hennebry (2012), Nakache and D'Aoust (2012), and Tilson (2009) argue that the permanent residency option could be a solution to the plight of lower skilled temporary foreign workers since they would then have the right to permanently settle in Canada. This right might reduce the precariousness and vulnerability that non-citizens face (Basok, 2004; Goldring, 2010; Goldring & Landolt, 2011; Preibisch & Hennebry, 2011; Sharma, 2001). The option of permanent residency for temporary foreign workers has been available in Manitoba for over a decade. Indeed, recent statistics indicate that since 2006 nearly 6,000 temporary foreign workers have become permanent residents (Government of Manitoba, 2015). The two-step immigration process, however, problematizes the manner in which migrant workers negotiate their workplace experiences if they wish to settle permanently with their families in Manitoba.

The Meat-Processing Industry and Foreign Workers in Manitoba

Employers in the North American meat-processing industry began restructuring their operations in the late 1960s and early 1970s, when they moved production facilities away from larger urban areas into rural regions. Locating their plants closer to cattle-producing regions allowed these operators to reduce animal transportation costs. Moreover, by hiring non-unionized workers, they reduced their labour costs as well. As conveyor-operated carcass disassembly lines became the norm, plants decreased in number and increased in size (Novek, 1992). High employee turnover and small rural labour pools, however, meant that employers had difficulty recruiting adequate numbers of workers. In the 1970s, officials in American meat-processing plants solved their employment problems by hiring both legal and illegal immigrants, workers who were predominately Latin Americans (Parrado & Kandel, 2008). These employees settled in communities that were not considered to be traditional immigrant destinations (Dalla & Christensen, 2005; Stanley, 1992; Stull & Broadway, 2004). Canadian meat processors did not have access to a large and ready supply of immigrant workers, especially in rural regions, because federal immigration policy prioritizes highly skilled immigrants who typically settle in urban regions (Broadway, 2007). However, as Michael Broadway (2013) remarks, some Canadian meat-processing companies did access immigrant and refugee workers who were already in Canada prior to the availability of temporary foreign workers (see also Novek, 1992; Charlebois & Summan, 2014).

Since the late 1980s, restructuring of the hog-processing industry in Manitoba has resulted in the closure and relocation of several plants as well as an increase in capacity of two slaughter-processing plants and one ham-processing plant (Honey, 2014). The larger of the two plants has the capacity to process 4.5 million hogs yearly by operating two shifts and employing over 2,300 workers. This plant is located in the small city of Brandon, an agricultural centre for its surrounding rural communities. Brandon's population in 2011 was 46,061 residents (Statistics Canada, 2012). The second facility has the capacity to process 1.4 million hogs per annum and requires about 900 workers for its operation (Honey, 2014). It is located in a rural town with approximately 3,000 residents; thus, I identify this small community as Prairieville as a means to preserve the anonymity of the temporary foreign workers I interviewed. The administrators of each of these companies found difficulty in securing enough local workers to run their operations, a problem common throughout the meat-processing industry. Indeed, upon opening in 1999, the Brandon facility experienced unsustainable employee turnover rates. Company officials raised wages and widened recruitment to include the Atlantic Provinces, but still struggled to find adequate numbers of employees in Canada.

In 2001, the managers of the Brandon plant considered hiring temporary foreign workers through the TFWP's lower skilled stream (Bird, 2001; Bucklaschuk, Moss, & Annis, 2009). The SLSO program, which was in its infancy at the time, represented a new mechanism for Canadian employers needing to expediently hire labour in occupations that required a minimum skill level associated with a high school diploma or on-the-job training. Under the SLSO program, the Brandon company officials initiated recruitment in Mexico, and the first group arrived in early 2002. They have since hired temporary foreign workers from China, Colombia, El Salvador, Honduras, Mauritius, and Ukraine. After the Prairieville plant managers witnessed the relative success of the company in Brandon, they also began using the Stream for Lower Skilled Occupations program to satisfy their need for workers. In addition to changing their recruiting practices, officials of both companies adjusted their workplace practices to address the needs of employees who were almost entirely foreign-born and had not yet acquired fluency in English. Company managers offered language interpretation for their training and orientation sessions, and provided workplace documents in multiple languages. The United Food and Commercial Workers Canada (UFCW) union, which represents workers at both companies, has assumed a central role in providing services to temporary foreign workers. Union officials had the UFCW's collective agreement translated into multiple languages and began offering services to members in multiple languages. The union also provides English-language training classes to temporary foreign workers and ensures that both the Brandon and Prairieville companies participate in Manitoba's Provincial Nominee Program.

The unprecedented growth in diversity and population resulting from the arrival of temporary foreign workers fundamentally changed the demographic characteristics of the communities in which the plants are located (Bucklaschuk, Moss, & Annis, 2009; Moss, Bucklaschuk, & Annis, 2010). Prior to the arrival of temporary foreign workers, the communities had low annual immigration levels. In 2001, Brandon received only 69 immigrants. Yet, a decade later, that number multiplied twenty fold. Prairieville's immigration rates were not even large enough to report until 2010, when it received nearly 200 immigrants. In 2012, Prairieville ranked high on a list of Manitoba's top immigrant destinations (Government of Manitoba, 2013). The population growth in both communities put pressure on social services, housing availability, and the education system. For example, beginning in 2005, the Brandon School Division saw an exponential increase in the enrolment of students requiring courses in English as an Additional Language and had to hire more teachers and expand physical space to accommodate them (Moss, Bucklashuk & Annis, 2010). To cope with increasing demands on Brandon's infrastructure and to develop adequate social support services for the incoming immigrant population, city officials initiated early collaborative and community-wide information sharing. They endeavoured to encourage communication among multiple sectors, including employers, service providers, and policy makers. By creating innovative community-based services, such as language co-operatives for translation and interpretation services, city officials have enabled service providers to prepare for population changes and cope with some of the challenges posed by a growing and diverse population (Bucklaschuk & Moss, 2008; S. Trudel, personal communication, Nov. 29, 2012).

The increase in immigration levels in both communities is largely a result of the permanent settlement of temporary foreign workers through the Provincial Nominee Program. Interviewees indicate that many workers in the hog-processing industry come to Manitoba with the intention of staying permanently. Such intention is often shaped by employers' suggestions of potential permanent residency during recruiting campaigns and job interviews in source countries. Approximately 80 per cent of temporary foreign workers who apply to the PNP are successful (Government of Manitoba, 2015). Once they obtain permanent residency, they frequently initiate the process of moving their families to Manitoba. While, initially, temporary foreign workers seek work in Canada and other countries because of limited employment opportunities, low wages, and unstable work conditions at home, the possibility of permanent residency extends to them the chance to establish desirable lifestyles for themselves and their families. Thus, in Manitoba, the Stream for Lower Skilled Occupations program is both an immigration pathway for foreign workers and a viable labour solution for employers.

In general, when meat producers recruit workers through the SLSO program, they are able to reduce their employee turnover, since the conditions of work permits restrict temporary foreign workers' mobility. Moreover, because the government issues work permits for specified periods, worker turnover becomes increasingly predictable for employers. Within the context of Manitoba, the opportunity for operators in the hog-processing industry to assist in "converting" temporary foreign workers to permanent residents through the PNP offers a potential long-term solution to labour demands. In fact, out of the 10 former temporary foreign workers interviewed for the study, only three workers left the hog-processing industry for other employment after they had received permanent residency. For the administrators of the Brandon and Prairieville companies, the combined policies of the Provincial Nominee Program and the Stream for Lower Skilled Occupations program have yielded a two-step migration process that has enabled them to retain workers. Thus, the two programs have provided Manitoba's hog processors a seemingly permanent strategy to secure a committed labour force.

Injury, Pain, and Silence: The Workplace Experiences of Temporary Foreign Workers

The commitment of temporary foreign workers to their work is, in large part, borne of the policies that bind them to their employer and of the roles their employers play in sponsoring applications for permanent residency through the Provincial Nominee Program. Workers' non-citizen status precludes their access to social supports and limits their ability to exercise the same rights enjoyed by citizen workers. They have little recourse to address the challenges they encounter in their workplaces (Preibisch & Otero, 2014).

Those in the hog-processing industry in Manitoba, however, have the protective benefits of United Food and Commercial Workers Canada, which is not the case for many other temporary foreign workers in Canada (Alberti, Holgate, & Tapia, 2013; Gabriel & Macdonald, 2014; Hanley, Shragge, Rivard, & Koo, 2012). Despite the benefits provided by a strong labour union, temporary foreign workers in Manitoba still struggle to cope with and treat workplace injuries as they negotiate a tenuous two-step immigration process.

Work in the hog-processing industry is physically demanding and workers are subject to strain and injury, especially at industrial facilities, such as the plants in Brandon and Prairieville (Charlebois & Summan, 2014; Novek, 1992). Indeed, the meat-processing industry is included among the kinds of labour that have the highest risk of worker injury (Novek, 1992; Stanley, 1992). Between 2003 and 2013, statistic for industries covered by the Workers' Compensation Board revealed that the mean injury rate (both time loss and no time loss) in the meat-processing industry in Manitoba was 20.1 injuries per 100 full-time workers (Safe Work Manitoba, 2014). In comparison with a mean rate of 13.6 for all manufacturing jobs in the province and an overall rate of 7.9 for all industry sectors over the same time period, meat processing ranks as one of the most injury prone sectors.

High injury rates are due to the fact that workers perform repetitive tasks using sharp tools in cold conditions. Moreover, they are exposed to chemical and biological agents. These hazards can be compounded by worker inexperience and inadequate training. According to some interviewees, temporary foreign workers begin work in departments based upon management's need to fill openings, rather than their levels of skill and experience. For example, in spite of the fact that many temporary foreign workers from the Philippines had previous meat-cutting experience and thought they had been hired because of their skills in deboning meat carcasses, when they began working in Prairieville they were assigned to departments such as sanitation or packaging. Marlon[2] explains that he was hired as a meat cutter and states that "when I arrived here I expected to be [...a] de-boner [...] because I'm a meat cutter. But [management] put me in the packaging [...]." Those who have previous meat-cutting experience feel that their skills are being wasted. Meat cutting requires extreme precision and knowledge, but even when temporary foreign workers have these skills, they are not being utilized. Instead, employers sometimes assign positions requiring skills in meat cutting to workers who have no previous experience. Isabel is one of these. Initially, she was scared to work with the knives and had to learn safety techniques and develop skills on the shop floor. The problem that results from a mismatch between skills, experience, and job placement is a compounding of the potential for injury in the workplace.

The kinds of jobs meat-processing employers expect workers to perform include the following: killing animals and removing their entrails, cutting the carcasses into segments using mechanized knives, packaging meat, and sanitizing equipment. In an automated hog-butchering plant, a conveyor belt carries the carcasses and segments through the processing system at high speeds, which requires workers stationed on disassembly lines to perform the same specialized task quickly and repeatedly throughout the duration of their shifts. Joseph describes this repetitive work as the "same job, same job, everyday." Many workers have difficulties adjusting to the speed and repetition. Michael, who worked as a meat cutter in the Philippines, compares his former job to his job in the hog-processing plant, and remarks:

> Back in the Philippines [...] you do it manually, pig by pig, from start to the end. Here, it's [...done] very different. You are using machine [...and] conveyor. [The carcass] will just pass by [...and] you [are] not doing the full hogs. It's [...] just like a train [...], section by section.

Meat-processing jobs demand high levels of training because they require meat cutters to work with precision, efficiency, and speed. In spite of initial orientation sessions, it is difficult even for skilled meat cutters to anticipate the realities of the labour requirements before they enter the shop floor and commence working. While the orientation includes safety and sanitation procedures and correct workplace habits, interviewees indicate that it did not prepare them for the physical demands of the job. Ana describes the discrepancy between her expectations and the realities of the workplace and explains that, in spite of the fact that plant managers warned workers during orientation sessions that the job would be hard, she says, you don't realize how hard it is. Like, you think hard job is to be standing there. And then we don't realize the size of the company and like for us it was like unbelievable when we came and they kill 16,000 pigs in a day. So we didn't realize, I don't think anyone realized how hard it can be.

Many temporary foreign workers reported that they were unprepared for the intensity of the work involved in processing thousands of hogs in a shift or keeping up with the high speed of the conveyor system. Nor were they prepared for the smell of animal by-products and the cold temperature in the plant.

Participants also related that during the first few weeks of their new jobs they doubted they would be able to continue, since they could not imagine how they could endure the pain caused by standing in one spot all day, from lifting heavy boxes, or from holding knives and repeatedly performing the same motion to cut the carcasses. The cold temperature of the plants also contributed to their initial trepidation. Diego's account of his first days of work summarizes the sentiments that many others also felt:

> The first week I started work I felt a bit [...] desperate. Because when [management] assigned the area I had to work nobody had told, and I didn't know, what the temperature was going to be like there. I remember the first day [...], I just went like this, with pants and short sleeved shirt. I didn't know I was going to [...] an area where the temperature is minus 16 or minus 12 degrees. The first week, I thought, wow, what I am doing here? I would've been better in my country. [...] After a while I got used to the cold.

Other temporary foreign workers also expressed thoughts of returning home, admitting that they questioned their decision to come to Canada to work in the hog-processing industry. Like Diego, Javier panicked during his first week of work and doubted that he could continue. He recalls:

> I wanted to come back to my country. I thought this is not for me. I never had, I don't have this kind of experience. I didn't like it at all, I think nobody likes it. Yeah, I wanted to come back. Yeah and my

> thoughts were, I hope this time pass quickly [...] as quickly as possible so I have the chance to [go] back.

Many workers coped with the difficulty of their first weeks not just by hoping for the time to pass quickly, but also by focusing on the financial gains their employment would yield.

When asked if they suffered injuries and pain, many participants said "of course"; these experiences were inevitable in their jobs. Muscle strain was one of the common injuries among workers, especially during their first few weeks on the job when they had to adjust to the physical intensity of such demanding labour. Regardless of their previous work experience, all of the temporary foreign workers I interviewed admitted to having struggled to cope with the new working conditions and, even though their employers instructed them on proper ways to hold the knives and correct posture during heavy lifting, the realities of the job required them to repeat the same motions for the duration of their shifts, which resulted in pain and discomfort. Nearly all of the participants cited injury to and pain in their wrists, fingers, hands, and arms. When Michael was asked to describe his first few months of work, he spoke of the difficulty, stating:

> I could not even close my hands when sleeping. My fingers are not, cannot be closed. Even those friends of mine that [are] using the knife, it's hard [for them] to close [their hands]. It's painful. For the last eight weeks, my middle finger could not close.

Many participants described similar experiences of being unable to open and close their hands; others related that they had developed back pain or swelling in their arms. Some participants developed fevers and illness from the shock of cold temperatures in the plant, and some lost sleep at night due to the pain in their bodies. Isabel was one of these workers. She said: "It's very cold inside and sometimes our bodies are very painful and sometimes I cannot sleep well at the night." While the workers interviewed spoke of varying injuries and discomfort, only a few experienced injuries that were debilitating in the short term. The extent to which injuries are a normalized part of their workplace, however, remains a troubling aspect of temporary foreign workers' employment experiences in meat-processing plants.

While many participants spoke about their own and others' experiences with pain and injuries, they referred to pain and injuries as things they overcame, and avoided dwelling on their first few weeks of work. Ruth Simpson and her colleagues (2014) suggest that people working in occupations such as meat processing attempt to make sense of their work by invoking notions of sacrifice and accepting that the physical demands are inherent in the job. The participants in my study acknowledged the difficulty of their work, but during the interview, few complained about their circumstances; rather, they reflected that the magnitude of difficulty had been beyond their expectations when they accepted employment. They experienced a sense of physical and mental relief at the end of a shift, but felt that the pain was something they had to overcome. Indeed, the interviewees at both plants discussed their strategies for pain management as merely getting used to it. As Carla explained: "You get over everything. It's a matter of habit. You've gotta get used to it. Maybe it took me over a year.... [Now] the work feels softer and softer, easier to be doing the same thing." Participants identified components of their pain-management regimens, such as exercises like stretching, taking vitamins, and seeking other forms of therapy, but their pain persisted and was often not properly treated. For example, when Juan reported that he was experiencing numbness and limited mobility in his hands and arms, his supervisor merely told him to increase his work speed. After this incident, he said, he began referring to the plant as "hell" and sought ways to mitigate, yet live with, the pain. Participants indicated that they continue to work through their injuries because they both accepted it as part of the job and worried that pursuing medical treatment might threaten their chances of accessing the Provincial Nominee Program.

Workers do not often report their injuries to supervisors or managers for fear of possible consequences, which is a consistent finding in the literature on migrant workers (Basok, 2002; Preibisch & Hennebry, 2011). In fact, none of the temporary foreign workers I interviewed pursued formal workplace injury reporting or raised the issue with anyone other than their co-workers; many expressed their trepidation about pursuing treatment that might result in time off. When I asked Maria if she went to a doctor about her arm pain, she said no, because her employer does not approve of employees taking time off work for doctor appointments. Nor did David seek treatment for his excruciating pain, because, as he explained, "I had to pass the tests so I didn't say anything to the supervisor. I think it's three months that we are on our probation to see if we could stay at the company." Whether or not his employment would have been terminated had he reported an injury is unknown; his fears were fostered by rumours that shape how workers address their injuries. Employers' control over immigration opportunities caused workers to remain silent about injuries and to continue working rather than risk being denied applications for permanent residency. When Ana had a workplace accident, she sought treatment but was informed by a health practitioner that reporting the injury might compromise her opportunity to stay in Canada. Instead, her employer assigned her to lighter duties but still required her to come to work. Juan recalls conversations with co-workers about how reporting an injury could compromise immigration plans. As Juan explains, employers do not explicitly say they will deny opportunities to temporary foreign workers

> but we're not going to press our luck [...]. Sometimes we're in real pain, but we keep working. I haven't seen it happen or whatever, but you kind of feel like if you start complaining they're not going to like it. So you're like, okay, I better keep quiet and keep working. That's it. Zone out and keep doing whatever it is.

Whether the workers' fears are real or imagined, the possibility of losing opportunities for permanent residency is enough to keep them from reporting injuries. Worker compliance thus guarantees that the managers of hog-processing plants have access to a productive workforce whose members take little time off.

In general, migrant workers do not wish to return to their home countries; rather, they plan to seek permanent residency, although they realize that their situations are precarious and that there are many rules to follow. As Diego says, in the context of coping with the difficulties of his work, "I've got to hang in there whatever happens. I've gotta do whatever I've gotta do,

I'm not going back." All of the participants expressed a sense of self-sacrifice and determination in the narratives of their workplace experiences and centred on their goals of achieving permanent residence status and family reunification.

Although employment in the hog-processing industry is injurious, relatively few temporary foreign workers left the meat-processing industry upon achieving permanent resident status. At the time of the interviews, those who had received permanent status or citizenship stayed in their jobs for at least four years. As previously mentioned, only three of the workers I interviewed had left the plant to pursue other employment or to further their education. Seven of the workers who stayed at their jobs explained that their respective employers offered steady incomes and provided good benefits while requiring minimal English language levels. Some temporary foreign workers are not confident in their ability to find better forms of employment than those they have in the hog-processing industry, so they choose to remain in a demanding and a potentially debilitating occupation. Others are motivated to leave but are unable to find alternative employment in rural communities.

In contrast to these reports, some of the workers I interviewed concluded that the hog-processing plants were actually good places to work. Some participants stayed because, regardless of their injuries and pain, they felt a sense of gratitude to the company officials for bringing them to Canada. Carlos felt a sense of obligation to give much of his time and energy back to the company, since his employers covered his transportation costs when he came to Canada and have paid him relatively well since his arrival. Javier echoed the same sentiment, saying: "I think the company has done very good thing for us [...]. I'm very grateful to them. They gave me the opportunity to train and I work very hard for them. [I] think I pay off. I gave them like four years of my life for that." The reasons other foreign workers stayed at the plants after achieving permanent residence status are diverse, but most reasons centred on notions of indebtedness or lack of alternative employment opportunities. Either way, the managers of the two Manitoba hog-processing plants have gained dedicated employees and have eliminated their immediate concerns about high rates of attrition in their workforce.

Conclusion

While plant owners in Manitoba's hog-processing industry initially struggled to secure a committed labour force, they have now found it in many temporary foreign workers. Employers have benefitted from both the Temporary Foreign Worker Program and the Provincial Nominee Program. The fact that many of these workers wish to settle permanently in Manitoba is the reason that they suffer through injuries throughout the duration of their work permit. In some cases, workers remain in the hog-processing industry once they have made the transition from temporary to permanent residency status.

Since the Manitoba government has included temporary foreign workers in its Provincial Nominee Program with few exceptions, the province is often viewed as an atypical case when scholars consider what policy changes might be made to mitigate the vulnerability that workers with non-citizen status encounter (Carter, 2012; Nakache & D'Aoust, 2012). The case of Manitoba demonstrates that provincial immigration policy combined with the efforts of a dedicated union can benefit temporary foreign workers by including them in collective agreements and by giving them access to language and immigration support. Temporary foreign workers can then plan for a future in Canada with their families as they work toward becoming permanent residents.

In spite of the increases in opportunities for temporary foreign workers to attain permanent residency status through PNPs, studies of their employment in the hog-processing industry in Manitoba reveal that the two-step immigration process can, in fact, exacerbate an already unequal power relationship between temporary foreign workers and their employers. Thus, caution is warranted when policy makers, advocates, and researchers consider the utility of two-step immigration systems as a means of reducing the vulnerability of temporary foreign workers. As Goldring and Landolt (2011) suggest, increasing the security and legality of status for workers should lead to their "improved work outcomes, based on expanded rights and protections, other factors being equal" (p. 327). Yet, they state that, in actuality, the effects of vulnerability and non-citizen status are not easily overcome. The practices and relations that temporary foreign workers experience while they have non-citizen status have long-term negative consequences on health and social and economic outcomes that do not necessarily disappear upon achieving permanent residency (Landolt & Goldring, 2013; McLaughlin & Hennebry, 2013; Preibisch & Otero, 2014). To alleviate some of the adverse experiences, it is important to ensure the active engagement and involvement of advocates, such as labour unions, in addition to challenging the continued practice of employer-tied work permits in the Temporary Foreign Worker Program.

Notes

1. Beginning in the fall of 2014, the federal government overhauled the Temporary Foreign Worker Program, eradicating streams based on skill level and instead defining streams by wage level. This chapter and the research project on which it is based were completed prior to the TFWP overhaul.
2. All interview participants have been assigned pseudonyms to ensure anonymity.

References

Alberti, G., Holgate, J., & Tapia, M. (2013). Organising migrants as workers or as migrant workers? Intersectionality, trade unions and precarious work. *The International Journal of Human Resource Management, 24*(22), 4132–4148.

Basok, T. (1999). Free to be unfree: Mexican guest workers in Canada. *Labour, Capital and Society, 32*(2), 192–222.

Basok, T. (2002). *Tortillas and tomatoes: Transmigrant Mexican harvesters in Canada.* Montreal, QC: McGill-Queen's Press.

Basok, T. (2004). Post-national citizenship, social exclusion and migrants' rights: Mexican seasonal workers in Canada." *Citizenship Studies, 8*(1), 47–64.

Bird, B. (2001, Sept. 11). Maple Leaf looks to Mexico. *Brandon Sun.* pp. A1, A2.

Broadway, M. (2007). Meatpacking and the transformation of rural communities: A comparison of Brooks, Alberta and Garden City, Kansas." *Rural Sociology, 72*(4), 560–582.

Broadway, M. (2013). The world "meats" Canada: Meatpacking's role in the cultural transformation of Brooks, Alberta. *Focus on Geography, 56*(2), 47–53.

Bucklaschuk, J., & Moss, A. (2008). Settlement: Considerations for temporary foreign workers in Brandon and area. RDI Temporary Foreign Worker Dialogue Group Discussion Paper #2. Brandon, MB: Rural Development Institute, Brandon University.

Bucklaschuk, J., Moss, A., & Annis, R. (2009). Temporary may not always be temporary: The impact of "transitional" foreign workers and increasing diversity in Brandon, Manitoba. *Our Diverse Cities, 6*(Spring), 64–70.
Carter, T. (2012). Provincial nominee programs and temporary worker programs: A comparative assessment of advantages and disadvantages in addressing labour shortages. In P. Lenard & C. Straehle (Eds.), *Legislated inequality: Temporary labour migration in Canada* (pp. 178–201). Montreal, QC: McGill-Queen's University Press.
Champlin, D., & Hake, E. (2006). Immigration as industrial strategy in American meatpacking. *Review of Political Economy, 18*(1), 49–70.
Charlebois, S., & Summan, A. (2014). Abattoirs, meat processing and managerial challenges: A survey for lagging rural regions and food entrepreneurs in Ontario, Canada. *International Journal of Rural Management, 10*(1), 1–20.
Dalla, R., & Christensen, A. (2005). Latino immigrants describe residence in rural midwestern meatpacking communities: A longitudinal assessment of social and economic change. *Hispanic Journal of Behavioral Sciences, 27*(1), 23–42.
Gabriel, C., & Macdonald, L. (2014). "Domestic transnationalism": Legal advocacy for Mexican migrant workers' rights in Canada. *Citizenship Studies, 18*(3–4), 243–258.
Goldring, L. (2010). Temporary worker programs as precarious status: Implications for citizenship, inclusion and nation building in Canada. *Canadian Issues/Thèmes canadiens*, Spring, 50–54.
Goldring, L., & Landolt, P. (2011). Caught in the work–citizenship matrix: The lasting effects of precarious legal status on work for Toronto immigrants. *Globalizations, 8*(3), 325–341.
Government of Canada, Employment and Social Development Canada. (2013). *Hiring temporary foreign workers for lower-skilled occupations.* ESDC. Retrieved from http://www.esdc.gc.ca/eng/jobs/foreign_workers/lower_skilled/index.shtml
Government of Canada, Citizenship and Immigration Canada. (2013). *Facts and figures 2012—Immigration overview: Permanent and temporary residents.* Retrieved from http://www.cic.gc.ca/english/resources/statistics/facts2012/index.asp
Government of Manitoba, Manitoba Immigration & Multiculturalism. (2013). *Manitoba immigration facts: 2012 statistical report.* Retrieved from http://www.gov.mb.ca/labour/immigration/pdf/manitoba_immigration_facts_report_2012.pdf
Government of Manitoba, Manitoba Immigration & Multiculturalism. (2015). Manitoba provincial nominee program, 2014 data. Personal communication.
Hanley, J., Shragge, E., Rivard, A., & Koo, J. (2012). "Good enough to work? Good enough to stay!" Organizing among temporary foreign workers. In P. Lenard & C. Straehle (Eds.), *Legislated inequality: Temporary labour migration in Canada* (pp. 245–271). Montreal, QC: McGill-Queen's University Press.
Hawthorne, L. (2010). How valuable is two-step migration? Labor market outcomes for international student migrants to Australia. *Asian and Pacific Migration Journal, 19*(1), 5–36.
Helly, D., Depatie-Pelletier, E., & Gibson, A. (2014). Lessons from Canada: The economic necessity to make all guestworker regimes "2-step immigration programs facilitating just-in-time integration and circular migration." Working Paper #5. Retrieved Sept. 23, 2014 from http://www.carfms.org/sites/default/files/Helly,%20Depatie-Pelletier%20&%20Gibson_CARFMS%202014.pdf

Hennebry, J. (2009). Mobile vulnerabilities, transnational risks: Temporary agricultural migrants in Ontario. *International Settlement Canada, 22*(3), 10–15.

Hennebry, J. (2012). Permanently temporary? Agricultural migrant workers and their integration in Canada. IRPP Study 26. Montreal, QC: Institute for Research on Public Policy.

Honey, J. (2014). *Manitoba pig and pork industry 2013.* Winnipeg, MB: Department of Agribusiness and Agricultural Economics, University of Manitoba.

Landolt, P., & Goldring, L. (2013). The social production of non-citizenship: The consequences of intersecting trajectories of precarious legal status and precarious work. In L. Goldring & P. Landolt (Eds.), *Producing and negotiating non-citizenship: Precarious legal status in Canada* (pp. 154–174). Toronto, ON: University of Toronto Press.

McLaughlin, J., & Hennebry, J. (2013). Pathways to precarity: Structural vulnerabilities and lived consequences for migrant farmworkers in Canada. In L. Goldring & P. Landolt (Eds.), *Producing and negotiating non-citizenship: Precarious legal status in Canada* (pp. 175–194). Toronto, ON: University of Toronto Press.

Moss, A., Bucklaschuk, J., & Annis, R. (2010). Small places, big changes: Temporary migration, immigration, and family reunification. *Canadian Issues/Thèmes canadiens,* Spring, 33–36.

Nakache, D., & D'Aoust, S. (2012). Provincial/territorial nominee programs: An avenue to permanent residency for low-skilled temporary foreign workers? In P. Lenard & C. Straehle (Eds.), *Legislated inequality: Temporary labour migration in Canada* (pp. 158–177). Montreal, QC: McGill-Queen's University Press.

Novek, J. (1992). The labour process and workplace injuries in the Canadian meat packing industry. *Canadian Review of Sociology/Revue canadienne de sociologie, 9*(1), 17–37.

Parrado, E., & Kandel, W. (2008). New Hispanic migrant destinations: A tale of two industries. In D. Massey (Ed.), *New faces in new places: The changing geography of American immigration* (pp. 99–123). New York, NY: Russell Sage Foundation.

Pratt, G. (2012). *Families apart: Migrant mothers and the conflicts of labor and love.* Minneapolis, MN: University of Minnesota Press.

Preibisch, K. (2007). Local produce, foreign labor: Labor mobility programs and global trade competitiveness in Canada. *Rural Sociology, 72*(3), 418–449.

Preibisch, K. (2010). Pick-your-own labor: Migrant workers and flexibility in Canadian agriculture. *International Migration Review, 44*(2), 404–441.

Preibisch, K., & Hennebry, J. (2011). Temporary migration, chronic effects: The health of international migrant workers in Canada. *Canadian Medical Association Journal, 183*(9), 1033–1038.

Preibisch, K., & Otero, G. (2014). Does citizenship status matter in Canadian agriculture? Workplace health and safety for migrant and immigrant laborers. *Rural Sociology, 79*(2), 174–199.

Safe Work Manitoba. (2014). *The Manitoba workplace injury statistics report, 2000–2013.* Retrieved from http://safemanitoba.com/sites/default/files/resources/annualinjurystats2000.2013 v3.1.pdf

Satzewich, V. (1991). *Racism and the incorporation of foreign labour: Farm labour migration to Canada since 1945.* New York, NY: Routledge.

Sharma, N. (2001). On being not Canadian: The social organization of "migrant workers" in Canada. *Canadian Review of Sociology/Revue canadienne de sociologie, 38*(4), 415–439.
Sharma, N. (2006). *Home economics: Nationalism and the making of "migrant workers" in Canada*. Toronto, ON: University of Toronto Press.
Sharma, N, (2012). The "difference" that borders make: "Temporary foreign workers" and the social organization of unfreedom in Canada. In P. Lenard & C. Straehle (Eds.), *Legislated inequality: Temporary labour migration in Canada* (pp. 26–47). Montreal, QC: McGill-Queen's University Press.
Simpson, R., Hughes, J., Slutskaya, N., & Balta, M. (2014). Sacrifice and distinction in dirty work: Men's construction of meaning in the butcher trade. *Work, Employment and Society, 28*(5), 754–770.
Stanley, K. (1992). Immigrant and refugee workers in the midwestern meatpacking industry: Industrial restructuring and the transformation of rural labor markets. *Review of Policy Research, 11*(2), 106–117.
Stasiulis, D., & Bakan, A. (2005). *Negotiating citizenship: Migrant women in Canada and the global system*. Toronto, ON: University of Toronto Press.
Statistics Canada. (2012). *Focus on geography, 2011 Census*. Analytical Products, 2011 Census Statistics Canada Catalogue No. 98-310-XWE2011004. Ottawa, ON: Author.
Stull, D., & Broadway, M. (2004). *Slaughterhouse blues: The meat and poultry industry in North America*. Belmont, CA: Wadsworth/Thomson Learning.
Tilson, D. (2009). *Temporary foreign workers and non-status workers*. 40th Parliament, 2nd Session. Report of the Standing Committee on Citizenship and Immigration. Ottawa, ON: House of Commons Canada.
Torres, S., Spitzer, D., Hughes, K., Oxman-Martinez, J., & Hanley, J. (2012). From temporary worker to resident: The LCP and its impact through an intersectional lens. In P. Lenard & C. Straehle (Eds.), *Legislated inequality: Temporary labour migration in Canada* (pp. 227–244). Montreal, QC: McGill-Queen's University Press.

SIX

WORKING AWAY

Exploring the Lived Experiences of Farm Owner-Operators with Off-Farm Employment in Alberta

Zane Hamm

Introduction

The Alberta government has long maintained that denying farm workers various employment rights is intended to preserve the institution of the family farm; yet, competition from agribusinesses has a greater impact on small farms than farm owners' relationships with hired workers. This chapter explores the struggles of farming families in the face of increasing corporate influence and industrialization of agricultural production. Family farm owners and operators have complex relationships with paid employment: some are employers of seasonal and/or year-round employees, and, simultaneously, some farm owner-operators may be employees who take off-farm work to cope with the ever-present "economic stress and threat of economic disaster" (Gordon, 1998, p. 149). Investigating this latter role offers an important, but little researched, perspective on agricultural employment. Commonly held beliefs about off-farm work imagine men leaving the farm to work in the oil-and-gas industry while women work close to home as cashiers, servers, nurses, and teachers. Such a patriarchal and stereotypical view is inaccurate and obscures the gendered dimension and impact of off-farm work (Heather, Skillen, Cross, & Vladicka, 2012).

This chapter examines off-farm work to identify its prevalence among men and women, to understand its impact on owner-operators and their communities, and to explore the relationship of farm work with off-farm employment in Alberta's oil-and-gas industry. It presents results drawn from dialogue with members of farming communities and from interviews with farm owner-operators (whose names have been substituted with pseudonyms) to reveal the complex interplay of social, political, and economic factors in off-farm work. The experiences shared in this exploratory study provide evidence that the decisions of owner-operators are shaped by their context and gender (Heather et al., 2012; Kubik & Moore, 2002; Roppel, Desmarais, & Martz, 2006b), while acknowledging that there is no "average" farm or rural community (Bollman & Smith, 1988).

Political, Social, and Economic Terrain and the Challenge of Rural Community Sustainability

Canadian researchers have identified complex and often inter-related economic, environmental, political, and social factors that impact farming and rural development in Alberta, including the farm owner-operator's sense of community belonging, as well as class and gender ideologies (Ableman, 2005; Heather, Skillen, Young, & Vladicka, 2005; Kubik, 2004; Reimer, Burns, & Garneau, 2007). Of particular concern to policy makers and farmers is the emergence of labour shortages in agriculture due to the rapid growth in Alberta's oil-and-gas industry coupled with the growing problems of rural out-migration (Lall, Selod, & Shalizi, 2006; Lyson, 2004; Mündel, 2007). Rural out-migration has social and economic impacts, such as the destabilization of home environments, decreased access for rural residents to education and health care, increased health risks such as exposure to higher-risk work environments, and long-term negative impacts on food systems and food security (Epp, 2007; FOA, 1995; McCullum, 2006; Williams, 2007).

Some farmers also face increasing economic pressure. As Bob Barnetson notes in Chapter 1, the number of Alberta farms has declined while the physical size, capitalization, and gross receipts of these farms has increased. A decrease in the number of farms has also meant a decrease in the number of farm operators in Alberta, a change that mirrors global trends of increasing farm outputs and declining farm populations (Barkley & Barkley, 2013; Statistics Canada, 2012a). Although the number of Alberta owner-operators is declining, the proportion of female operators increased by 29 per cent in 2011 (Alberta Agriculture and Rural Development, 2013). Canada's 2011 Census of Agriculture indicates that farm owner-operators have become increasingly reliant upon income and remittances from off-farm employment and businesses (Statistics Canada, 2012a). Danysk (1995) claims that Alberta farmers have long sought to increase their incomes through off-farm employment. Likewise, Bollman and Smith (1988) maintain that current trends in off-farm work by farm owner-operators are part of an historical pattern of integration of farm enterprises, farm families, and the non-farm economy; yet, farm families may never have been truly self-sufficient.

Despite the media's bucolic representations of family farms, farming is a "pressure laden, complicated business filled with economic risk" (Gordon, 1988, p. 143). Moreover, competition with agribusiness operators puts pressure on small producers to increase the size of their operations (Roppel et al., 2006a). As a result, farm families are "increasingly integrated into the off-farm economy" (Bollman & Smith, 1988, p. 185) by an ongoing cost-price squeeze, wherein expenses rise faster than revenue (Mitchell, 1975). In 2011, 52.0% of all Alberta farm operators had off-farm jobs or businesses (an increase of 40.1% since 1991), although the off-farm work of spouses and children may not be fully captured in this data (Statistics Canada, 2012a). Overall, the largest increase has been in full-time, off-farm employment. The numbers of hours of off-farm employment has increased over the past decade, while the hours of on-farm employment has declined (Statistics Canada, 2012a). In 2006, the number of farm operators working more than 40 hours a week on average on their farm operations was 43.6%; in 2011, that number decreased to 37.8% (Statistics Canada, 2011). The proportion of female farm owner-operators who work off-farm is higher than the proportion of male owner-operators who do so, although female owner-operators are more likely to be employed off-farm on a part-time basis and work fewer off-farm hours than the men. Nonetheless, 11.1% of the female farm owner-operators reported more than 40 hours a week of off-farm employment compared with 20.6% of the male operators (Statistics Canada, 2012b). In addition to paid on-farm work and off-farm work, female farm operators often also care for family and community members (Heather et al., 2012; Roppel, 2006a).

Statistics Canada identifies the opportunity for farm owner-operators to find off-farm work in Alberta's job market as a factor that "lures farmers from the land" (Statistics Canada, 2006b). Age is also a factor. Of farm operators under 35 years of age, 32.8% work off-farm for more than 40 hours a week. The percentage decreases, however, as the age of workers increases. Only 27.9% of farm operators between 35 and 54 years of age work full time off-farm, and 12.8% of operators over 55 years of age (Statistics Canada, 2012a). Nationally, the largest increases in the proportion of farm operators working off-farm are in Alberta and Saskatchewan (Statistics Canada, 2006a). Farm owner-operator Anna notes that young rural residents see their futures in the "oil patch" and take advantage of family connections to access these high-salary positions. Today, more of these individuals pursue paid employment (often in the oil-and-gas sector), and fewer are willing and able to perform farm and other low-paying jobs (Cross & Bowlby, 2006; Epp, 2007; Ferrao, 2006).

Off-farm employment is one form of employment-related geographic mobility (ERGM), which refers to extended travel from places of permanent residence for the purpose of and as part of employment (Green, 2004; Temple Newhook et al., 2011). Such travel includes lengthy daily commutes as well as more extended, work-related periods of absence from home to locations elsewhere in the province, country or world, which means that journeys between work and home are often becoming increasingly sustained and complex in terms of time consumption, distance travelled, stops along the way, and time spent away from home (Clark, 2000; Heisz & LaRochelle-Côté, 2005a, 2005b; Pisarski, 2007; Statistics Canada, 2008). Examples of ERGM in agriculture are found among foreign national labourers who work for months or years in Alberta under the auspices of the Seasonal Agricultural Worker Program or the Temporary Foreign Worker Program (Preibisch, 2010). Workers from within Alberta as well from other provinces also engage in ERGM when they reside in work camps located near oil-sands deposits around Fort McMurray or work with mobile crews in the oil-and-gas industry (De Guerre, 2009; Hiller, 2009). The effects of ERGM on "sending" regions include population loss, economic dependency on migrant work, and changes in community dynamics (Pisarski, 2007; Temple Newhook et al., 2011; Ferguson, 2011). Scholarly study of owner-operators who take on off-farm employment has been limited and identifies mixed outcomes. Off-farm employment brings money into rural communities. Yet, employment migration can also result in diminished local labour forces, gender pressures, and negative impacts on families (Epp, 2007; Kubik & Moore, 2002; Lall, Selod, & Shalizi, 2006; McCullum, 2006). The oil price crash of 2015–2016 is also changing off-farm employment prospects for many farm operators related to oil-sands production.

Tensions in Contemporary Farming

There has been little research that examines the effects of off-farm employment on owner-operators or their communities. Jon Hall (2014) documents some of the different ways farmers engage in off-farm work. One Albertan poultry farmer may work through the winter as a mechanic while another farmer may work full time in the oilfield. The demands on such labourers require emotional adjustments, especially for farmers who never imagined that off-farm work was essential to cover their living expenses and allow them to "afford to grow food to feed people'" (Hall, 2014, p. 61). Nonetheless, these farmers remain hopeful that their children will have the resources to "do something with the land" (p. 67). Other farmers see off-farm employment as a way to leave agriculture. For example, Roy, a welder, chose to leave a family farm rather than support the farm with off-farm work, because he believes that "there's no future in farming"; thus, he balances work with "better opportunities, education...options" for his children.

Sheryl, a new farm owner in southern Alberta who works off-farm, believes that old farmhouses will "die and wither away" and that the land will be auctioned off. She expects that the next generation will choose farming as a livelihood, but realizes that young people "need to make a lot of money first" to allow them to farm. Sheryl's brother, who was, initially, discouraged from farming, now works in the oil-and-gas industry, but hopes to return to farming with the "millions [he will make] up north." Sheryl also notes that small oil-and-gas companies now provide employment in the area, monitoring gas wells. The relationship between the agricultural and oil-and-gas industries (and perhaps the dependence of the former on the latter) is a recurring theme. Kate, a farm and land owner who rents out her land and works in an urban setting, notes that rural young people who leave post-secondary education to seek off-farm employment (often in occupations related to oil and gas) may lack training and credentials for future employment. Yet, not all off-farm work is in the oil-and-gas sector. For example, Ella, a stay-at-home parent, takes on casual labour, such as bookkeeping, and helps to run a local farm store.

While census data demonstrates women's contributions to farm viability through on-farm and off-farm work, such data does not capture the full spectrum of women's contributions to their farms or rural communities. There are often critical barriers that preclude public recognition of women's contributions to agriculture. Smith (1988) identifies structural barriers, such as unequal ownership, and social factors, such as patriarchal attitudes in the family and broader community. Indeed, much of women's labour is obscured by terms such as "farm women" and "farm wife," which imply similarity in female farm operators' experiences and difficulties, and which discount the many ways women support the farm both "as an enterprise and as a household" (Smith, p. 170). Yet, performing complex roles as they work in the household, in the community, and on and off the farm, farm wives contribute to the social and economic value of their farms (Heather et al., 2012; Kubik & Moore, 2005; Smith).

Women's attitudes about themselves and toward other women also pose barriers to public recognition of their contributions. For example, farm women take pride in their ability to manage heavy workloads both on and off the farm; yet, "doing it all" and "being a good woman" often comes at the cost of women's health and well-being (Heather et al., 2012). A woman's need to be flexible and available for farm work also contributes to her sense of uncertainty (Kubik & Moore, 2005) and impacts how and when she can work off-farm (Heather et al., 2012). Respondents noted that the levels of women's involvement with farm operations vary from highly involved to none whatsoever. Anna states that among the women who are highly involved, some operate highly mechanized tractors and are at the centre of planning and managing the farm. Indeed, she notes that large farms are often run by highly educated women who work off-farm or apply their knowledge and skills to the "business of farming." Further, Anna asserts that while women used to work to help cover farm bills or pay for the family's extracurricular activities, they now sometimes have professional off-farm careers as, for example, corporate executive officers or crop technicians.

Yet, there is diversity in farm women's experiences. Furthermore, off-farm employment may also be, at least partly, a choice for some. Farm owner-operator Kate recalled that a farm wife who sought off-farm work to provide financial support to a farm during a crisis chose to continue such employment even when farm conditions improved. Kate also noted that some women work at local grocery stores for minimum wage, in part, to be available for child-rearing and other family tasks during times when the men are away due to employment in $150,000-a-year jobs in the oil sector. However, with the oil price collapse in 2015, these employment prospects have been adversely affected. Given the significance of women's contributions to and multiple roles on the farm, they are often partners in the farming operation, even though such partnerships are not reflected in formal ownership agreements. Gender still impacts expected roles, the division of labour, and decision-making power (Gerrard & Woodland, 2012). The family farm is a form of production that relies on contributions from all members. Ownership and titles are often complex and may not reflect actual contributions of labour and capital (Hedley, 1982 in Smith, 1988). For example, though farm woman may be contributing to the daily operations of the farm, they are often not legal owners. Further, the labour or financial support contributed by women and older children is often not part of a formal calculation.

The effects on farm families and communities when men and women take on supplementary off-farm work are profound. Anna explains that when men work off-farm for long stretches of time, the "wife is left making decisions," which can give rise to domestic and personal tensions. Moreover, the physical demands of farming—which Anna describes as "more than a full-time job"—can be stressful, and not every woman can find "a partner who is attentive to off-farm work, the farm, and the children." The money earned from off-farm income also shapes family life in complex ways. When off-farm income allows the family to purchase non-essential material goods, such as recreational vehicles and firearms, and to increase their access to non-essential services such as the "trendiest haircuts," such purchases may result in habitual desires to acquire material possessions despite the fact that the family has high, farm-related debt. Anna also describes the expansion of women's work on- and off-farm as increasing their physical mobility while, at the same time, reducing the time they have to spend with their families and friends.

Salaried employment for both men and women who take on off-farm work may also shift the "constellation" of roles on a farm and impact dynamics among extended families. Anna notes that the high prices of agricultural land may cause two or three siblings to farm together, which creates the potential for conflict. She explains that when a sibling (most often a brother) whose work in the oil-and-gas sector supports the farm operation "returns home and questions how decisions [were] made" in his absence, his sense of entitlement to decision making may cause resentment among the siblings and their partners who operate the farm on a day-to-day basis. The potential for family discord (one of many examples of the kinds of problems that result from off-farm labour) draws our attention to the relationship between the agricultural and oil-and-gas industries. Respondents noted that, in addition to financially sustaining farms, oil-and-gas jobs were attractive in and of themselves. For example, Anna's former students have reported to her that their employment in the oil-and-gas industry provides them with higher wages in half a day than she makes in a full day of teaching. The students' "parents don't mind because they know there's better money in that [kind of employment] than farming." Another benefit comes from the camaraderie among "the guys on the rigs"; they take care of new employees who come from the same rural community. Kate admits that "there's no way that [wages in] agriculture can compete with those salaries." Opportunities for employment in the oil-and-gas industry fluctuate, however, and are subject to boom and bust cycles such as the oil price collapse in 2015. Kate emphasizes that while farm owners' passions might be for farming and they recognize that off-farm salaries often sustain the family farm, "the road doesn't necessarily lead back there." She adds that "[p]eople who have grown up on farms are in high demand as labourers." Anna observes that, in the oil-and-gas sector, the availability of jobs, such as driving trucks, often depends on "who you know." In other words, farm-family networks, which increasingly cover both agricultural and oil-and-gas sectors, can privilege farmers who have access to them. Yet, as Kate explains, the presence of the oil-and-gas work in rural Alberta also stimulates demand for secondary services, such as food, lodging, and services to maintain and repair vehicles, work equipment, and machinery, which allows people to "stay closer to where they grew up." These jobs, however, often drive up wages, which affect farmers' ability to attract and retain farm workers.

The oil-and-gas industry has also had a profound effect on the cost of agricultural land in Alberta. According to Kate, land that was worth $50,000 four years ago is now worth $400,000. Now, wealthy oil-and-gas employees are more able to afford to purchase additional land, and this new demand continues to drive up the price of agricultural land. Despite the recent collapse in oil prices in 2016, agricultural land prices are likely to be driven higher as global food commodity prices rise and make agricultural land situated in relatively stable jurisdictions more desirable for investors. One respondent observed that many farmers cannot compete for the land that is necessary to achieve the requisite economies of scale associated with larger operations in the current market, and they "can't survive" without a major source of off-farm income. Oil pump jacks on farm land, which can bring in $50,000 a year, can be the equivalent of an off-farm income. Yet, oilfield activity is associated with air, water, and soil pollution, which can directly compromise the agriculture value of the land (Epp, 2012). To add to the difficulties, both agriculture and the oil-and-gas industry use similar infrastructure and resources, such as roads, water, and unskilled labour and, thus, may end up competing with one another. Kate notes that although oil-and-gas companies may invest in infrastructure in a region or community, they also use and strain "the systems that once sustained the agricultural industry."

Some participants also described Alberta farmers as "competitive" and "ambitious." Kate explains that for a new farmer or operator who has not inherited a farm, competition for agricultural land has driven up prices. Further, financial gain may drive decisions, with some farmers deciding to sell their land to foreign-owned companies with an office in Alberta rather than pass the land on to their children through inheritance. Kate also notes that individual farmers "50 [years old] and under" try to rent or buy from neighbours to establish their land base, but they are in competition with successful farms that benefit from three generations of one family working together to support the farm. These intergenerational farms are often supported by at least one or two family members "under 50" years of age, who work off-farm to support the enterprise. While the increasing size of Alberta farms may seem to indicate a thriving agricultural sector, Stirling (2007) cautions that large wealthy farms are not necessarily a sign of healthy rural life. Large farms can indicate high debt loads and lack of support for small-scale agriculture in the face of increasing competition and corporate models of production.

According to Kate, "highly mechanized and tech-driven farming" is now "capital intensive" and requires farmers to provide a "lot of up-front investment." The resulting debt load drives people off farms, she continues, and forces small farm owners to compete with foreign investors and "Hutterites, Mennonites, Chinese...[who] band together and invest." The cost pressures associated with farming and the availability of lucrative off-farm employment for some farmers have clear implications for labour and mobility. Financial and social pressures on farmers to increase the size of their farms and improve the quality of their lives, according to Anna, may drive farmers to borrow "extreme sums of money." Lifestyles, she goes on to explain, have become "so much more materialistic" than they were in previous decades. "Farmers now aren't satisfied with 'good quality machinery...grain and cattle.' They want to expand. They want the same house as in the city...the holidays, the toys, the trailer." Increasingly, large farms and escalating lifestyle costs create the need for high-wage jobs and the amount of time that farm owners and operators must spend doing off-farm work. Such work is often found in the oil-and-gas industry. Anna offers an extreme example of the time spent away from the farm in the case of a farm operator in her area who has worked "100 days on" in the oil field. The partial or full absence of owner-operators may require farm owners to hire managers and many so-called family farms to hire employees. In addition to existing competition posed by farming collectives, Anna also cited members of traditional Mennonite communities as an important source of the hired labourers necessary to support local farming operations in east central Alberta. Labour is in itself an important source of the income that members of farming collectives use for land purchases, which drives owner-operators to seek off-farm work in order to compete. The existing pattern is a complex feedback loop in labour mobility.

Another tension Kate describes is vertical integration, which occurs when company owners who sell seed, chemicals, and farm machinery control the market and information flow. As Kate observes, it is the company owners who then "own" this information and control the education and materials that farmers receive about farm inputs and products. Yet, she explains, farmers' "wisdom and local knowledge [is also] part of a changing rural context." Moreover, local knowledge, which means wisdom that is gained through years of experience and a deep understanding of agriculture in a particular context (people and place), is crucial to understanding the current context of farming. This local knowledge is a vital accompaniment necessary to balance the technological approaches to farming and to assess the relevance of new sectors and how they impact the local rural communities. Kate maintains, however, that when farmers' experience and in-depth local knowledge is not recognized as relevant, the "loss of confidence and identity has a huge impact" on these farmers. Not all farmers willingly embrace farm consolidation, off-farm employment, and vertical integration. Indeed, Kate asserts, some farmers' responses might be characterized as a "trauma response...a loss of what would have been, and a loss of the narrative of the agricultural community or farming culture where it was intergenerational, stable, with a certain ethic or pride." Kate's observations demonstrate that farming is part of a complex identity that is rooted in history and a sense of pride in rural community and food production. In other words, people's decisions to farm (to grow food, to support a farm enterprise, or to care for land) are not just economic ones—they are often driven by deep attachments to family and place. Farm owner-operators' decisions to work off-farm, but to support a farm financially, are impacted by the increasingly high costs of land and farm inputs, as well as low financial returns in agriculture. For example, when Kate decided to purchase her family's farm land and take out a loan to support the farm operation, she reasoned that the decision to finance the farm would enable her parents to continue a traditional way of life that has long been considered noble, "enabling the person who is still farming that land to continue to do that with some dignity." This ownership continues the stewardship of land that has been in the family for generations. She explains that she feels "an obligation to the place and people in [her] family that invested in that place and made it their own...I don't want to be the person who completely walks away." Her commitment to stewardship informs "who farms the land and the type of agriculture" she will support. In other words, her interest is to support a family farm and small-scale agriculture with an emphasis on healthy food production that supports a local rural community base, rather than large-scale agribusiness and high chemical inputs. She poignantly depicts the tensions inherent in the financial and personal investment required to continue to farm, but affirms her commitment to maintain the farm land and her family's agricultural roots. In her words: "These are decisions that I can live with, at least for now."

Conclusion

This exploration of the lived experiences of farm owner-operators with off-farm work emphasizes both the complexity of agricultural employment in Alberta and the need for additional research. Currently, the majority of farmers engage in some off-farm employment; however, their individual experiences differ based upon their need and, or, desire for employment and the opportunities available to them. The drop in oil prices in 2015–2016 may have profound impacts on what employment prospects, if any, are available to them in Alberta's oil-and-gas industry. Typically, owner-operators appear to undertake off-farm employment primarily as a strategy to cope with financial pressure. Some farm owner-operators also seek additional income, status, or the psychological rewards that off-farm work provides. A small number of owner-operators may also see off-farm employment as a step toward exiting the agricultural labour sector. Farmers use off-farm employment to generate additional income in order to maintain the financial viability of their farms, or as an alternative or complement to efforts to minimize labour costs, a strategy Barnetson identifies in Chapter 1.

There is evidence to support the stereotypical images of men working off-farm some distance from home in highly remunerative work in the oil-and-gas industry, and images of women taking local lower-wage and/or part-time work to maintain home life on the farm. Yet, off-farm employment (and, more broadly, employment-related geographic mobility) is a highly diverse and contingent undertaking. While many men do take jobs in the oil-and-gas sector, there is variation in the skill requirements and duration of these jobs as well as in the type of migration involved, such as daily commuting in lieu of long-term relocation. Additional research to document off-farm work and identify patterns would provide useful insight into the realities of this labour mobility, which is often related to oil and gas, and into the impacts on sustaining agriculture in Alberta. Of particular relevance in 2016 is the need for research on the impacts of boom and bust cycles on off-farm employment. Furthermore, understanding off-farm employment opportunities available to farmers may lead to further investigation of how close community bonds or "membership" in family or locale-specific networks affect the opportunities for off-farm work available to owner-operators and how they secure such work. Additional research is also necessary to increase an understanding of family dynamics, and how decisions about off-farm work that are made by family members affect not only nuclear families, but also extended families.

The off-farm employment of women appears to be affected by gendered expectations. While many women choose to take jobs within or close to their home communities, a choice that may be shaped by non-economic considerations, there is, likewise, significant diversity among their reasons for taking on additional work and among the kinds of positions they assume. The jobs that are available to female owner-operators and those they are qualified to perform range from highly skilled and well-paid occupations, such as nursing, teaching, and financial or scientific specialization, to low-skill, poorly paid positions as, for example, cashier, server, cleaner, and child-care provider. Women's degrees of engagement in both farming and off-farm work (full time versus part time) and duration (short term versus long term) also differ, depending upon the individual, the opportunities, and competing priorities. Again, further research to document and categorize this work and the factors contributing to it would be useful. Such research might also seek to identify the non-remunerative forms of work that female owner-operators contribute to their farms and their communities.

The reliance of farm owner-operators on off-farm income also means that individuals earning such income may feel entitled by virtue of their financial contribution to exert additional influence on their family members when making decisions about farm management. The change in the balance of power brought about by off-farm employment can lead to marital and family discord and may also affect farm management strategies and employment choices. This area offers a rich source to understand the ways family dynamics affect employment-related geographic mobility. Preliminary research also suggests that an examination that is limited to the legal ownership of farms may fail to fully reveal the power dynamic of family farm operations. The research also identifies dynamics and tensions in the relationship between Alberta's agricultural and oil-and-gas industries and reveals that some farm owner-operators depend on employment in the oil-and-gas industry to maintain the financial viability of their farms. Indeed, work in the oil-and-gas industry may be particularly attractive to farmers because of its seasonal nature; that is, there is more work available during the winter when frozen ground increases vehicular access to remote sites. The corollary is that farmers are able to "balance" this labour and be on the farm during the growing season. Yet, the availability of jobs in the oil-and-gas industry tightens the rural labour market and, consequently, drives up the cost of hiring farm workers. The oil-and-gas industry also competes with agriculture for inputs such as fresh water and fuel, while also posing environmental threats to agricultural production, such as soil, water, and air contamination, and access to infrastructure like roadways. While employment in the oil-and-gas industry may maintain the viability of some farms, it takes people away from communities, both temporarily and permanently, and thereby exacerbates rural out-migration. In addition, the supplementary income off-farm employment brings into rural communities has a significant impact on the agricultural community. Farmers supported by off-farm income are able pay a premium for agricultural land or can access large bank loans to purchase land, which drives up land prices and may limit the ability of an individual owner-operator to expand.

References

Abelman, M. (2005). *Fields of plenty: A farmer's journey in search of real food and the people who grow it*. San Francisco, CA: Chronicle Books.

Alberta Agriculture and Rural Development. (2013). *Agriculture statistics yearbook 2012*. Edmonton, AB: Author.

Barkley, A., & Barkley, P. (2013). *Principles of agricultural economics*. London, UK: Routledge Taylor & Francis.

Bollman, R., & Smith, P. (1988). Integration of Canadian farm and off-farm markets and the off-farm work of farm women, men, and children. In G.S. Basran & D.A. Hay (Eds.), *The political economy of agriculture in western Canada* (pp. 185–203). Toronto, ON: Garamond Press.

Clark, W. (2000). Traffic report: Weekday commuting patterns. *Canadian Social Trends*, Spring, 18–22.

Cross, P., & Bowlby, G. (2006). The Alberta economic juggernaut: The boom on the rose. *Canadian Economic Observer*. Ottawa, ON: Statistics Canada. Catalogue no. 11–010.

Danysk, C. (1995). *Hired hands: Labour and the development of prairie agriculture, 1880–1930*. Toronto, ON: University of Toronto Press.

De Guerre, K. (2009). *Temporary foreign workers in Alberta's oil sector* (Report No. 54). Working Paper. Sussex Centre for Migration Research: University of Sussex.

Epp, R. (2007). Farming out our future. *Alberta Views*, Oct., 38–41.

Epp, R. (2012). Off-road democracy: The politics of land, water and community in Alberta. In D. Taras & C. Waddell (Eds.), *How Canadians communicate politically* (pp. 259–279). Edmonton, AB: Athabasca University Press.

FAO. (1995). *Food and Agriculture Organization: Gender, Migration, Farming Systems & Land Tenure Module*. Retrieved from http://www.fao.org/docrep/x0252e/x0252e04.htm

Ferguson, N. (2011). From coal pits to tar sands: Labour migration between an Atlantic Canadian region and the Athabasca oil sands. *Just Labour: A Canadian Journal of Work and Society*, 17/18, 106–118.

Ferrao, V. (2006). Recent changes in employment by industry. *Perspectives*, Jan., 5–10.

Gerrard, N., & Woodland, A. (2012). Gender politics and rural women: Barriers to and strategies for enhancing resiliency. In B. Leipert, B. Leach, & W. Thurston (Eds.), *Rural Women's Health* (pp. 269–287). Toronto, ON: University of Toronto Press.

Gordon, E. (1988). Stress in the farm family: Implications for the rural human service worker. In G.S. Basran & D.A. Hay (Eds.), *The political economy of agriculture in western Canada* (pp. 143–154). Toronto, ON: Garamond Press.

Green, A. (2014). Is relocation redundant? Observations on the changing nature and impacts of employment-related geographical mobility in the UK. *Regional Studies*, *38*(6), 629–641.

Hall, J. (2014). *Preparing for the Andrew project: The experience of Alberta farmers in the recent development of small-acreage farms* (Unpublished MBA project). Cape Breton University, Sydney, NS.

Heather, B., Skillen, D.L., Cross, J., & Vladicka, T. (2012). Being a good woman: The gendered impacts of resturcturing in rural Alberta. In B. Leipert, B. Leach, &

W. Thurston (Eds.), *Rural women's health* (pp. 253–269). Toronto, ON: University of Toronto Press.

Heather, B., Skillen, L., Young, J., & Vladicka, T. (2005). Women's gendered identities and the restructuring of rural Alberta. *Sociologica Ruralis*, *45*(1–2), 86–89.

Heisz, A., & LaRochelle-Côté, S. (2005a). Getting to work. *Canadian Social Trends*, Winter, 14–17.

Heisz, A., & LaRochelle-Côté, S. (2005b). Work and commuting in census metropolitan areas, 1996–2001. Ottawa, ON: Statistics Canada.

Hiller, H. (2009). *Second promised land: Migration to Alberta and the transformation of Canadian society*. Montreal, QC: McGill-Queen's University Press.

Kubik, W. (2004). Women's contradictory roles in the contemporary farm economy. *Prairie Forum*, *29*(2), 245–251.

Kubik, W., & Moore, R. (2005). Women's diverse roles in the farm economy and the consequences for their health, well-being, and quality of life. *Prairie Forum*, *27*(1), 115–129.

Kubik, W., & Moore, R. (2005). Health and well-being of farm women: Contradictory roles in the contemporary economy. *Journal of Agricultural Safety and Health*, *11*(2), 249–256.

Lall, S., Selod, H., & Shalizi, Z. (2006). Rural-urban migration in developing countries: A survey of theoretical predictions and empirical findings. Washington, DC: The World Bank Development Research Group.

Lyson, T. (2004). *Civic agriculture: Reconnecting farm, food and community*. Lebanon, NH: University Press of New England.

McCullum, H. (2006). *Fuelling fortress America: A report on the Athabasca tar sands and US demands for Canada's energy*. Ottawa, ON: Canadian Centre for Policy Alternatives.

Mitchell, D. (1975). *The politics of food*. Toronto, ON: James Lorimer.

Mündel, K. (2007). *Walking through your old way of thinking: The learning dimension of farmers' transitions to sustainable agriculture* (Unpublished doctoral dissertation). University of Toronto, Toronto, ON.

Pisarski, A. (2007). Commuting in America. *Issues in Science and Technology*, Winter, 76–80.

Preibisch K. (2010). Pick-your-own-labour: Migrant workers and flexibility in Canadian agriculture. *International Migration Review*, *44*(2), 404–441.

Reimer, B., Burns, M., & Gareau, P. (2007). Ethnic and cultural diversity in rural Canada: Its relationship to immigration. In B. Reimer (Ed.), *Our diverse cities: Rural communities* (pp. 30–35). Toronto, ON: Metropolis Centre.

Roppel, C., Desmarais, A.A., & Martz, D. (2006a). *Farm women and Canadian agricultural policy*. Ottawa, ON: Status of Women Canada.

Roppel, C., Desmarais, A.A., & Martz, D. (2006b). *Farm women and Canadian agricultural policy: Executive Summary*. Ottawa, ON: Status of Women Canada.

Smith, P. (1988). Murdoch's, Becker's, and Sorochan's Challenge: Thinking again about the roles of women in primary agriculture. In G.S. Basran & D.A. Hay (Eds.), *The political economy of agriculture in western Canada* (pp. 157–174). Toronto, ON: Garamond Press.

Statistics Canada. (2006a). *Snapshot portrait*. Retrieved from http://www.statcan.gc.ca/ca-ra2006/articles/snapshot-portrait-eng.htm

Statistics Canada. (2006b). *Increasing share of female operators*. Retrieved from http://www.statcan.gc.ca/ca-ra2006/analysis-analyses/alberta-eng.htm#r4

Statistics Canada. (2008). *Commuting patterns and places of work of Canadians, 2006 Census*. Ottawa, ON: Author.

Statistics Canada. (2011). *Farm and farm operator data*. Retrieved from http://www.statcan.gc.ca/pub/95-640-x/2012002/prov/48-eng.htm

Statistics Canada. (2012a). *2011 Census of Agriculture*. Ottawa, ON: Author.

Statistics Canada. (2012b). *Snapshot of Canadian agriculture*. Ottawa, ON: Author.

Stirling, B. (2007). In perpetuity: Rail and community in the prairies. In M. Knuttila & B. Stirling (Eds.), *The prairie agrarian movement revisited: Centenary Symposium on the Foundation of the Territorial Grain Growers Association* (pp. 263–273). University of Regina, SK: Canadian Plains Research Center.

Temple Newhook, J., Neis, B., Jackson, L., Roseman, S. Romanow, P., & Vincent, C. (2011). Employment-related mobility and the health of workers, families, and communities: The Canadian context. *Labour/Le Travail*, 67, 121–155.

Williams, C. (2007). Fuelling the economy. *Perspectives*, May, 16–24.

SEVEN

FARMING THE CONSTITUTION

The Illegality of Excluding Alberta Farm Workers from Labour and Employment Legislation

Jennifer Koshan, Gianna Argento, Delna Contractor, Brynna Hambly (Takasugi), Paul Kennett, C.F. Andrew Lau, J. Graham Martinelli, Robin C. McIntyre, Nelson Medeiros, Heidi Rolfe, and Kay Elizabeth Turner

Workers have generally used two strategies to protect their interests: political action to achieve minimum protections and compensation schemes, and collective action to negotiate contractual rights such as better pay and job security (Tucker, 2006). In Alberta, four statutes have resulted from these efforts. Minimum standards and compensation are protected under the Employment Standards Code, Occupational Health and Safety Act, and Workers' Compensation Act, while the right to take collective action without employer interference is protected under the Labour Relations Code.

From the early 1900s, when this legislation was introduced in Alberta, until recently, farm workers were excluded from all four legislative regimes, either in whole or in part. This exclusion left them without the protections that most other workers enjoy and contributed to the precarious nature of their work (Vosko, 2006). While other Canadian jurisdictions historically excluded farm workers from similar protections, they have, for the most part, amended their legislation to rectify this inequity. Even in an overall context of "farm worker exceptionalism" (Tucker, 2012, citing Schell, 2002), Alberta has been an outlier in Canada for its comprehensive failure to protect farm workers, and was likely in breach of international standards for agricultural workers as well.

This chapter explores the strategy of "farming" the Canadian Charter of Rights and Freedoms as a basis for challenging these exclusions. The analysis was developed in a constitutional clinical project at the University of Calgary Faculty of Law in the winter of 2014 (Martinelli & Lau, 2014; Medeiros & McIntyre, 2014; Takasugi, Contractor, & Kennett, 2014; Turner, Argento, & Rolfe, 2014). At that time, the Progressive Conservatives had been in power in Alberta for over 40 years and the prospects for success in lobbying the government to include farm workers in the legislation were slim. The New Democrats took power in the spring of 2015 in Alberta, and one of the first laws the new government passed was Bill 6, the Enhanced Protection for Farm and Ranch Workers Act (2015). Our analysis shows that Alberta had a constitutional obligation to enact this law, because the exclusion of farm workers from employment and labour legislation violated farm workers' rights to freedom of association, security of the person, and equality under the Charter. Our review of the case law and secondary literature helps to identify the nature of the violations, and the weakness of the arguments available to the province to justify these violations under section 1 of the Charter. We conclude by examining the benefits and challenges of relying on legal strategies to achieve the protection of farm worker interests.

The Legislation and Some History and Comparisons

Alberta began excluding farm workers from labour and employment legislation with the introduction of the Workmen's Compensation Act of 1908. Section 10 of that Act excluded farm workers from compensation by employers for workplace injuries. As successive Alberta governments enacted broader standards for workers, legislators continued to exclude farm workers from these protections. Similar exclusions of farm workers originally existed in other Canadian provinces and at the federal level in employment insurance legislation. Beginning in the 1960s, other jurisdictions began to repeal the exclusions, making Alberta an outlier in Canada (Barnetson, 2009; Fudge, 2012; Tucker, 2006, 2012).

The Employment Standards Code (ESC) is the successor to a number of employment welfare statutes enacted in the 1930s and 1940s in Alberta, and farm workers were excluded from these statutes from the outset (see, for example, the Hours of Work Act, 1936, section 3; and the Labour

Welfare Act, 1943, section 3). The ESC today generally provides minimum protections for Alberta workers. Until Bill 6 was enacted, the ESC exempted persons employed on a farm or ranch from minimum wage, hours of work, and vacation protections, and exempted farm workplaces from restrictions on child labour. Bill 6 repealed the exemptions, but the original law remains in force while the government consults with stakeholders to develop regulations, which may continue to exempt some farm and ranch workers from particular protections in the ESC. Some other provinces, such as Ontario, exempt agricultural workers from some employment standards protections (Tucker, 2012; Exemptions, Special Rules and Establishment of Minimum Wage, O Reg 285/01). In other provinces, including Manitoba, coverage is tailored to certain factors, such as when farm work is undertaken by non-family members and when it is performed in climate-controlled facilities (Employment Standards Regulation, Man Reg 6/2007).

Alberta's Occupational Health and Safety Act (OHSA) creates minimum workplace standards designed to protect the health and safety of workers in the province. Government officers have the power to inspect worksites and investigate serious injuries or accidents, and workers have the right to refuse unsafe work without adverse job consequences (OHSA, sections 8, 19, 35). Before Bill 6, the OHSA only applied to a small range of farming and ranching operations—those involving the processing of food, greenhouses, mushroom and sod farms, nurseries, landscaping, and pet breeding and boarding (OHSA, section 1(s), Farming and Ranching Exemption Regulation, Alta Reg 27/95, sections 1, 2, 3). With Bill 6, Alberta became the last province to amend its occupational health and safety legislation to cover agricultural workers. However, Bill 6 stipulates that the exemption from the OHSA will still apply to family members and unpaid workers on farms and ranches. The government will also develop specific occupational health and safety technical standards for the farm and ranch industries.

Under the Workers' Compensation Act (WCA), workers who suffer workplace injuries are entitled to receive compensation and benefits through a no-fault insurance scheme funded by levies on employers. These benefits include income replacement, medical aid, and vocational rehabilitation for workers and their dependents. Receiving these benefits correspondingly disentitles workers and their dependents from suing employers for compensation. Most agricultural industries in Alberta were exempted from mandatory coverage from the early 1900s until Bill 6 came into effect in January 2016. While employers in the farming industry previously could opt into voluntary coverage for their workers, as Bob Barnetson reveals earlier in this volume, only about 7.5 per cent of employers did so. Workers' compensation coverage is now mandatory for farm and ranch industries in Alberta, with the exception of family members and unpaid workers.

The Labour Relations Code (LRC) gives workers in Alberta the right to form trade unions without employer interference, to collectively bargain with employers to gain job security and other benefits, and to withhold their labour under certain conditions. Before Bill 6 was enacted, persons employed on farms or ranches were completely excluded from the LRC (section 4(2)(e)) and, unlike many other excluded groups of workers in Alberta, are not covered under alternate labour relations statutes. The exclusion of farm workers from labour relations legislation dates back to the 1940s when labour laws were first enacted in Alberta (see, for example, the Labour Welfare Act, 1943, section 3; and the Alberta Labour Act, 1947, section 3). While other provinces originally exempted farm workers from labour legislation, Alberta became the exception once Ontario provided some protections for its farm workers following the *Dunmore* case, which will be discussed below. Pending government consultations following Bill 6, the exemption will remain in force until specific regulations are developed for farm and ranch industries under the LRC.

The historical legislative exclusions of farm workers in Alberta are each problematic in and of themselves, but the cumulative impact of the exclusions must also be considered. The exclusions meant that the government did not monitor working conditions on farms or protect farm workers from having to work long hours or in circumstances unfit for children, which could entail or create unsafe work conditions that workers could not refuse. If farm workers were then injured on the job, they typically could not claim workers' compensation or rehabilitation benefits. Nor could they organize collectively to advocate for improvement to their working conditions without being at risk of (further) adverse job consequences. The province's exclusion of farm workers from employment and labour laws resulted in several corresponding advantages to farm owners: In their roles as employers, they could set wages and hours of work that were most advantageous to them, they could employ child labourers, and they could require dangerous and demanding tasks of their workers without fear that these workers would complain to regulatory bodies. They could also avoid payment of levies for workers' compensation. Finally, they could avoid dealing with collective associations of farm workers.

What have been the rationales for maintaining this entrenched tradition of exploitation in agricultural workplaces? Historically, the government's justifications for the exclusions were to keep agricultural production high and food prices low, to accommodate the unpredictability of the harvest season, their fears of socialism and aggressive unions, and, according to Barnetson (2009), the insistence of both farm owners and government that so-called family farms are not a suitable environment for the protections that are appropriate for other industries. Concerns about the family farm also animated the discussions of Bill 6, leading to an amendment that continues to exempt family members and unpaid workers from the changes to the OHSA and WCA (an exemption that may also be maintained through the pending regulations for the ESC and LRC). Many of these rationales, Barnetson explains, are an articulation of the "agrarian myth," which promotes the notion of farming as a "virtuous activity" requiring "personal sacrifice" and justifying a lack of regulation so as not to imperil farms (2009, p. 65). Alberta's Progressive Conservatives, the ruling party until spring 2015, also derived a large portion of their electoral support from rural constituencies (Barnetson, this volume). Both the Progressive Conservatives and the right-wing Wildrose Party vehemently opposed Bill 6, and mobilized public opposition against the Bill and the New Democrats. Accordingly, the political consequences of reforming labour and employment laws in ways that farm owners consider adverse have also been factors in maintaining and advocating for the exclusions.

It is important to place these historical justifications in a modern context. A large portion of the agricultural industry in Alberta now consists of sophisticated, mechanized operations that require a staff much larger than that comprising members of the farm owners' families (Barnetson, 2009, 2012). Over time, Alberta farms are increasing in size and decreasing in number, in keeping with national and global trends toward corporatization of farming (Preibisch, 2009). The overall number of paid farm employees has decreased, yet the number of paid weeks of employment per farm has increased, leading Barnetson to suggest an increased reliance on paid labour in Alberta (this volume). These realities undermine many of the traditional rationales used to justify the exclusions of farm workers, as we discuss below.

The Constitutional Violations

The Canadian Charter of Rights and Freedoms is part of Canada's constitution. Under the principle of constitutional supremacy, all laws in Canada must comply with the Charter or they will be declared of no force or effect (Constitution Act 1982, section 52). Charter analysis entails a two-step process: (1) consideration of whether laws violate particular Charter rights, and, if so, (2) consideration of whether those violations can be justified under section 1 of the Charter, which permits governments to place limits on rights when those limits are reasonable and demonstrably justified in a free and democratic society.

Sections 2(d), 7, and 15 of the Charter are the most pertinent to the legality of excluding farm workers from Alberta's labour and employment legislation. We begin our analysis with section 2(d), which is only relevant in the labour relations context, followed by discussion of sections 7 and 15, which are more broadly relevant.

Freedom of Association: Section 2(d) of the Charter

Section 2(d) of the Charter protects freedom of association as a "fundamental freedom." In one of the Supreme Court of Canada's most recent decisions in the labour relations context, it interpreted section 2(d) as protecting the right of workers to join with others to form associations; to pursue other constitutional rights; and to meet the power and strength of other groups or entities on more equal terms (*Mounted Police Association of Ontario v. Canada (Attorney General)* [hereafter *Mounted Police*], 2015, para. 66).

The Supreme Court decisions of *Ontario (Attorney General) v. Fraser* [hereafter *Fraser*], 2011, and *Dunmore v. Ontario* (Attorney General) [hereafter *Dunmore*], 2001, are the leading cases on the legality of excluding farm workers from labour relations legislation. In *Dunmore*, farm workers in Ontario, though historically excluded from labour codes, were included for a brief time via the Agricultural Labour Relations Act, 1994 (ALRA) while the New Democratic Party (NDP) was in power. Under the ALRA, farm workers had the right to form trade unions and to collective bargaining rights. When the NDP lost power to the Conservatives, Ontario once again excluded farm workers from labour legislation via the Labour Relations and Employment Statute Law Amendment Act, 1995 (LRESLAA).

In *Dunmore*, the LRESLAA was found to be unconstitutional on the grounds that it infringed the freedom of association of farm workers. The Supreme Court held that a violation of section 2(d) will occur where exclusion from a protective regime amounts to substantial interference with the effective exercise of freedom of association. The unique vulnerability of farm workers as an economically disadvantaged group, often working in isolated settings, close to their employers meant that they could not form trade associations or have meaningful negotiations with their employers unless they had legislative protection. The Court struck down the exclusion of farm workers from labour relations legislation and indicated that, at a minimum, the government was required to enact a regime that protected "freedom to assemble, to participate in the lawful activities of the association and to make representations, and the right to be free from interference, coercion and discrimination in the exercise of these freedoms" (*Dunmore*, para. 67).

In *Fraser*, the Supreme Court re-examined the circumstances of farm workers in Ontario under new legislation that was enacted following *Dunmore*. Adhering very closely to the minimum requirements from *Dunmore*, the Agricultural Employees Protection Act, 2002 (AEPA) provided farm workers with only some rights, including "the rights to form and join an employees' association, to participate in its activities, to assemble, to make representations to their employers through their association on their terms and conditions of employment, and the right to be protected against interference, coercion and discrimination in the exercise of their rights" (AEPA, section 1(2)). The United Food and Commercial Workers and individual farm workers challenged the legislation after an attempt to collectively bargain with a large agricultural producer reached an impasse and where no remedy was available that would force the employer to bargain in good faith.

The claimants argued in *Fraser* that the new legislative scheme "substantially interfere[d] with the right to associate to achieve collective goals" including the right to collectively bargain, which had been found to be protected under section 2(d) of the Charter in *Health Services and Support-Facilities Subsector Bargaining Assn v. British Columbia* [hereafter *Health Services*], 2007. In *Fraser*, the Court appeared to re-articulate the test for a section 2(d) violation in a way that created a more stringent standard than *Dunmore*'s substantial interference: "whether the impugned law or state action has the effect of making it *impossible* to act collectively to achieve workplace goals" (para. 46; emphasis added). This standard could not be met on the evidence in *Fraser*; the Court found that the claim was "premature" because the workers had not given the legislation a sufficient chance to operate (para. 116). The majority emphasized that while section 2(d) protects "good faith bargaining on important workplace issues," it does not guarantee access to a particular model of labour relations or bargaining process (paras. 40, 47). Only Justice Abella, writing in dissent, accepted the claimants' argument that the AEPA impeded meaningful collective bargaining and therefore violated section 2(d) of the Charter.

The *Fraser* decision has been critiqued (e.g., Faraday, Fudge, & Tucker, 2012; Fudge, 2012; Lynk, 2012), but the loss to farm workers in that case does not undermine the constitutional illegality of excluding Alberta farm workers from labour legislation. The situation in Alberta is more similar to *Dunmore* than to *Fraser*, as farm workers have been entirely excluded from the ambit of the Labour Relations Code, thereby completely precluding them from taking any collective action or participating in any process of collective bargaining. Additionally, the Supreme Court has given new life to section 2(d) of the Charter following *Fraser*, extending it to include the right to strike (*Saskatchewan Federation of Labour v. Saskatchewan* [hereafter *Saskatchewan Federation of Labour*], 2015) and clarifying that the test for a violation of section 2(d) remains one of substantial interference, not impossibility (*Mounted Police*, 2015). The complete exclusion of Alberta's farm workers from the Labour Relations Code prior to Bill 6 substantially interfered with the meaningful exercise of their associational rights and, arguably, violated section 2(d) of the Charter.

Nevertheless, *Fraser* shows that Alberta might legitimately respond to this Charter violation with legislation similar to Ontario's Agricultural Employees Protection Act, which offers less fulsome protection for farm workers. The AEPA has not led to any collective agreements in the agricultural sector in Ontario, and there is not yet precedent for a government obligation to protect farm workers under the more robust Wagner model of labour relations, which gives exclusive bargaining rights to unions with majority workplace support (Fudge, 2012). Section 2(d), therefore, must be recognized as a somewhat limited protection of farm workers' rights in the labour context, although still an important one.

Right to Life, Liberty and Security of the Person: Section 7

Section 7 of the Charter provides that: "Everyone has the right to life, liberty and security of the person and the right not to be deprived thereof except in accordance with the principles of fundamental justice." This is a two-part right, and to be successful claimants must prove both (1) a deprivation of life, liberty and/or security of the person, and, (2) that this deprivation was contrary to the principles of fundamental justice.

Security of the person protects against state interference with a person's bodily integrity and serious state-imposed psychological stress (*R. v. Morgentaler* [hereafter *Morgentaler*], 1988; *New Brunswick (Minister of Health & Community Services) v. G(J)*, 1999; *Canada (Attorney General) v. Bedford* [hereafter *Bedford*], 2013). Security of the person is engaged in the case of Alberta farm workers because the province's under-regulation of farm workplaces has made their jobs substantively more dangerous than they would be if the government provided farm workers with legislative protections. This argument is particularly strong in the case of the Occupational Health and Safety Act, given the historical exclusion of most farms and ranches from mandatory workplace safety standards and inspections, and the inability of most farm and ranch workers to refuse unsafe work. In the case of the Employment Standards Code, the exclusions resulted in a lack of protection for children, and a lack of regulation of hours and time away from work, all of which have contributed to the creation of unsafe workplaces for farm workers. Under the Labour Relations Code, the argument is more indirect—specifically, that lack of union oversight has led to unsafe workplaces with no avenues of complaint for farm workers, who are precarious workers unlikely to assert their own interests (Tucker, 2006).

It is important to note that injuries and fatalities are disproportionately suffered by farm workers. Farm workers face exposure to harmful chemical and biological agents, an increased likelihood of workplace injury due to fatigue from long work days, physically demanding and repetitive tasks, use of hazardous equipment, and exposure to potentially dangerous livestock, as well as the risks inherent in unsafe transportation, inadequate sanitation, and working alone (Barnetson, 2012; Tucker, 2006). When compared with other industrial sectors in terms of absolute numbers of fatalities, agriculture is the most dangerous occupation (Pickett, Hartling, Brison, & Guernsey, 1999). Significantly, over 20 per cent of such fatalities involve children (Calgary Workers' Resource Centre, 2012). On average, 17 fatalities occur every year on Alberta farms, including three children per year (Alberta Agriculture and Rural Development, 2013).

Exclusion from the relevant statutes could be seen as a government-created risk of harm to farm workers' physical and psychological security of the person. The reasoning in *Bedford* strongly supports this argument. In that case, the Supreme Court struck down provisions of the Criminal Code regulating prostitution, finding that the government's regulatory scheme increased the dangers of engaging in sex work and, thereby, violated sex workers' security of the person rights. The exclusion of farm workers from the Occupational Health and Safety Act, the Employment Standards Code, and the Labour Relations Code prior to Bill 6 was similar: Excluding them from protective regimes substantively increased the workplace danger on farms and ranches. As long as the government action could be shown to have a sufficient causal connection with the risks to security of the person flowing from the exclusions, the government's obligation not to violate section 7 of the Charter would be engaged, and any arguments that the risks were more attributable to the actions of third parties or to farm workers' choice of employment could be refuted (*Bedford*, 2013). Arguments that the government bears no positive obligation to protect farm workers could also be refuted on the basis that once a government decides to provide benefit-conferring legislation, it must to do in compliance with the Charter (*Chaoulli v. Quebec (Attorney General)* [hereafter *Chaoulli*], 2005; *Dunmore*, 2001; *Vriend v. Alberta* [hereafter *Vriend*], 1997). This reasoning could also form the basis for a right to life argument under section 7, because the exclusions placed farm workers at greater risk of suffering fatal injuries (*PHS Community Services Society v. Canada (Attorney General)* [hereafter *PHS*], 2011; *Carter v. Canada (Attorney General)* [hereafter *Carter*], 2015).

Another issue engaging the section 7 rights to life, liberty, and security of the person arose under the Workers' Compensation Act prior to Bill 6. Delay in access to health care may result in detrimental physical and psychological effects that violate security of the person (*Chaoulli*, 2005; *Morgentaler*, 1988). Injured workers covered under the WCA likely have priority access to medical care and diagnostic tests, because health-care providers receive financial incentives to provide expedited services (Workers' Compensation Board, 2010 at 11). The exclusion of farm workers from the Workers' Compensation Act resulted in diminished quality and speed of health care as well as disentitlement to other services that are provided by the Workers' Compensation Board such as vocational rehabilitation (WCA; section 25). Farm workers, therefore, may have experienced both physical and psychological detriment as a result of the exclusion of mandatory WCB coverage, violating their right to security of the person.

The second part of the section 7 analysis asks whether the violations of life, liberty and/or security of the person are contrary to the principles of fundamental justice. These principles have been described as relating to the basic tenets of our legal system and can be procedural as well as substantive (*Re BC Motor Vehicle Act*, 1985). The principles of fundamental justice most relevant to the exclusion of farm workers from the ESC, LRC, OHSA, and WCA are that laws cannot be arbitrary, overbroad, or grossly disproportionate.

According to the Supreme Court: "A law is arbitrary where it bears no relation to, or is inconsistent with, the objective that lies behind [it]" (*Chaoulli*, 2005: para. 129; see also *Bedford*, 2013). The exclusion of agricultural workers under the OHSA prior to Bill 6 could be seen as arbitrary because the overall objective of that Act—to keep workers safe in their workplaces—is inconsistent with exempting farm and ranch workers from workplace protections (Barley, 2008). The fact that some farm and ranch workers were historically included under the OHSA also suggests a degree of arbitrariness. Similar reasoning applies to the exclusions from hours of work and child labour protections under the Employment Standards Code and from union oversight under the Labour Relations Code: Such exclusions were arbitrary in light of the overall protective goals of the legislation.

Also relevant is the purpose of the exclusions themselves. For example, the purpose of the Workers' Compensation Act exclusion was generally thought to be the protection of financial interests of agricultural industries by relieving them from mandatory participation in the workers' compensation scheme. Nevertheless, the exclusion may have been more harmful than beneficial to employers, since an injured farm worker not covered by the WCA could bring a claim in negligence, resulting in potential financial liability for the farm owner. This result occurred after the workplace death of farm worker Kevan Chandler, forcing the employer to declare bankruptcy after reaching settlement of a negligence claim launched by Mr. Chandler's widow (Barley, 2008; Barnetson, 2013). The exclusion of agricultural industries from the Workers' Compensation Act was thus arbitrary in light of its own purpose.

A second relevant principle of fundamental justice under section 7 of the Charter is overbreadth. A law will violate the principles of fundamental justice if the means used by the state are broader than necessary for the legislative objectives to be achieved (*Bedford*, 2013; *Carter*, 2015; *R. v. Heywood*, 1994). It bears repeating that one of the main objectives of the farm worker exclusions has been the protection of family farms; such farms tend to be small and are said to be unable to afford to meet the financial and administrative requirements of the ESC, LRC, OHSA, and WCA (Barnetson, 2009). This rationale is overbroad, however, because the exclusions impacted the rights of far more farm workers than those on family farms. As Barnetson discusses earlier in this volume, farm work is being performed less on small family farms and more in large industrial operations. The label "family farm" may also be inaccurate to the extent that it implies small size, given that some family-run farms are actually quite large in scale(see also Preibisch, 2009). The Supreme Court in *Dunmore* found the exclusion of all farm workers from Ontario's labour legislation to be overbroad on this basis, noting that some provinces have tailored their exclusions to small or family-run farms. If the government's concern is to protect family farming operations, there are narrower means of meeting this goal than blanket exclusions. This is recognized in Bill 6, with its continued exemptions for family members and unpaid workers in some circumstances.

The third relevant principle of fundamental justice is gross disproportionality. A law is grossly disproportionate when its negative effect on individuals is out of all proportion to the purpose of the measure (*Bedford*, 2013). In this case, the purpose of the exclusions—protection of the interests of small farm owners—is, arguably, grossly disproportionate to their negative effects—the potential physical and psychological injuries and risk of death the exclusions have caused to farm workers. In particular, evidence that children were injured or killed as a result of the exclusions would make it exceedingly difficult for Alberta to argue that the harm to individuals is a proportionate price to pay for financial relief to farm owners.

The grossly disproportionate impact on individual rights was the basis for finding that prostitution laws violated the principles of fundamental justice (*Bedford*, 2013), as did the federal government's failure to permit the continued existence of a safe injection site in Vancouver (*PHS*, 2011). Most recently, the criminal prohibitions on assisted death were found to be overbroad because they went further than necessary to protect the vulnerable (*Carter*, 2015). The outcomes of these other Charter challenges provide strong support for the position that the exclusion of farm workers from the relevant legislation violated their rights to life and security of the person in a manner contrary to the principles of fundamental justice.

The Right to Equality: Section 15

Section 15(1) of the Charter provides that "Every individual is equal before and under the law and has the right to the equal protection and equal benefit of the law without discrimination and, in particular, without discrimination based on race, national or ethnic origin, colour, religion, sex, age or mental or physical disability." Section 15 protects against both direct and indirect discrimination, whether intentional or unintentional, and its focus is on substantive rather than formal equality (*Andrews v. British Columbia* [hereafter *Andrews*], 1989; *Eldridge v. British Columbia (Attorney General)*, 1997; *Vriend*, 1998).

The first step of the test for a violation of section 15(1) requires proof of differential or adverse treatment that is based on at least one of the grounds enumerated in section 15(1) or an analogous ground (*R. v. Kapp* [hereafter *Kapp*], 2008; *Withler v. Canada (Attorney General)*, 2011). Farm workers were directly subject to differential treatment under the relevant legislation prior to Bill 6: They were excluded from protections and benefits that other workers receive. However, the basis for that differential treatment does not fit within any of the grounds explicitly enumerated in section 15(1), which requires consideration of whether occupational status as an agricultural worker is an analogous ground. The exclusions also may have indirectly differentiated on the basis of immigration status and ethnicity, given their disproportionate impact on migrant workers.

The Supreme Court has stated that an analogous ground is one that is based on "a personal characteristic that is immutable or changeable only at unacceptable cost to personal identity" as well as "characteristics... that the government has no legitimate interest in expecting us to change to receive equal treatment under the law" (*Corbiere v. Canada*, 1999, at para. 13). Although a majority of the Court has not yet adopted the position that occupational status is an analogous ground, this argument has found support amongst some members of the Court. In her concurring opinion in *Dunmore*, Justice L'Heureux-Dubé found that the occupational status of agricultural workers constituted an analogous ground because these workers face historic disadvantage and lack political power, and the government had no legitimate interest in expecting them to change their employment status to obtain equal treatment given the sense of identity and self-worth that flows from employment. The poor socio-economic circumstances of agricultural workers also supported the finding that they could change their occupation only at great cost, which is a useful finding to offset any government arguments based on "choice" of occupation. The majority of the Court declined to express an opinion on the analogous ground issue in *Dunmore*, deciding the case on freedom of association under section 2(d) of the Charter instead.

In *Fraser*, the Court had to address section 15(1) given its dismissal of the farm workers' section 2(d) claim. Justices Rothstein and Charron rejected the discrimination argument based on their finding that occupational status as an agricultural worker was not shown to meet the test for analogous grounds on the evidence before them. Similarly, in *Baier v. Alberta* the Court rejected a section 15(1) challenge based on occupational status more generally, stating that it did not have any basis for finding that this was an analogous ground "on the evidence presented" (2007, at para. 64). These cases leave some space for arguing that occupational status as a farm worker qualifies as an analogous ground, if strong evidence of the systemic marginalization and exploitation of farm workers was presented. Faraday (2012), however, reminds us that evidence of this kind of marginalization was, in fact, presented in *Fraser*, yet ignored by the Court.

The second relevant ground flows from the fact that many farm workers are international migrants on temporary work permits under the Temporary Foreign Worker Program (TFWP) or Seasonal Agricultural Worker Program (Preibisch, 2009). In this context, excluding farm workers adversely impacts them based on their immigration status. Immigration status is not an enumerated ground under section 15(1), but the Supreme Court has already accepted citizenship as an analogous ground (*Andrews*, 1989), so this would not be a major hurdle in the requirement to prove differential treatment based on a protected ground. Ethnicity might also be seen as a relevant ground given that many migrant farm workers are racialized (Faraday, 2012; *Peart v. Ontario (Community Safety and Correctional Services)* [hereafter *Peart*], 2014).

Because the legislation does not explicitly single out migrant farm workers for differential treatment, however, it may be more challenging to show that the exclusions created distinctions based on immigration status and ethnicity. It is worthwhile to examine how Alberta's legislative exclusions interacted with the vulnerabilities and disadvantages that migrant farm workers already experience. Some of these disadvantages are attributable to the federal government, including the inability of migrant farm workers to gain permanent resident status and to work outside the agricultural sector, or even for a different employer, given the closed nature of their work permits. Other disadvantages are attributable to farm owners, including their recruitment of migrant farm workers to the most precarious forms of farm work, and their housing of workers in substandard conditions, often in isolated settings without access to services. Migrant farm workers are reluctant to make complaints to their employers and to refuse unsafe work, and are vulnerable to deportation following termination by their employers and to mistreatment in their countries of origin upon return (Faraday, 2012; *Peart*, 2014; Preibisch, 2012; Tucker, 2006; *United Mexican States v. British Columbia (Labour Relations Board)*, 2014). This set of circumstances has resulted in uniquely adverse impacts, including lack of freedom and increased risks to health and safety that are even more egregious than those experienced by other farm workers and by migrant workers in other fields. Alberta's legislative exclusions therefore effectively created differential treatment based on immigration status and ethnicity (*Peart*, 2014; Preibisch & Otero, 2014).

The historical exclusions of farm workers can also be analyzed using an intersectionality or combination of grounds approach (*Falkiner v. Ontario (Ministry of Community and Social Services)*, 2002). Intersectionality recognizes that there are multiple aspects of farm workers' identities, including their occupational and immigration status and disadvantaged socio-economic position, that converge to create a unique experience of discrimination. It is also important to note the role of law in constructing the differential and disadvantageous treatment of farm workers on these intersecting grounds (Faraday, 2012).

Once distinctions based on enumerated or analogous grounds are established, the second step under section 15(1) requires proof that the distinctions are discriminatory. The test for discrimination has changed over time, and its current content is somewhat unsettled. In *Kapp* (2008), the Supreme Court unanimously framed the test as requiring proof that the distinction results in the perpetuation of prejudice or stereotyping against the claimant group. In *Quebec (Attorney General) v. A.* (2013), several members of the Court acknowledged that a focus on prejudice (the holding of pejorative attitudes) and stereotyping (attributing characteristics to individuals based on group membership rather than actual needs and circumstances) may capture only discriminatory attitudes. They indicated that consideration of the perpetuation of disadvantage more broadly is also required in order to capture the effects of discriminatory conduct. An approach focusing on historical disadvantage was accepted by a unanimous Supreme Court in its most recent decision on section 15(1), although the Court continues to import considerations of arbitrariness into its analysis (*Kahkewistahaw First Nation v. Taypotat*, 2015). Discrimination analysis thus involves examination of how the challenged laws perpetuate prejudice, negative stereotypes, and arbitrary imposition of disadvantage, as well as how they perpetuate historical inequities.

Farm workers have traditionally been regarded as disadvantaged workers. As the Supreme Court recognized in *Dunmore*: "they are poorly paid, face difficult working conditions, have low levels of skill and education, low status and limited employment mobility" (2001, at para. 165). These historical disadvantages are even more pronounced in the case of migrant farm workers. Alberta's perpetuation of these disadvantages by excluding farm workers from the ESC, LRC, OHSA, and WCA therefore constituted discrimination. The exclusions have had the following effects: farm workers have had limited access to minimum standards of employment; they have been subject to the risks inherent in dangerous, unregulated workplaces; they typically have not been entitled to compensation or rehabilitation for their injuries; and they have not been able to organize collectively to make their working conditions less precarious. The disadvantaging effects of Alberta's historical treatment of farm workers are most apparent when the cumulative impact of the legislation is considered, but the disadvantage flowed from each statute separately as well.

Another way of framing the discrimination argument is that Alberta's traditional rationales of minimizing financial and regulatory costs on family farms and of maintaining their unique characters are based on stereotypical assumptions about the nature of agricultural operations that do not reflect the needs and circumstances of many farm workers, and are thus arbitrary. To the extent that Bill 6 continues to exempt only family members and unpaid workers, the government could be seen to have corrected this element of arbitrariness, however.

The province's historical exclusion of farm workers from the relevant legislation could also be seen as having been based on the prejudicial view that they were not worthy or deserving of the protections to which other workers are entitled, or that they were less likely to fight their exploitation than other workers, because of lack of capacity, resources, and labour mobility. This argument would be particularly strong in the case of migrant farm workers (Preibisch, 2012; Tucker, 2006). The wholesale exclusion of farm workers prior to Bill 6 thus resulted in the perpetuation of disadvantage and prejudicial and stereotypical attitudes about farm workers.

There are, however, Supreme Court judgments that present some challenges to the argument that government exclusion of farm workers from labour and employment legislation is discriminatory. In *Fraser*, the majority of the Court found that the farm workers' section 15(1) claim was premature, stating that, "on the record before us, it has not been established that the regime utilizes unfair stereotypes or perpetuates existing prejudice and disadvantage" (2011, at para. 116). In *Health Services*, while a majority of the Court found a violation of section 2(d) of the Charter, it rejected the claim that the legislation violated section 15(1) because it discriminated against a particular group, health-care workers. According to the majority, "the differential and adverse effects of the legislation on some groups of workers relate essentially to the type of work they do, and not to the persons they are" (2007, at para. 165). The outcomes in both *Fraser* and *Health Services* could be attributed to inadequate evidentiary records, but they are still cautionary tales about the difficulties inherent in enforcing government obligations not to discriminate in the context of labour and employment laws.

There are also cautionary tales beyond the Supreme Court. In *Peart* (2014), the Ontario human rights tribunal dismissed a complaint by farm workers about their exclusion from provincial legislation requiring a coroner's inquest following fatal workplace accidents in the mining and construction industries. The tribunal found that the exclusion had an adverse impact on migrant farm workers on the basis of their race and immigration status, but that the exclusion was not discriminatory when considering the government's purpose for singling out mining and construction workers. The evidence established that workers in those industries faced a greater risk of workplace fatalities from a greater range of sources than migrant farm workers, and the tribunal held that the government's preferential treatment did not perpetuate stereotyping or indicate that the lives of migrant farm workers were less worthy of protection when looked at in that context. Although the *Peart* decision is not binding in Alberta, it illustrates the difficulties in the current approach to discrimination law, where courts and tribunals may focus too heavily on the government's intentions rather than the adverse effects of its exclusionary treatment of particular workers.

Overall, the strongest Charter arguments for government obligations to include farm workers under labour and employment legislation lie under section 2(d) in relation to the Labour Relations Code, and under section 7 in relation to the Occupational Health and Safety Act, Employment Standards Code, and Workers' Compensation Act. Discrimination arguments are also available for all four statutes, if occupational status as farm workers were recognized as a protected ground under section 15(1) of the Charter, and if the exclusions were seen to result in the perpetuation of disadvantage, prejudice or stereotyping.

International Law

International law also supports the argument that governments are obligated to include farm workers under labour and employment legislation. Conventions of the International Labour Organization (ILO) ratified by Canada guarantee freedom of association, the right to workplace protections, and equality among workers (Convention (No. 87) Concerning Freedom of Association and Protection of the Right to Organize; Promotional Framework for Occupational Safety and Health; Discrimination (Employment and Occupation) Convention), as does the Declaration on Fundamental Principles and Rights at Work. The Supreme Court relied on international instruments in *Dunmore*, *Health Services*, and *Saskatchewan Federation of Labour*, although it must be recognized that the Court can use international law selectively. In *Fraser*, it declined to refer to a decision of the ILO's Committee on Freedom of Association that the Agricultural Employees Protection Act's regime for Ontario farm workers violated ILO principles on collective bargaining, and even in *Dunmore* the Court mentioned only aspects of international law that were consistent with its relatively narrow definition of freedom of association (Fudge, 2012). The views of the ILO Committee on Freedom of Association recently received a more positive reception in *Saskatchewan Federation of Labour*, where a majority of the Supreme Court relied on international human rights law as a "magnetic guide" supporting the right to strike (2015, at para. 63).

Although this analysis suggests that Alberta's historical exclusion of farm workers violated their Charter rights, the government always has the opportunity to justify infringements under section 1 of the Charter.

Justifying Violations under Section 1

Section 1 stipulates that the Charter "guarantees the rights and freedoms set out in it subject only to such reasonable limits prescribed by law as can be demonstrably justified in a free and democratic society." In order to justify a limit on the rights and freedoms of farm workers, Alberta would need to prove that the exclusions have a pressing and substantial objective, that they are rationally connected to that objective and minimally impair the rights or freedoms in question, and that there is proportionality between the salutary and deleterious effects of the exclusions and the rights violations (*R. v. Oakes*, 1986). Failure at any stage would defeat the province's case.

It is rare for section 1 arguments to fail at the pressing and substantial objective stage, although there is precedent for the proposition that cost and administrative convenience alone cannot justify a Charter violation short of a fiscal crisis (*Nova Scotia (Workers' Compensation Board) v. Martin*, 2003; *Newfoundland (Treasury Board) v. N.A.P.E.*, 2004). In *Dunmore*, the Supreme Court accepted Ontario's stated rationale for excluding agricultural workers from labour legislation—protection of the unique nature of family farms and farm productivity—as a pressing and substantial objective. According to the Court, "the fact that Ontario is moving increasingly towards corporate farming and agribusiness does not...diminish the importance of protecting the unique characteristics of the family farm; on the contrary, it may even augment it" (2001, at para. 52). This was not seen as an economic rationale by the Court, which construed family farming as a way of life more than a commercial enterprise. If Alberta had put forward a similar argument and evidence in the event of a Charter challenge to the exclusion of farm workers from the relevant statutes, it is likely the courts would have followed *Dunmore* to find a pressing and substantial objective.

The second stage of analysis under section 1 requires consideration of whether the government's means of achieving its objectives are rational or, conversely, whether the law is arbitrary. The arguments outlined earlier regarding the arbitrariness of the exclusions under section 7 of the Charter would be relevant at this stage, as would the arguments under section 15(1) relating to the underlying stereotypical assumptions about farm workers. The historical exclusion of farm workers could be seen as arbitrary in light of the exclusions' inconsistency with the overall objectives of the legislation, which include protecting associational rights, employment standards, workplace safety norms, and appropriate compensation for injured workers.

Further to this argument, the Court held in *Dunmore* that a purely economic rationale for excluding farm workers did not meet the rational connection test in light of the fact that most other employers in Ontario had to cope with the costs of inclusion of their workers under labour relations regimes. This reasoning shows that Alberta's historical exclusion of farm workers was arbitrary, given the inclusion of most other workers (and indeed some farm and ranch workers) in labour and employment statutes.

On the other hand, in *Dunmore* the Court found that the exclusion of farm workers from labour legislation was rationally connected to the objective of protecting family farms, as unionization might "threaten the flexibility and cooperation that are characteristic of the family farm" (2001, at para. 54). This rationale was not applicable in the case of larger farming operations, however, where preserving flexibility for employers was said to be irrational and, in fact, coercive. Bill 6 recognizes that the exclusions of farm workers from the relevant legislation are only rational and justifiable to the extent that they relate to family farms.

At the minimal impairment stage, the focus of analysis would be whether Alberta impaired the rights or freedoms of farm workers more than was reasonably necessary to achieve its objectives. In *Dunmore*, the Supreme Court held that Ontario could not justify "the categorical exclusion of agricultural workers where no satisfactory effort has been made to protect their basic right to form associations" (2001, at para. 59). The exclusion of farm workers from Ontario's labour code impaired their section 2(d) rights more than reasonably necessary in two ways: by excluding all agricultural sectors from the right to associate, and by denying every aspect of the right to farm workers. The Court noted that other provinces, such as Quebec and New Brunswick, had tailored the exclusion of farm workers to farms with small numbers of employees. This reasoning provides a strong basis for finding that the total exclusion of farm workers from the Labour Relations Code in Alberta historically could not be justified. For similar reasons, the exclusions of farm workers from the Employment Standards Code, the Occupational Health and Safety Act, and the Workers' Compensation Act would likely have failed the section 1 justification test, although those exclusions were not fully categorical: Farm workers have always had some entitlements under the ESC and, if farm owners opted in, under the WCA. Moreover, some farm and ranch workers were included under the OHSA even before Bill 6. Following Bill 6, because the exclusions have been restricted to family members and unpaid workers on farms and ranches, the government would likely be seen as minimally impairing farm workers' rights.

What about the claim that education and training are reasonable alternatives to the inclusion of farm workers in the legislation? This argument was made by Alberta in response to the recommendations of Judge Peter Barley following the Kevan Chandler fatality inquiry. Judge Barley recommended that Alberta should include paid farm workers under the OHSA and should develop training programs to minimize the risks of farm work (Barley, 2008). In response, the government at the time established a Farm Safety Advisory Council, a body that, with only one farm worker representative, recommended education and training for farm safety issues rather than legislative action (Farm Safety Advisory Council, 2012). If the government had been called upon to justify this response under section 1 of the Charter, it would have been required to produce evidence that these strategies have reduced the rates of injury and death to farm workers, and would have been required to explain why voluntary workplace safety measures were appropriate for farm workers when they are mandatory for most other industries. Similarly, if the government had tried to justify the alternative of opt-in coverage under the WCA as reasonable, farm workers could have pointed to the small number of farm owners who actually opted in, leaving many farm workers without protection.

In the case of the Employment Standards Code, it is difficult to envision any justification the government might make for the exclusion of farm workers from the child labour protections. However, Alberta might establish seasonally based limits in relation to farm workers' hours of work as a reasonable alternative to their complete exclusion from protection in this area, or limit the exclusion to family members as Manitoba has done. Indeed, for all of the statutes, exclusions restricted to small farms or to family members and unpaid workers is a significantly less impairing means of meeting the government's objectives, which Bill 6 has done for the OHSA and WCA. Other provinces have similarly tailored their legislation without imperilling their agricultural industries.

The final stage of section 1 justification analysis requires consideration of the proportionality between the salutary and deleterious effects of the law and the rights violations. This factor has traditionally not been determinative, but the Supreme Court gave it new life in the *Alberta v. Hutterian Brethren of Wilson Colony* case, where the Court noted that it "allows for a broader assessment of whether the benefits of the impugned law are worth the cost of the rights limitation" (2009, at para. 77). The salutary effects, or benefits, of the exclusions of farm workers from the ESC, LRC, OHSA, and WCA were that farm owners had the freedom to regulate their workplaces in ways that were most appropriate to their specific business—they were not required to deal with collective action, to apply minimum workplace norms and safety standards, or to pay into workers' compensation schemes. The deleterious effects of the exclusions were that farm workers died or were injured in higher numbers than in other occupations; they had no access to workers' compensation or expedited health and rehabilitation services; and they had no meaningful ability to achieve better workplace conditions collectively, solely because of their occupational status. These harms would be particularly hard to justify when inflicted on migrant farm workers and child labourers. It would, therefore, have been very difficult for the province to assert that the benefits of the historical exclusions for farm owners outweighed the severely detrimental effects that the rights violations had on farm workers.

Conclusion

There are strong arguments that the historical exclusions of farm workers from the Employment Standards Code, the Labour Relations Code, the Occupational Health and Safety Act, and the Workers' Compensation Act unjustifiably violated the Charter. It may well be that Alberta's new government was recognizing its constitutional obligations when it passed Bill 6, for the most part repealing the exclusions. Interestingly, however, the government did not clearly invoke its Charter obligations as the impetus for Bill 6, which may have helped to offset the opposition's and the public's criticism of the Bill (Alberta Hansard, 29th Legislature, 1st Session (2015–2016)).

The government's enactment of Bill 6 without being ordered by the courts to do so is nonetheless a very positive development. Constitutional litigation is complex, expensive, and takes time to resolve, and farm workers may have been too marginalized and dispersed to mount litigation without the strength of union support (Barnetson, 2009; Tucker, 2006). Moreover, litigation of farm worker rights has had limited success in the past, especially in the context of collective bargaining, which has led some critics to question its utility (Fudge, 2012). At the same time, the experience in Ontario, where successive governments enacted and then withdrew labour protections for farm workers, reminds us that governments and laws change. Litigation may remain a necessary strategy for enforcing farm workers' rights in future, depending on which party is in power.

It must also be recognized that inclusion in the legislation is only the first step. Regulations are still being developed, and they may continue to exclude some farm workers in ways that engage their Charter rights. Moreover, Tucker (2006) has noted enforcement difficulties with respect to employment protections, which may present an ongoing challenge that would need to be addressed by farm workers and their representatives. This need for vigilance around enforcement may be facilitated by permitting unionization in farm workplaces. Collective representation can lead to the acquisition and enforcement of protective provisions in collective agreements (e.g., those related to wages and hours of work) that could be enforced through the labour arbitration process. At the same time, farm workers may face difficulties in organizing in spite of Bill 6, particularly in workplaces in which there are many migrant farm workers, in light of the precarious nature of their employment circumstances. The experience of Ontario farm workers under the AEPA following *Dunmore* and *Fraser* also illustrates that protection of representation rights without legislated collective bargaining rights and the right to strike may not lead to significant changes in working conditions for farm workers (Fudge, 2012). The government would do well to heed the lessons from these cases when it is developing regulations under the LRC.

In spite of these enforcement challenges and the work still to be done to implement Bill 6, the inclusion of farm workers in labour and employment legislation is a crucial first step that was long overdue in Alberta.

References

Cases, International Materials, and Legislation

Agricultural Employees Protection Act, 2002, SO 2002, c 16.
Agricultural Labour Relations Act, 1994, SO 1994, c 6.
Alberta, Legislative Assembly, *Alberta Hansard*, 27th Leg, 3rd Sess (24 March 2010) at 1848.
Alberta, Legislative Assembly, *Alberta Hansard*, 29th Leg, 1st Sess (2015–2016)
Alberta Labour Act, SA 1947, c. 8.
Alberta v. Hutterian Brethren of Wilson Colony, 2009 SCC 37.
Andrews v. British Columbia, [1989] 1 SCR 143.
Baier v. Alberta, 2007 SCC 31.
Bill 6, the Enhanced Protection for Farm and Ranch Workers Act, 29th Legislature, 1st Session (2015).
Canada (Attorney General) v. Bedford, 2013 SCC 72.
Canadian Charter of Rights and Freedoms, Part I of the Constitution Act, 1982, being Schedule B to the Canada Act 1982 (UK), 1982, c 11.
Carter v. Canada (Attorney General), 2015 SCC 5.
Chaoulli v. Quebec (Attorney General), 2005 SCC 35.
Corbiere v. Canada, [1999] 2 SCR 203.
Dunmore v. Ontario (Attorney General), 2001 SCC 94.
Eldridge v. British Columbia (Attorney General), [1997] 3 SCR 624.
Employment Standards Code, RSA 2000, c E-9.
Employment Standards Regulation, Alta Reg 14/1997.
Employment Standards Regulation, Man Reg 6/2007.
Exemptions, Special Rules and Establishment of Minimum Wage, Ontario Regulation 285/01.

Falkiner v. Ontario (Ministry of Community and Social Services), 2002 59 OR (3d) 481 (CA).
Farming and Ranching Exemption Regulation, Alta Reg 27/95.
Health Services and Support-Facilities Subsector Bargaining Assn v. British Columbia, 2007 SCC 27.
Hours of Work Act, SA 1936, c 5.
International Labour Organization, Convention (No. 87) Concerning Freedom of Association and Protection of the Right to Organize, 68 UNTS 17 (1948).
International Labour Organization, Declaration on Fundamental Principles and Rights at Work IHRR 285 (1999).
International Labour Organization, Discrimination (Employment and Occupation) Convention (No. 111), 25 June 1958, 42nd ILC.
International Labour Organization, Promotional Framework for Occupational Safety and Health, 15 June 2006, No. 87, Geneva, 95th ILC Session.
Kahkewistahaw First Nation v. Taypotat, 2015 SCC 30.
Labour Relations and Employment Statute Law Amendment Act, 1995, SO 1995, c 1.
Labour Relations Code, RSA 2000, c L-1.
Labour Welfare Act, SA 1943, c 5.
Mounted Police Association of Ontario v. Canada (Attorney General), 2015 SCC 1.
Newfoundland (Treasury Board) v. N.A.P.E., 2004 SCC 66.
New Brunswick (Minister of Health & Community Services) v. G(J), [1999] 3 SCR 46.
Nova Scotia (Workers' Compensation Board) v. Martin, 2003 SCC 54.
Occupational Health and Safety Act, RSA 2000, c 23.
Ontario (Attorney General) v. Fraser, 2011 SCC 20.
Peart v. Ontario (Community Safety and Correctional Services), 2014 HRTO 611.
PHS Community Services Society v. Canada (Attorney General), 2011 SCC 44.
Quebec (Attorney General) v. A., 2013 SCC 5.
Re BC Motor Vehicle Act, [1985] 2 SCR 486.
R. v. Heywood, [1994] 3 SCR 761.
R. v. Kapp, 2008 SCC 41.
R. v. Morgentaler, [1988] 1 SCR 30.
R. v. Oakes, [1986] 1 SCR 103.
Saskatchewan Federation of Labour v. Saskatchewan, 2015 SCC 4.
United Mexican States v. British Columbia (Labour Relations Board), 2014 BCSC 54.
Vriend v. Alberta, [1998] 1 SCR 493.
Withler v. Canada (Attorney General), 2011 SCC 12.
Workers' Compensation Act, RSA 2000, c W-15.
Workmen's Compensation Act, RSA 1908 c 12.

Secondary Sources

Alberta Agriculture and Rural Development. (2013). *Industry Profiles: Agricultural Industry*. Edmonton, AB: Author. Retrieved Feb. 12, 2015 from http://eae.alberta.ca/documents/profiles/industry-profile-agriculture.pdf

Barley, P. (2008). *Report to the Minister of Justice and Attorney General, Public Fatality Inquiry, Kevan Chandler*. Okotoks, AB: Author.
Barnetson, B. (2009). The regulatory exclusion of agricultural workers in Alberta. *Just Labour: A Canadian Journal of Work and Society, 14*, 50–74.
Barnetson, B. (2012). No right to be safe: Justifying the exclusion of Alberta farm workers from health and safety legislations. *Socialist Studies, 8*(2), 3–29.
Barnetson, B. (2013). The most unsafe workplace in Alberta. *Alberta Views, 16*(4), 28–32.
Calgary Workers' Resource Centre. (2012). *Regulatory weaknesses in Alberta's employment legislation and their impact on the economic well-being of vulnerable workers*. Calgary, AB: Author.
Faraday, F. (2012). Envisioning equality: Analogous grounds and farm workers' experience of discrimination. In F. Faraday, J. Fudge, & E. Tucker (Eds.), *Constitutional labour rights in Canada: Farm workers and the Fraser case* (pp. 109–138). Toronto, ON: Irwin Law.
Faraday, F., Fudge, J., & Tucker, E. (Eds.). (2012). *Constitutional labour rights in Canada: Farm workers and the Fraser case*. Toronto, ON: Irwin Law.
Farm Safety Advisory Council. (2012). *Recommendations to the Minister of Alberta Agriculture and Rural Development: Enhanced farm safety education and training*. Edmonton, AB: Author. Retrieved Feb. 12, 2015 from http://www1.agric.gov.ab.ca/$Department/deptdocs.nsf/all/aet13518/$FILE/farm-safety-report-02-2012.pdf
Fudge, J. (2012). Constitutional rights, collective bargaining and the Supreme Court of Canada: Retreat and reversal in the *Fraser* case. *Industrial Law Journal, 41*(1), 1–29.
Lynk, M. (2011). Labour rights are human rights: Labour rights under the Charter after Fraser. In *The Labour Movement After Fraser: Report of a Seminar held May 30, 2011 on the Supreme Court of Canada Decision AG of Ontario v. Fraser* (pp. 34–38). Ottawa, ON: Canadian Foundation for Labour Rights.
Martinelli, G., & Lau, A. (2014). Challenging the farm work exclusions in the employment standards code. ABlawg Blog. Retrieved Feb. 12, 2015 from http://ablawg.ca/2014/05/27/challenging-the-farm-work-exclusions-in-the-employment-standards-code/
Medeiros, N., & McIntyre, R. (2014). The constitutionality of the exclusion of farm industries under the Alberta Workers' Compensation Act. ABlawg Blog. Retrieved Feb. 12, 2015 from http://ablawg.ca/2014/05/14/the-constitutionality-of-the-exclusion-of-farm-industries-under-the-alberta-workers-compensation-act/
Pickett, W., Hartling, L., Brison, R., & Guernsey, J. (1999). Fatal work-related farm injuries in Canada, 1991–1995. *Canadian Medical Association Journal, 160*(13), 1843–1848.
Preibisch, K. (2009). Local produce, foreign labor: Labor mobility programs and global trade competitiveness in Canada. *Rural Sociology, 72*(3), 418–449.
Preibisch, K. (2012). Development as remittances or development as freedom? Exploring Canada's temporary migration programs from a rights-based approach. In F. Faraday, J. Fudge, & E. Tucker (Eds.), *Constitutional labour rights in Canada: Farm workers and the Fraser case* (pp. 81–108). Toronto, ON: Irwin Law.
Preibisch, K., & Otero, G. (2014). Does citizenship status matter in Canadian agriculture? Workplace health and safety for migrant and immigrant laborers. *Rural Sociology, 79*(2), 174–199.

Schell, G. (2002). Farmworker exceptionalism under the law: How the legal system contributes to farmworker poverty and powerlessness. In C. Thompson Jr. & M. Wiggins (Eds.), *The human cost of food: Farmworkers' lives, labor, and advocacy* (pp. 139–166). Austin, TX: University of Texas Press.

Takasugi, B., Contractor, D., & Kennett, P. (2014). The statutory exclusion of farm workers from the Alberta Labour Relations Code. ABlawg Blog. Retrieved Feb. 12, 2015 from http://ablawg.ca/2014/05/02/the-statutory-exclusion-of-farm-workers-from-the-alberta-labour-relations-code/

Tucker, E. (2006). Will the vicious circle of precariousness be unbroken? The exclusion of Ontario farm workers from the Occupational Health and Safety Act. In L. Vosko (Ed.), *Precarious employment: Understanding labour market insecurity in Canada* (pp. 256–276). Montreal, QC: McGill-Queen's University Press.

Tucker, E. (2012). Farm worker exceptionalism: Past, present, and the post-Fraser future. In F. Faraday, J. Fudge, & E. Tucker (Eds.), *Constitutional labour rights in Canada: Farm workers and the Fraser case* (pp. 30–56). Toronto, ON: Irwin Law.

Turner, K., Argento, G., & Rolfe, H. (2014). Alberta farm and ranch workers: The last frontier of workplace protection. ABlawg Blog. Retrieved Feb. 12, 2015 from http://ablawg.ca/2014/04/28/alberta-farm-and-ranch-workers-the-last-frontier-of-workplace-protection/

Vosko, L. (2006). Precarious employment: Towards an improved understanding of labour market insecurity. In L. Vosko (Ed.), *Precarious employment: Understanding labour market insecurity in Canada* (pp. 3–39). Montreal, QC: McGill-Queen's University Press.

Workers' Compensation Board. (2010). *Physician's Reference Guide*. Edmonton, AB: Author. Retrieved from http://www.wcb.ab.ca/pdfs/providers/C459_physicians_reference_guide.pdf

EIGHT

BC-GROWN

Examining the Place-Embeddedness of Managed Migration and Farm Labour Markets in British Columbia

Kerry Preibisch

Introduction

Canadian growers have used institutionalized programs of "managed migration" to meet their labour demands since 1966, when Canada launched the Seasonal Agricultural Worker Program (SAWP). For the next three decades, the SAWP operated as one of only two mechanisms authorizing the employment of international migrants to fill jobs characterized as low skill in the Canadian labour market, with the other dedicated to live-in caregivers performing domestic work. It was not until 2002 that a federal initiative permitted all employers experiencing labour shortages in low-wage jobs, regardless of sector, to hire international migrants. Despite the fact that agricultural producers in Canada had privileged access to international migrants for low-wage work for 36 years prior to other employers, this was not true in all provinces. In British Columbia, Canada's third largest agricultural labour market, the provincial government did not allow growers to access migrants through the SAWP until 2004. Despite this late entry into the market for international labour, BC growers made up for lost time and, by 2014, the province employed over 6,000 international migrants in agriculture, ranking as the third-highest provincial employer behind Ontario and Quebec (Employment and Social Development Canada, 2014). This chapter analyzes the development of migrant employment in BC agriculture since 2002, tracing the rapid incorporation of Mexican migrants under the SAWP. I situate international migrant workers on temporary work permits as a discernible type of labourer, whose particular relations to employers and to labour markets are structured by the managed migration programs that authorize their employment. Using Luin Goldring and Patricia Landolt's (2011) concept of precarious legal status, I show how authorized status for migrant farm workers in British Columbia intersects with precarious work in agriculture. Finally, I use the narratives of BC growers to highlight how the precarious status of international migrants enables labour hyper-productivity within BC's food system. The chapter is based on a transnational ethnography of the social relations among those involved in agriculture in Canada. It outlines the international labour migration of agrifood workers in British Columbia, based on research that I undertook in that province and in Mexico with migrants, migrant- and/or labour-rights activists, growers, and civil servants (see Preibisch & Otero, 2014). It draws, in particular, from the in-depth interviews I conducted with these latter two groups between 2006 and 2009.[1]

The Seasonal Agricultural Worker Program in BC

Agriculture in British Columbia has long relied on low-wage labour supplied by workers with less-than-full citizenship status. From the turn of the century until the 1930s, these workers comprised thousands of indentured Chinese labourers; during the Second World War, they were interned Japanese-Canadians, German prisoners of war, and conscientious objectors; and, during the immediate postwar period, they were Polish war veterans and displaced persons (Lanthier & Wong, 2002; Mann, 1982; Satzewich, 1991; Wong, 1988). In the 1960s, growers also employed international migrants from the southern United States, the Caribbean, and Portugal, many of whom were not authorized to work in Canada (Satzewich, 1991; Wall, 1992; Wong, 1988). Throughout the 20th century, these migrant farm workers, many of them racialized as non-whites (or in the case of the Doukhobors, as religious radicals), worked in an ethnically, racially, and religiously diverse agricultural labour force alongside new immigrants and Canadian-born citizens who had migrated to farms in British Columbia from places of economic disadvantage, such as reserves of First Nations people, Quebec, and the Maritimes (Basok, 2002; BC Human Rights Commission, 1983; Lanthier & Wong, 2002; Satzewich, 1991).

The Seasonal Agricultural Worker Program, which authorizes foreign nationals to work on Canadian farms, is constituted by bilateral agreements between the Canadian government and government officials in participating migrant-sending countries. The Seasonal Agricultural Worker Program is available only to employers who seek to fill jobs in primary agriculture and in production in specific commodity sectors, for a maximum of eight months per worker per year. By 2012, the Canadian government approved almost 30,000 men and women from Mexico and 12 Caribbean countries to work on temporary contracts in a range of agrifood operations as diverse as cucumber greenhouses in Ontario and apiaries in Alberta. In spite of the fact that BC's Department of Agriculture had received requests from the province's growers since the 1950s (Lanthier & Wong, 2002), it refused them access to the Seasonal Agricultural Worker Program until 2004 (Muñoz & Manuel, 2011). Employers in Ontario and Quebec were the first beneficiaries in 1966, followed by Alberta and Manitoba (1992), Prince Edward Island and New Brunswick (2001), Saskatchewan (2003) and Nova Scotia (also 2004) (Muñoz & Manuel, 2011).

British Columbia's late arrival to the SAWP can be explained in part by the availability of immigrant workers. In 1967, changes to Canada's immigration policy, which eliminated discrimination based on race, religion, or national origin, resulted in increased immigration from India. The 1970s and 1980s saw heavy Punjabi immigration to British Columbia (Johnson, 1988). Because many of the sponsored new immigrants had little education and limited skills in English yet well-developed skills in farming, they found work in agriculture. The BC Public Service Agency estimated that by 2003, Indo-Canadians accounted for 98 per cent of the province's 6,000 farm workers, the majority of which were recent immigrants (BC Public Service Agency, 2003; Runsten, Hinojosa Ojeda, Lee, & Mines, 2000). The fact that most of them were also women—many over 50 years of age when British Columbia adopted the Seasonal Agricultural Worker Program—reflects gendered norms of mobility inscribed in Canadian immigration policies and in Punjabi transnational communities (Fairey et al., 2008; Walton-Roberts, 2003).

The local availability of citizen and immigrant workers was, initially, an obstacle to the success of BC agricultural producers, who lobbied provincial and federal authorities for access to international migrants. In the early 2000s, the newly elected provincial government continued to view the Seasonal Agricultural Worker Program as a politically sensitive topic. As one grower representative recalled,

> The Liberal government was fairly new and had spent a lot of time getting into power, and then we come along and say "oh, by the way, we want to import foreign workers like everybody else does in Canada." It was just...you couldn't even start a conversation. In fact, we were told when we met with ministers and deputies, don't even bother bringing it up; they don't want to talk about it.

By the mid-1990s, however, a shift in federal immigration policy to an emphasis on economic migrants (people viewed to have skills, experience, or capital to contribute to Canada's economy) resulted in a reduction in family-class immigrants (close relatives of citizens and permanent residents whose immigration is supported by their family in Canada), and gave credence to growers' half-century-old complaints about labour shortages. One grower explained the reasons for these shortages, recalling that

> immigration from India was quite high up until the mid-1990s, when it just died off....We'd have so many workers, young workers that could handle the physical work. So the immigration slowed down. The second thing was that the people that had been working for many years just got older and older and they couldn't do it anymore and then the next generations were Canadian-born and they went into different fields, into construction or professional fields. We started running out of labour in the mid '90s. Our costs were going really high. There weren't enough workers and there were times we couldn't get our crops harvested on time.

While federal government restrictions on the admission of the parents and grandparents of immigrant workers bolstered the growers' arguments about a labour shortage, provincial statistics indicated that the number of employees bonded by licensed farm labour contractors (brokers who provide

Table 8.1 Number of Temporary Foreign Worker Positions on Positive Labour Market Opinions in Agricultural Occupations, British Columbia

	2004	2005	2006	2007	2008	2009	2010	2011	2012
SAWP	47	855	1,605	2,890	3,795	3,695	3,535	3,985	4,980
Agricultural Stream		0	0	0	0	0	0	380	880
Higher-skilled		25	35	80	60	30	50	50	70
Lower-skilled		10	100	405	1,040	425	410	285	110
Total	47	890	1,740	3,375	4,895	4,150	3,995	4,700	6,040

Source: Employment and Social Development Canada, 2014.

labourers to agricultural producers) was virtually unchanged from 1999 to 2003 (Moore, 2004). Despite a lack of numerical evidence of a labour shortage, employers in the agricultural industry, with support from BC's Minister of Agriculture, John van Dongen, and Canada's Minister of Human Resources and Skills Development, Joe Volpe, (both Liberals), convinced the BC Premier's Office to extend the Seasonal Agricultural Worker Program to the province. In 2004, the federal government created a new Memorandum of Understanding with Mexico to allow BC growers to hire migrant farm workers and created a similar agreement in 2008 with government officials in the Caribbean.

BC growers' use of international migrants under the Seasonal Agricultural Worker Program increased rapidly, from 47 in 2004 to just fewer than 5,000 by 2012 (see Table 8.1). In addition, employers in BC's agrifood sector also hired international migrants through the Stream for Low-wage Positions (formerly the Low-skilled Workers Pilot Project) as indicated in the fourth row of Table 8.1. Until 2010, producers qualifying for the SAWP were able to hire workers under this newer initiative. The federal government then obliged employers who were eligible to hire international migrants to use a new Agricultural Stream (indicated in the second row of Table 8.1) that aligned terms and conditions of work between the Stream for Low-wage Positions and the Seasonal Agricultural Worker Program.

The rapid and sustained rise of migrant employment in British Columbia, shown in Table 8.1, reflects the satisfaction of growers with the

Seasonal Agricultural Worker Program. One grower claimed the program is "the only thing that saved us in BC." Another employer claimed, "this [program] has been a life saver for us." Stan Vander Waal, owner of Rainbow Greenhouses, told a BC newspaper in 2008 that the program was "working fantastic....It's the best thing we ever did" (*Chilliwack Times*, 2008). Such testimonies, alongside the precipitous employment of migrants since 2004, reveal the desirability of migrant workers as a source of labour for BC agricultural producers. In the following section, quoting the growers I interviewed to illustrate, I position international migrants as constituting a distinct workforce with specific relations to the labour market and to employers.

International Migrants on Temporary Work Permits as a Discernible Type of Labour

Over the 20th century, when many other groups of workers secured basic labour rights and protections, the availability of socially and politically subjugated, racialized sources of labour contributed to maintaining farm work as a low-wage, hazardous, and unprotected occupation that people with other employment options or access to social protection chose to avoid (Basok, 2002; Satzewich, 1991). When the Minimum Wage Act was passed in BC in 1925, its tacit purpose was to allow employers who had high paying jobs to offer to attract privileged members of the labour force and to push Asians into occupations like agricultural jobs, which were not covered by the Act (Lanthier & Wong, 2002). In the 1960s, the BC Federation of Labour urged growers to improve the working conditions for their employees and condemned the continued and systematic exploitation of those in the agricultural labour force (Lanthier & Wong, 2002). A 1983 report of the BC Human Rights Commission documented the dreadful conditions farm workers experienced in the province, including poverty wages, deplorable housing, chemical exposure, lack of drinking water and sanitation facilities, and unsafe transportation (BC Human Rights Commission, 1983). In noting that most farm workers were members of ethnic minorities, the report was also a landmark in recognizing systemic legislative racism. Yet, in 2008, similar conditions still existed as a result of government policies that allowed the erosion of employment protections and were lax in the enforcement of safety procedures and policies in agriculture (Fairey et al., 2008). Indubitably, labour shortages in agriculture persist in contemporary times because most farm work in British Columbia remains a 4-D job: dirty, difficult, dangerous, and demeaning. To describe its status in the labour force, one grower stated: "Farm work is right at the bottom of the barrel," and added, "it's looked down on in society."

Most jobs in the agrifood sector exhibit many, if not all, of Goldring and Landolt's (2011) indicators of precarious work (Preibisch & Otero, 2014). The first indicator is that few farm workers have union representation and even those who have voted for union certification have seen their efforts aggressively countered by management (Russo, 2012). The second indicator is that, with the exception of international migrants, farm workers tend to work without employment contracts, which leads to the third indicator: the uncertain and often illegal terms and conditions of work. Most farm workers in British Columbia, with the exception of legalized migrants, are seasonal day labourers employed by farm labour contractors, who, reputedly, have a long history of exploiting farm workers and violating employment standards and safety regulations (Fairey et al., 2008; Moore, 2004). The fourth indicator of precarious work is that farm workers have little ability to predict or to control schedules that are prone to seasonal variation and hours that are inconsistent, demanding, and unconventional (Lanthier & Wong, 2002; Sergeant & Tucker, 2009). In addition, with the exception of authorized international migrants, whose employers are required to pay hourly wages, most farm workers are paid by piece. Due to these and other contributory factors, immigrant farm workers in British Columbia often lack secure incomes and earn less than the minimum wage (Fairey et al., 2008). They are also denied overtime pay and other common employment benefits, such as paid statutory holidays, paid rest periods, and paid annual vacation.

The BC government eroded farm workers' wages in 2003 through policy changes that included eliminating the requirement that employers retain records of wages paid to the employees of farm labour contractors, which exempted employers from liability for unpaid wages (Fairey et al., 2008). Governmental policy changes also reduced by approximately 4 per cent the minimum piece rates payable to farm workers by deeming piece rates to include statutory holiday and annual vacation pay. They also excluded farm workers who are paid by the hour from statutory holiday pay and annual vacations, reduced by half the minimum hours that contractors were required to pay workers transported to farms, and, subsequently, excluded farm workers from all overtime requirements (Fairey et al., 2008). As G. Moore (2004) points out, measures such as the inclusion of statutory holiday pay and vacation pay in a wage rate are abnormal and unique to hand harvesters (farm workers who harvest fruits, berries, and vegetables by hand) and reduced their already low-wage rates. Between 2001 and 2015, minimum piece rates for hand harvesters increased by a mere 7.5 per cent while the general minimum wage rose 30.6 per cent and food prices in the province increased by more than a third (Pabla & Fairey, 2015). Not only has the BC government kept farm workers' wages low and unstandardized, but it has also prevented these labourers from receiving benefits, which is another indication of precarious work.

The fact that employers can shift farm workers' places of work among multiple sites is a further indicator of precarious work and is, likely, the most significant occupational hazard for those contracted by farm labour contractors (Preibisch & Otero, 2014). The grisly, tragic crash of a multi-passenger motor vehicle in 2007, which killed three farm workers and critically injured another eight, ultimately led to a coroner's inquest and subsequent recommendations for farm labour transportation. Nonetheless, almost a fifth of farm vehicles inspected between 2007 and 2010 on average still did not meet the requirements of provincial authorities (see Hartman, 2010). Moreover, that average has increased since inspections have dropped off. A final indicator of precarious work is that farm workers receive payment for their work in cash. According to regulations set by BC Employment Standards, farm labour contractors have been required to pay their employees through direct deposit since 2007; yet, highly unequal power relations permit contractors to coerce farm workers by, for example, pressuring them to return portions of their wages in exchange for the records of employment they need to obtain off-season Employment Insurance benefits (BC Ministry of Labour, 2011; Moore, 2004; Otero & Preibisch, 2010). Another kind of coercion, which contractors have purportedly used to discipline workers and their families, is to cease to pick them up and transport them to the day's work.

Agricultural labour thus persists as a form of precarious work in British Columbia. Although technological innovations have removed some of the drudgery, most farm work continues to be physically demanding and involve climatic extremes, whether labourers perform their jobs in open fields or in hot greenhouses. Farm work is also dangerous (Preibisch & Otero, 2014). In British Columbia, although the injury rate for agriculture as a subsector remains relatively stable between 2009 and 2013, it remains higher than the injury rates for all other types of labour combined (WorkSafeBC, 2015). In periods of high production, growers require their employees to work extended hours, and overtime on weekends. As a result of highly skewed employment relations between farm workers and the growers or labour contractors that employ them, workers are subject to considerable labour control, manifested in aggressive management and, increasingly, digital surveillance. New and old technologies of labour control have contributed to an intensification of production in contemporary agriculture throughout the global North (Basok, Bélanger, & Rivas, 2014; Hennebry et al., 2014; Paciulan & Preibisch, 2013; Rogaly, 2008; Rye & Andrzejewska, 2010).

The persistence of precarious employment conditions in agriculture is linked to an increasingly competitive environment that has emerged during four decades of neoliberal globalization. The dramatic rise in global trade in food and agricultural products; new forms of intellectual property and institutional structures of governance; the expansion of supermarkets; and the growing concentration, integration, and globalization of value chains are among the processes that have radically restructured the agrifood sector (Busch, 2010; Carton De Grammont & Lara Flores, 2010; Du Toit & Ewert, 2002; McMichael, 1996). British Columbia has not been exempt from these changes, which in turn have effected considerable change in production. One notable manifestation is that, since the late 1990s, greenhouses in British Columbia have grown increasingly in size and are now more technology- and capital-intensive operations than ever before. Moreover, the industry has expanded its presence into the United States and Mexico in order to ensure a consistent supply to the supermarkets that dominate food retail (Mendis, 2007). These changes have particularly hit smaller producers. For example, one grower of field vegetables reported the following:

> We started harvesting broccoli in June and it was coming in from the US and landing here at about $10, so we put our price at $9. Initially [the supermarkets] bought it. Then all of a sudden I've got 10,000 cases sitting in my cooler and they weren't buying. Their ad says "broccoli crowns BC grown" but we hadn't shipped anything to them, nor had anybody else, so where are they getting it from? Washington. They did that with broccoli, corn, and a couple of other products: buying it out of the [United] States, advertising it as BC grown. They cut a deal: Washington dumps it here cheap but [the supermarket] keeps their own prices higher.

In addition to the consolidation of food retail in Canada and trade liberalization, the proliferation of private and public standards for food safety and quality has imposed further challenges on growers. Thus, in the highly competitive environment in which BC growers operate, international migrants represent a feasible and flexible labour force, stemming from their precarious legal status.

Goldring and Landolt (2011) use the term "precarious legal status" to encapsulate "the multiple and variable forms of 'less than full status,'" including the absence of "key rights or entitlements usually associated with the full or nearly full status of citizenship and permanent residence" (p. 328) in the neoliberal context of global migration governance and the restructuring of work. International migrants on temporary employment authorization have precarious legal status based on the following criteria: They lack permanent residence and permanent work authorization, they depend on a third party for their residence and employment rights, they are deportable, and they have restricted or no access to public services and protections available to permanent residents and citizens (see also Hennebry & McLaughlin, 2012). Perhaps the key element structuring precarious legal status for migrants under the Seasonal Agricultural Worker Program and Stream for Low-wage Positions is the condition that limits their employment authorization to a single, designated employer. While in theory migrants are permitted to find new employers, most do not know they have this right. For those who do know, they are unlikely to exercise this right because of the logistical impediments involved as well as well-grounded fears that such actions might spark reprisals from the home country officials who administer their future job placements. Under the Seasonal Agricultural Worker Program, migrants depend on origin country government officials to approve their employment in Canada. Employers, however, have the power to let migrants go and hire different migrants each year. Under the Seasonal Agricultural Worker Program, the government also allows employers to apply to transfer migrants to a second, named employer when, for example, production in one commodity is scarce and plentiful in another. These are employer-driven, government-mediated transfers in which migrants have little say. Often, employers "loan" migrants to a neighbouring employer requiring labour without authorization. This situation, in which a migrant is working for someone other than their named employer without a government-authorized transfer, violates their employment status in Canada and their right to workers' compensation if they become ill or injured. Migrants under the Stream for Low-wage Positions experience a further layer of precariousness with the federal restriction that came into effect on April 1, 2011, on the number of years they can work in Canada. While migrants under the Seasonal Agricultural Worker Program can ostensibly work in Canada year after year, providing they have a job and government officials who will approve their placement, migrants authorized under other managed migration streams lose the right to work in Canada after accumulating four years of employment. This cumulative duration rule may induce migrants to accept extended hours and workweeks in order to make the most of their time-limited tenure in the Canadian labour market.

Migrants' lack of labour mobility is further compounded by housing arrangements. The Seasonal Agricultural Worker Program requires employers to provide accommodation, and such living arrangements not only extend employers' control over farm workers' behaviour beyond the sphere of work, they also serve to foster paternalistic, personal labour relations (Preibisch, 2004; Satzewich, 1992; Wall, 2002). Employers' desires for captive, on-hand, and accessible members of a workforce was reflected in the alacrity with which BC growers sought to change provincial and municipal regulations that initially prevented the construction of on-site housing (Sustainable Agriculture Management Branch, 2009). Migrants' dependence on their individual employers for immediate and future rights to work in Canada, not to mention a place to live, creates a "regime of deportability" in which even *the threat* of deportation is a highly effective tool for labour discipline (Basok et al., 2014; Preibisch, 2004). Finally, precarious legal status is exemplified in the fact that migrant farm workers have restricted or no access to a range of public services and protections available to permanent residents and citizens. For example, international migrants on temporary work permits pay into Employment Insurance, but cannot access most of the benefits associated with this government program. Moreover, international migrants must rely on private medical insurance for their first three months of employment in British Columbia before they qualify for publicly funded provincial insurance, regardless of the fact that not all health-care providers recognize private insurance (Otero & Preibisch, 2010). Even migrant workers who qualify for publicly funded health care face considerable barriers to access presented by factors such as fears of reprisal, lack of transportation to a health facility, and limited ability to communicate due to their lack of skills in English (Preibisch & Hennebry, 2012). In addition to migrants' unique relationship to the rights or entitlements associated with citizenship or permanent residence, the architecture and operation of Canada's programs of managed migration structure their vulnerability in other distinct ways, which Patricia Tomic and Ricardo Trumper amply document later in this volume.

Precarious legal status is institutionalized in the managed migration programs that engender a hyper-productive source of labour that feeds into producers' strategies to respond to the flexibility demanded by the globalization of agriculture. During interviews, growers emphasized that the productivity of international migrants is greater than that of citizen and immigrant farm workers. Growers attributed this capacity largely to the younger ages of Mexican workers when compared with citizen and immigrant farm workers. As one grower argued, "the Indo-Canadians that we have on the farm lately are older. They still work fine but they are older and most of your Mexican people that come up are in their 20s. So I don't have to tell you the difference in production; it's just natural." In a study of 200 international migrant and immigrant farm workers in 2010, Gerardo Otero and I found that, while almost 50 per cent of immigrant farm workers were 46 years old and older, only 13 per cent of Mexican migrant workers were in that age category (Otero & Preibisch, 2010).

Some growers assert that the high productivity of international migrant workers offsets the initial capital investments required to hire and transport them to British Columbia. The BC Seasonal Agricultural Worker Program requires employers to cover the costs of migrants' round-trip airfare from Mexico City to Canada and their transportation in Canada, and they must provide them with furnished accommodations. Employers can recover up to $826 for accommodations and $12 per day for meals (if provided) over the worker's residency. They must also pay workers no less than the equivalent of $10.33 per hour for every hour they work, even while harvesting on a piece-work basis, and they must guarantee them a minimum work week. Growers' cost-benefit analysis of migrants is illustrated by an industry representative who observes that the Seasonal Agricultural Worker Program "is more expensive for the operator" than hiring workers in Canada, but,

> now many [growers] tell me that that even though it's more expensive, it's actually, on a per unit basis, more cost effective, because the Mexican workers are very, very productive in terms of their work ethic. So even though [growers] are paying higher wages under the [program] contract and even though they have to pay the airfare and provide accommodations, that's all worth it because they are getting better productivity.

Another grower admitted: "I was paying $15/16 an hour [to Canadian workers] and you know these guys get $8/9 and they're worth double that but that's the Canadian minimum wage so we go on that." Thus, in a labour-scarce provincial economy of the mid-2000s, employing international migrants and paying them minimum wages allowed growers to extract profit through cheapening their workforce.

Growers also asserted that international migrants were more reliable than locally available workers. This perceived greater reliability flows from the unfree conditions arising from migrants' closed work permits, housing arrangements, and other aspects of the architecture and operation of managed migration programs, which, together, serve to ensure worker acquiescence. Prior to the Seasonal Agricultural Worker Program,

BC growers experienced high labour turnover and recruitment difficulties due to the poor working conditions on farms and the wage rates they offered to farm workers. Further exacerbation of these problems arose from the growth of the greenhouse industry that drew workers away from field crops. Other sources of labour in agriculture (e.g., aging immigrants, mothers, and students) are perceived as less reliable than international migrants precisely because they have physically proximate commitments to social reproduction, that is, family members within Canada. They can also withdraw from and re-enter the labour force more easily than workers in managed migration programs, in part because of the social cushioning of government-provided social protection (social assistance) or their social networks in Canada (family or friends who will support their unemployment). An industry representative attested to the greater dependability of a migrant labour force above citizen workers in a remark on the success of the Seasonal Agricultural Worker Program:

> The other big factor I hear about the SAWP is the consistency and reliability of having the workforce there. In many other cases there's a lot of what you think is your crew. They are there for three, four, or five days and then suddenly decide they don't like it and don't show up the next day and don't tell you they're not coming. Whereas the Mexicans are here with that work ethic and they're sending the money home so there's a motivation as to why they're doing it.

Mexican workers' "work ethic" was indubitably attributed to their acquiescence to labouring under difficult conditions and for long hours. Gerardo Otero and I found their daily hours of work to be considerably high; on average, they worked 12 hours a day, Monday to Friday, and eight hours Saturday and Sunday in periods of high production (Preibisch & Otero, 2014). Growers in British Columbia, as in other provinces, noted other advantages to the consistency of labour achieved through access to migrants under the Seasonal Agricultural Worker Program. Access to a captive source of labour has also enabled them to increase the flexibility of hours to locally available workers and to plan and expand their production operations (Preibisch, 2010).

Growers also cited advantageous forms of incentive and discipline as benefits that are made possible by the conditions of employment for a migrant labour force. For example, one operator in the Fraser Valley does not deduct rent from SAWP worker wages provided that they complete their contracts, but charges full rent to migrants who request to leave early. Some growers mentioned that they use migrants' deportability and their ability to choose migrants by name as mechanisms of labour control. BC growers employ such strategies because they want employees who are perceived to be compliant. As an anonymous BC grower claimed, "Indo-Canadians are too militant. Mexicans are much better in that respect" (qtd. in Mendis, 2007, p. 139). Whether this observation is accurate or not, the Seasonal Agricultural Worker Program structures worker discipline in unique ways. For example, in 2014, the BC Labour Relations Board ruled that Mexican government and consular officials had blacklisted Mexican SAWP workers suspected of being union sympathizers and barred their return to Canada (BC Labour Relations Board, 2014). Such strategies demand scrutiny, as does Mexico's recruitment of workers. In 2008, a Mexican civil servant, revealing that BC growers asked Mexican officials to select migrants with no prior employment history in Canada, provided this rationale:

> They want new people; they know [new migrants] don't know the language, that it's another country, that there are other customs as well. So there are ways of subjecting them to their will. They can't with [migrants who have] previous years in the Program because they know their rights and obligations.

Further, a 2010 report found that, in contrast with the Mexican population employed in Ontario through the Seasonal Agricultural Worker Program, the population in the British Columbia program shows high regional diversity, with an over-representation from the most populous, poorest states in Central and Southern Mexico, and a large percentage of people who spoke a Mexican native language, which is the criterion generally used to indicate indigeneity (Otero & Preibisch, 2010). While high diversity is due in part to the Mexican government's attempt to decentralize recruitment, Mexican civil servants have suggested that recruiting from various states including indigenous regions is intentional, for it creates "a cultural division as well, although they are Mexican."

Conclusion

Within the competitive atmosphere of neoliberal globalization, contemporary international and national immigration management creates multiple forms of legality and illegality that sustain employer strategies of flexibilization (Anderson, 2010; Goldring & Landolt, 2011; Sharma, 2006). As Bridget Anderson (2010) has argued, immigration policy functions both as a tap to regulate the flow of labour but also as a mould, to produce types of labourers with particular relations to employers and to labour markets. Indeed, according to Nandita Sharma (2006), border control practices are "less about restricting access to the territory of the national state than about differentiating those within it" (p. 144). Canada's Seasonal Agricultural Worker Program has been critical to providing the agricultural sector with a cheapened, productive, disciplined, and unfree source of labour since 1966 and, particularly, since the 1990s under the neoliberal restructuring of the global food system. In this chapter, I have outlined the incorporation of the program in British Columbia since 2004 and have demonstrated how international migrants have become a highly desired, valuable source of labour relative to locally available workers. British Columbia was one of the last provinces in Canada to take advantage of the Seasonal Agricultural Worker Program; yet, the growth of this program of migration governance has been rapid and sustained. As agrifood production becomes further embedded within global value chains under neoliberal globalization, competition increasingly rests on flexibility produced, in part, out of the precarious legal status of racialized, unfree labourers. In British Columbia, it is likely that employers who hire migrants provided under programs of managed migration will continue to see them as members of a prized labour force until a more productive, reliable, subjugated, and acquiescent source of farm workers can be found.

Notes

1. The data was gathered under grants funded by WorkSafeBC and SSHRC, much of it with my colleague Gerardo Otero. Some quotes have been edited for brevity with care to avoid distortion.

References

Anderson, B. (2010). Migration, immigration controls and the fashioning of precarious workers. *Work, Employment and Society, 24*(2), 300–317.

Basok, T. (2002). *Tortillas and tomatoes: Transmigrant Mexican harvesters in Canada.* Montreal, QC: McGill-Queens University Press.

Basok, T., Bélanger, D., & Rivas, E. (2014). Deportability, discipline, and agency: Migrant agricultural workers in southwestern Ontario. *Journal of Ethnic and Migration Studies, 40*(9), 1394–1413.

BC Human Rights Commission. (1983). *"What this country did to us, it did to itself": A report of the BC Human Rights Commission on the farmworkers & domestic workers.* Vancouver, BC: Human Rights Commission of British Columbia.

BC Labour Relations Board. (2014, Mar. 20). Decision No. B56/2014. Certain Employees of Sidhu & Sons Nursery Ltd. and Sidhu & Sons Nursery Ltd. vs. United Food and Commercial Workers International Union, Local 1518.

BC Ministry of Labour. (2011). Deductions from wages. Retrieved from https://www.labour.gov.bc.ca/esb/facshts/farm_worker.htm

BC Public Service Agency. (2003). *Multi-jurisdictional team raises employment standards for agricultural farm workers.* Vancouver, BC: Author.

Busch, L. (2010). Can fairy tales come true? The surprising story of neoliberalism and world agriculture. *Sociologia Ruralis, 50*(4), 331–351.

Carton De Grammont, H., & Lara Flores, S. (2010). Productive restructuring and standardization in Mexican horticulture: Consequences for labour. *Journal of Agrarian Change, 10*(2), 228–250.

Chilliwack Times. (2008, June 20). Farmworker exploitation. p. A1.

Du Toit, A., & Ewert, J. (2002). Myths of globalisation: Private regulation and farm worker livelihoods on western Cape farms. *Transformation: Critical Perspectives on Southern Africa, 50*(77), 77–104.

Employment and Social Development Canada. (2014). *Labour Market Opinion (LMO) Statistics — Annual Statistics.* Ottawa, ON: Author. Retrieved from http://www.esdc.gc.ca/eng/jobs/foreign_workers/lmo_statistics/annual-agriculture.shtml

Fairey, D., Hanson, C., MacInnes, G., Tigar McLaren, A., Otero, G., Preibisch, K., & Thompson, M. (2008). *Cultivating farmworkers' rights: Ending the exploitation of immigrant and migrant farmworkers in BC.* Vancouver, BC: Canadian Centre for Policy Alternatives; Justícia for Migrant Workers; Progressive Intercultural Community Services; BC Federation of Labour.

Goldring, L., & Landolt, P. (2011). Caught in the work–citizenship matrix: The lasting effects of precarious legal status on work for Toronto immigrants. *Globalizations, 8*(3), 325–341.

Hartman, C. (2010). Farm worker vehicle inspections update. Vancouver, BC: WorkSafeBC.

Hennebry, J., Grass, W., Williams, G., Williams, K., Walton-Roberts, M., Chikanda, A., & Crush, J. (2014). *Bilateral labour migration agreements, development and trade: Complexity, contradiction and coherence.* Research report for the Organisation for Economic Co-Operation and Development (OECD). Washington, DC: OECD.

Hennebry, J., & McLaughlin, J. (2012). The exception that proves the rule: Structural vulnerability, health risks and consequences for temporary migrant farmworkers in Canada. In C. Hughes & P. Lenard (Eds.), *Legislating inequality: Canada's Temporary Migrant Worker Program* (pp. 117–138). Montreal, QC: McGill-Queen's University Press.

Johnston, H. (1988). The development of the Punjabi community in Vancouver since 1961. *Canadian Ethnic Studies, 10*(2), 1–19.

Lanthier, M., & Wong, L. (2002). Ethnic agricultural labour in the Okanagan Valley: 1880s to 1960s: Victoria, BC: Royal BC Museum.

Mann, A. (1982). Kelowna's Chinatown. *Okanagan Historical Society Report*, 46, 20–28.

McMichael, P. (1996). Globalization: Myths and realities. *Rural Sociology, 61*(1), 25–55.

Mendis, A. (2007). *The greenhouse tomato industry in Delta, British Columbia* (Unpublished doctoral dissertation). University of British Columbia, Vancouver, BC.

Moore, G. (2004). *Hand-harvesters of Fraser Valley berry crops: New era protection of vulnerable employees.* Vancouver, BC: BC Federation of Labour.

Muñoz, C., & Manuel, L. (2011). Programa de trabajadores agrícolas temporales México—Canadá: Costos y benefícios. Washington, DC: George Washington University.

Otero, G., & Preibisch, K. (2010). *Farmworker health and safety: Challenges for British Columbia.* Vancouver, BC: WorkSafeBC.

Pabla, G., & Fairey, D. (2015, May 22). Unjust treatment of farm workers should end. Vancouver, BC: Canadian Centre for Policy Alternatives. Retrieved from https://www.policyalternatives.ca/publications/commentary/unjust-treatment-farm-workers-should-end

Paciulan, M., & Preibisch, K. (2013). Navigating the productive/reproductive split: Latin American transnational mothers and fathers in Canada's temporary migration programs. *Transnational Social Review: A Social Work Journal, 3*(2), 173–192.

Preibisch, K. (2004). Migrant agricultural workers and processes of social inclusion in rural Canada: Encuentros and desencuentros. *Canadian Journal of Latin American and Caribbean Studies, 29*(57–58), 203–239.

Preibisch, K. (2010). Pick-your-own labor: Migrant workers and flexibility in Canadian agriculture. *International Migration Review, 44*(2), 404–441.

Preibisch, K., & Hennebry, J. (2012). Buy local, hire global: Temporary migration in Canadian agriculture. In C. Hughes and P. Lenard (Eds.), *Legislating inequality: Canada's Temporary Migrant Worker Program* (pp. 48–72). Montreal, QC: McGill-Queen's University Press.

Preibisch, K., & Otero, G. (2014). Does citizenship status matter in Canadian agriculture? Workplace health and safety for migrant and immigrant laborers. *Rural Sociology, 79*(2), 174–199.

Rogaly, B. (2008). Intensification of workplace regimes in British horticulture: The role of migrant workers. *Population, Space and Place, 14*(6), 497–510.

Runsten, D., Hinojosa Ojeda, R., Lee, K., & Mines, R. (2000). The extent, pattern, and contribution of migrant labor in the NAFTA countries: An overview. Los Angeles, CA: North American Integration and Development Center.

Russo, R. (2012). *Solidarity forever, Canadians never: SAWP workers in Canada* (Unpublished doctoral dissertation). University of British Columbia, Vancouver, BC.

Rye, J., & Andrzejewska, J. (2010). The structural disempowerment of Eastern European migrant farm workers in Norwegian agriculture. *Journal of Rural Studies, 26*(1), 41–51.

Satzewich, V. (1991). *Racism and the incorporation of foreign labour: Farm labour migration to Canada since 1945*. New York, NY: Routledge.

Sergeant, M., & Tucker, E. (2009). *Layers of vulnerability in occupational health and safety for migrant workers: Case studies from Canada and the United Kingdom.* Toronto, ON: Comparative Research in Law and Political Economy.

Sharma, N., (2006). *Home economics: Nationalism and the making of "migrant workers" in Canada.* Toronto, ON: University of Toronto Press.

Sustainable Agriculture Management Branch. (2009). *Regulating temporary foreign worker housing in the ALR*. Victoria, BC: Ministry of Agriculture and Lands.

Wall, E. (1992). Personal labour relations and ethnicity in Ontario Agriculture. In V. Satzewich (Ed.), *Deconstructing a nation: Immigration, multiculturalism and racism in '90s Canada* (pp. 261–275). Halifax, NS: Fernwood.

Walton-Roberts, M. (2003). Transnational geographies: Indian immigration to Canada. *The Canadian Geographer/Le Géographe canadien, 47*(3), 235–250.

Wong, L. (1988). *Migrant seasonal agricultural labour: Race and ethnic relations in the Okanagan Valley* (Unpublished doctoral dissertation). York University, Toronto, ON.

WorkSafeBC. (2015). Agriculture Statistics (2010–2014). Vancouver, BC: Author. Retrieved from http://www2.worksafebc.com/portals/agriculture/statistics.asp

NINE

LABOURING IN THE "FOUR-SEASON PARADISE"

Workers and Agriculture in the Okanagan Valley

Patricia Tomic and Ricardo Trumper

Introduction

The Okanagan Valley in the southern interior of British Columbia is one of the premier agricultural areas of Canada. Indeed, agriculture has given the valley its identity since the 19th century, when British colonizers appropriated the land from the local Indigenous population and transformed it into cattle ranches. Agriculture has served to represent the Okanagan Valley as paradise. In this chapter we argue that the image of an idyllic playground of bucolic tranquility has been deceiving. We assert that this image has concealed the continuous exploitation of racialized and marginalized peoples labouring in the Okanagan Valley's agriculture. We show that until the end of the Second World War dispossessed Indigenous people and Chinese migrants constituted an important source of workers for the orchards. During the war, people of Japanese origin, displaced from the coast of British Columbia, and Doukhobor conscientious objectors were forced to labour on farms and in other related occupations. Until the end of the war, scientific racism served to justify the open exploitation of people of colour. We then turn to the short postwar years of a kinder, gentler Canada, when scientific racism was largely discredited, and when people from different parts of the world were able to immigrate to Canada. Here we discuss how Portuguese and Punjabi immigrants were attracted to the Okanagan Valley to provide labour for orchard production. Eventually, many of these labourers became farm owners or moved to other occupations. Racialized Québécois youth settled in the Okanagan Valley temporarily each year to cover the labour shortages that resulted during the peak periods of fruit production. Finally we describe how, in the current neoliberal era, racialized foreign migrant workers are brought to the Okanagan Valley year after year under the Seasonal Agricultural Worker Program (SAWP). Other temporary immigration schemes also contribute to resolve labour shortages in agriculture. These temporary foreign workers come mostly from Mexico and Jamaica, but also from countries like Guatemala and Peru. Neoliberalism has transformed the nature of the Valley's agriculture. Cherries for foreign markets, along with wine and tourism, have become central to the Okanagan economy. In this restructured economy, non-white workers remain hidden in the background while white employees create culinary experiences for tourists and interact with them in restaurants, wineries, and hotels as highly skilled wine makers, chefs, and winery owners who help reconstruct the image of the Okanagan Valley as a four-season paradise.

The Beginning

The Okanagan Valley, with its lakes and its orchards planted with Mediterranean fruits, lends itself to representations as an oasis in a Canada of harsh winters. In spite of this idyllic image, it is a semi-desert region. Until the 19th century, it was the home of the Syilx people, whom the British colonizers dispossessed in order to transform the land into large, privately owned cattle ranches (Lanthier & Wong, 2002). In the early 20th century, land speculators subdivided the large ranches into smaller acreages and began promoting the Okanagan Valley as an ideal environment for British "gentlemen farmers" (Barman, 1984; Koroscil, 2003). At that time, the production of apples, pears, and other soft fruit was the area's main economic activity. Promoters framed horticulture as "a beautiful art," a calling for Englishmen of "refinement, culture and distinction" (Dunae, 1981). A British farming guide published in 1909 described the lifestyle of the Okanagan Valley as an extension of life in Britain (Barman, 1984). The power, popularity, capital, and entrepreneurship of Lord Aberdeen, the seventh Governor General to represent Queen Victoria since Confederation, were also influential in establishing fruit cultivation as a desirable activity for upper-class entrepreneurs in the region (MacPhee, 1958 cited in Lanthier & Wong, 2002). The interrelated factors of whiteness, the fruit industry, and weather helped to foster a common view of the Okanagan Valley as a paradisiacal space. Indeed, due to the cultural activities practised by immigrants from Great Britain, which included golf, polo, and regattas, the region became known as an English gentlemen's space (Wilson, 2005). The lifestyle of these farmers and their families was not entirely idyllic, however. The time spent engaged in leisurely pastimes was balanced with periods of intense work in the orchards. Family members provided some of the labour, but racialized seasonal labourers formed a key part of the orchardists' workforce (Lanthier, 1984; Lanthier & Wong, 2002). Migrant Chinese and Indigenous workers initially filled the demands for hired help, especially at peak periods such as harvest time.

Male Chinese migrants, legally and informally prevented from working in many occupations in Canada, came to the Okanagan Valley to work for white families, not just as farm workers, but also as domestic servants. In 1901, the population was almost one-quarter Asian. Accordingly, in the Okanagan Valley, "Chinatowns" constituted a significant part of the urban landscape. First, a head tax and then the Chinese Exclusion Act condemned male members of the Chinese workforce to live permanently as bachelors. The Canadian government prevented them from reuniting with their families, and in a racist society mixed-marriage was seldom an option; thus, these men aged alone and eventually disappeared. Replacing the Chinese workforce required employers to find other sources of labour. During the Second World War, Canada's internment of Doukhobor conscientious objectors and persons of Japanese ancestry, robbed of their possessions and expelled from the coastal areas of British Columbia, provided a source of forced labour for railroad and road construction, and for agriculture (Lanthier, 1984; Lanthier & Wong, 2002; Wong, 1988). These workers satisfied farmers' desire for cheap labour in the Okanagan Valley and the nearby Similkameen Valley. Other racialized workers followed.

A Gentler Canada

The end of the Second World War brought about significant changes in Canada. Central to these changes were the implementation of Keynesian economics and the encouragement of Fordist industrialization, the development of a limited welfare system, and the growth of strong unions (Wells, 1995). Also key were the substantial challenges to scientific racism that fosters notions of the genetic superiority of some people over others (Gould, 1996; Rattansi, 2007) and served to justify employers' exploitation of workers of colour. Employing the "mosaic metaphor," government officials represented Canada as a multicultural nation (Day, 2000).

The postwar period also brought changes to the Okanagan Valley. Government programs and road construction ended the Valley's isolation. Retirees seeking affordable housing, mild sunny weather, recreation, rural scenery, and whiteness migrated to the region (Tomic, Trumper & Aguiar, 2005). Moreover, the rise of wages resulting from Fordist industrialization, the government's investments in roads (which permitted travel by car around the province), and the universalization of car use set the stage for the emergence of new forms of tourism and the institutionalization of vacations. The Okanagan Valley saw an increase in the number of campsites and motels for families arriving in their station wagons from outside the area. Tourism for these vacationers included visits to farm-stands, which were carefully designed places where tourists could buy fruit while they consumed an idealized orchard landscape. As early as 1979, a "Street Guide to the City of Kelowna" advertised the Okanagan Valley as "truly an all-year playground" (Street Guide, 1979). Forestry grew in importance and some manufacturing also emerged, which diminished agriculture's role in the region; yet agriculture remained economically important, for it was central to promoters' imagining and representation of the area.

As the provincial and federal governments implemented new programs to increase food production and improve the quality of its produce, the agricultural industry changed at an exponential rate. At the same time, the transformation of the discourse of race made it more difficult for government officials to discriminate against non-whites in immigration policy. Opportunities opened for non-whites beyond agriculture. These twin transformations exacerbated the problem of labour shortages in Okanagan orchards. For some time, employers dealt with the labour shortages within the logics of Canada's new de-racialized representations. In the 1950s, Canada and Portugal agreed on a program for the immigration of agricultural labourers. Portuguese immigrants, who had been previously labelled as undesirable immigrants, came to the southern Okanagan region with their families to fill jobs on farms. They lived in crowded, derelict houses and shacks, which often lacked indoor plumbing and running water. They took over the most strenuous jobs and laboured for poor pay (Russo, 2012). Around the same time, Punjabi immigration to Canada, which had been strenuously opposed since the early 19th century, substantially increased as immigration was becoming more permissive for non-whites. As Joy (1982) points out, despite widespread racism, these immigrants settled in the Okanagan Valley in the 1950s. In addition, the numbers of permanent immigrants in agricultural work grew as new immigration legislation, influenced by the discourse of a kinder multicultural Canada, promoted family reunification. Under the category Family Class, members of extended families were also able to immigrate. Consequently, in the Okanagan Valley, Portuguese and Punjabi immigrants and their families increased the number of labourers available for farm work.

As permanent residents, Portuguese and Punjabi immigrants could move freely from employer to employer in search of better or fairer working conditions. They could also move out of the region and work in activities outside agriculture. They were free to buy land if they had the means. Consequently, during the 1960s, the pool of poorly paid immigrant workers dried up (Russo, 2012). To resolve the agricultural labour shortage in the Okanagan Valley, government officials resorted to a program that recruited students from Quebec for seasonal migration. By representing the region as a sunny paradise that also offered a holiday resort experience, promoters and employers were able to entice young Quebecers to work in orchards. Continuity in the representation of the region as dominantly white, safe, friendly, and idyllic remained a key factor when attracting tourist-workers (Couture, 2009).

Québécois youth began coming to the Okanagan Valley for seasonal employment, travelling by bus or by hitchhiking (Lanthier, 1984; Lanthier & Wong, 2002; Wong, 1988), only to find that local residents racialized them, shunned them, and occasionally attacked them. Indeed, they were given pocketbooks called "Welcome to Kelowna" that warned them of potential racism in the area (Primeau, 1982). As Couture (2009) points out, British

Columbia's Human Rights Commission sent a researcher to analyze the situation in response to the frequency of racist incidents in the area. The researcher remarked that the Valley's racism was the worst he had encountered. In many cases, the accommodations were poor and the work conditions harsh. Thus, Couture (2009) asserts, Quebec youth faced not only poor and dangerous working conditions, but also racism coming from the local population and stress resulting from surveillance by the local RCMP who policed their everyday lives. The experiences of the young Quebec workers foreshadowed the current division of labour in agriculture, where employment, in fields and packinghouses, is mainly undertaken by racialized circular migrants who leave the Okanagan Valley at the end of the picking seasons.

The Neoliberal Turn: Cherries, Tourism, and Wine

In the 1980s, the short-lived Keynesian, de-racialized, and kinder Canada gave way to a new period of neoliberal capitalism. Neoliberalism significantly transformed Canada. Under neoliberalism, many of the policies and legislation that capital considered to be fetters to the action of the market have been eliminated or greatly reduced. Under neoliberalism there has been a process of de-unionization, minimization of the welfare component of the state, and a reduction of corporate taxes (Fowler, 2013). The neoliberal federal government has fostered an ethos of competition, individualism, and personal responsibility. A gradual end of the discourse of multiculturalism and of tolerance itself has facilitated the redirection of immigration legislation and policies toward decreasing the number of immigrants accepted under the Family Class category, while simultaneously building a discourse to justify a racialized system that favours employers' reliance on temporary migrants for jobs in low-paid and strenuous occupations.

Neoliberal changes in the Okanagan Valley have resulted in a remapping of the economy and society, the elimination of unionized blue-collar jobs, and the closing of important economic activities. Fordist factories and unionized mills are fewer now than before, while the implementation of free trade agreements has led to a readjustment of agriculture. With the creation of the Free Trade Agreement between Canada and the United

States in 1988, and the North American Free Trade Agreement in 1994, the agricultural industry became increasingly ruled by the market, which forces Canadian producers to compete with their American counterparts without custom or tariff protections (Hackett, 1996). As Roman and Velasco Arregui (2013) emphasize, free trade has been key in a neoliberal transformation of Canada propounded by a highly organized Canadian business elite. Free-trade practices have also had a negative impact on the Okanagan Valley's agricultural industry, which was previously dominated by relatively small orchardists who had little political power at the federal level.

In the past 30 years, agriculture in British Columbia has been challenged by global competition (Central Okanagan Economic Development Commission, 2012). Under the neoliberal policies of this period, the economic design of fruit production changed dramatically as the region's producers struggled for a share of the global market. Apple and pear growers have been particularly impacted by the competition of foreign producers. They have seen their industry decline due to increased competition with China, Washington State, South Africa, Chile, and Argentina. The area planted with apples and pears has fallen significantly. The number of acres dedicated to apple production declined in British Columbia by 40% in the first decade of the 21st century. In fact, the 2011 Census of Agriculture census shows that since 2006, the area in apples has decreased by 14%, while the acreage for sweet cherries and grapes has increased by 40% by 16%, respectively. In the Okanagan Valley, land ownership has become concentrated and capitalization has increased as fruit growers have adopted state-of-the-art technology and introduced new varieties of high-yield plants. Moreover, they have converted apple, pear, and soft fruit orchards to more profitable crops like cherries, grapes, and organic produce, which they sell globally and at seasonally operated vegetable and fruit stands, at local farmers' markets, and in specialty stores. In the free-trade, globalized, neoliberal world of the 21st century, cherry growers export directly to China, the United States, Taiwan, and Germany (Cherries to China, 2014; Couture, 2009). The cherry industry is now dominated by members of a small group of entrepreneurs competing worldwide, using advanced technology developed in laboratories in the Okanagan Valley and growing refined varieties of cherries that give them a competitive edge. In turn, growers have increased the acreage cultivated for grapes in response to the increase in worldwide wine consumption and the support of government policies that encourage grape production and other marketing activities.

Until the signing of the free trade agreements, growers cultivated Labrusca varieties, which are used to produce cheap table wine. In the 1980s, they replaced these varieties with European vinifera that is suitable for high-end wine production (Hira & Bwenge, 2011). This transformation enabled Okanagan-produced wine to be branded with a seal of quality, modernity, and European-ness to better compete with other world brands.

Entrepreneurs, local politicians, and planners have used images of orchards, vineyards, and wine as identity markers to rebrand the Okanagan Valley as a culturally hip, cosmopolitan, technologically progressive, and dominantly white region (Aguiar, Tomic, & Trumper, 2005). While the Okanagan Valley was previously a modest tourism region for vacationers, tourism has been transformed by the neoliberal turn. Boutique and four-star hotels, swanky bed-and-breakfast establishments, luxurious time-share condominiums, and a selection of expensive houses that are second homes for wealthy vacationers have replaced the budget motels that dotted the highways and rural thoroughfares in the past. As well, upscale bistros have displaced economical restaurants and diners. Many of these restaurants are located in wineries and are staffed with renowned chefs who proffer exquisite menus, purportedly featuring fresh local and organic ingredients that are produced in their own gardens or on local farms and purchased at the numerous farmer markets in the area. In fact, upscale, chic market cosmopolitan and close-to-nature tourism has become one of the most important economic activities in the Okanagan Valley. Those activities are closely connected to the region's agricultural sector. "Napa North" or the "four-season paradise," as the Okanagan Valley is branded, attracts 3.5 million visitors per year (TOTA, 2012).

Cyclical Racialized Migrant Labour

Youth from Quebec have continued to travel to the Okanagan after the neoliberal turn. In the past, they travelled to the area, to a large extent, out of economic need; yet, today they consider the travel experience as a combination of recreation and work. Leibel (2007) and Couture (2009) assert that since the 1990s, a sizable number of pickers have travelled for fun, adventure, and holidays, and have spent their summers working and touring. Each year, hundreds of Quebec youth continue to come to the Okanagan Valley where they move from south to north, as the fruit-picking season requires. Many of them come with tents, sleeping bags, and cooking utensils, and camp. Some of the orchardists provide camping grounds with limited facilities. In other cases, the pickers find their own accommodations. For instance, employers at Norton's Farm in Oliver recruit workers by advertising the jobs as a combination of strenuous work and a fun camping experience. Their website tells backpackers: "You will need a tent, sleeping bag, cooking utensils, working clothes (warm and cold), boots, and a bathing suit (there is a pool at the camp). The camp also has showers, flush toilets, stoves, fridges, microwaves, sinks, safe drinking water, couches and sometimes TV and movies" (Norton's Okanagan Harvest: World Class Cherries, n.d.). Other employers are less generous with facilities. In Oliver, city officials set up a rough camp to accommodate fruit pickers, mostly from Quebec. As in the past, Québécois pickers continue to be racialized. Nonetheless, Leibel (2007) points out, they continue to arrive each summer to work in the region.

The Okanagan Valley is attractive as a work and a tourist destination not only to Quebec youth, but also to young adults who come for working holidays from European countries, Australia, New Zealand, Japan, and South Korea. The BC Cherry Association actively seeks these young people to pick, sort, and pack fruit (BC Cherry Association, 2014). Okanagan farm owners also recruit tourist-workers, such as members of the World Wide Opportunities in Organic Farming (WWOOF), who work mainly on non-commercial, sustainable, organic farms in exchange for food and accommodation, but no wages (WWOOF, n.d.). These volunteers are marginal, however, to the labour force. Indeed, backpacking youth from Quebec and elsewhere are not numerous enough to meet the labour requirements of the agricultural sector in the Okanagan Valley.

Employers who operate orchards, vineyards, and wineries have found solutions to contemporary labour shortages by recruiting members of a new racialized and cyclical migrant labour (i.e., migrant workers who must leave every year by December 15 and return at some point the following year) who are highly productive, easy to discipline, and willing to work for low wages (Tomic, Trumper, & Aguiar, 2010). Specifically, employers utilize the Seasonal Agricultural Worker Program, which launched in Ontario in 1966 and then expanded throughout Canada. In British Columbia, it began in 2004 and rapidly became a fundamental source of labour in agriculture. The Seasonal Agricultural Worker Program (SAWP) operates under government-to-government agreements; it regulates and legitimizes temporary migration, providing employers in agriculture with workers at certain times of the growing season for specialized tasks. The SAWP allows employers to bring workers from Mexico and the Caribbean at the time they are needed and forces them to leave Canada once the jobs are completed. The maximum time these workers may stay in Canada is eight months, and all of them must leave by December 15.

The conditions under which Okanagan fruit growers hire such labourers bind them to such a degree that their employment may be considered a form of modern indenture (Baines & Sharma, 2002; Fairey et al., 2008; Sharma, 2006; Tomic & Trumper, 2012; Walia, 2010). The members of this labour force must be skilled, experienced, fully reliable, and disciplined; yet they are effectively powerless and disposable, and have no choice but to work long hours in harsh environments. Workers encounter obstacles if they wish to transfer to different employers and are not permitted to stay in Canada if they are not under contract to an employer. In contrast, the program authorizes employers to fire workers and return them to their home countries at will. In British Columbia, employers must provide housing for their workers, but at a cost to the workers. Workers have no power to determine the conditions or locations of their accommodations, which are often on employers' premises and under their surveillance. Although the program gives preference to labourers who are married and have children, the families of these employees are not allowed to accompany them to Canada. Thus, the Seasonal Agricultural Worker Program allows Canada to externalize labour costs, because the reproduction of the labour force remains the responsibility of the workers' countries of origin, including health services for their families and for the workers if they are sick or injured and unable

Table 9.1 Number of Temporary Foreign Worker Positions on Positive Labour Market Opinions in Agricultural Occupations, British Columbia

	2004	2005	2006	2007	2008	2009	2010	2011	2012
SAWP	47	855	1,605	2,890	3,795	3,695	3,535	3,985	4,980
Agricultural Stream		0	0	0	0	0	0	380	880
Higher-skilled		25	35	80	60	30	50	50	70
Lower-skilled		10	100	405	1,040	425	410	285	110
Total	47	890	1,740	3,375	4,895	4,150	3,995	4,700	6,040

Source: Employment and Social Development Canada, 2014.

to work. Individual employers and the Canadian state benefit from these bilateral agreements (Tomic, Trumper, & Aguiar, 2010).

The number of SAWP workers has increased exponentially since 2004, when 47 SAWP workers began to work in the province. In 2012, nearly 5,000 of the 6,040 agricultural migrant workers in British Columbia were hired under the Seasonal Agricultural Worker Program, and one-third of them worked in the Okanagan Valley (see Table 9.1).

The Seasonal Agricultural Worker Program is particularly well designed for fruit growers, because it allows them to hire workers for short periods. Many producers argue that these workers are crucial for their operations. The president of BC Fruit Growers' Association claims: "The Seasonal Agricultural Worker Program (SAWP) that allows fruit farmers to bring in foreign workers remains critical to the fruit growing industry in this region....Without this program, we would not be able to operate" (*Osoyoos Times* Staff, 2013). Employers in British Columbia's wine industry also hire migrant workers. In an article in the *Globe and Mail*, Stueck (2011) observes that Mexican labourers keep BC's wine flowing and estimates that around 40 per cent of the Mexican migrant labourers in the Okanagan toil in the wine industry.

The Seasonal Agricultural Worker Program is not the only scheme that provides low-paid, unfree, and racialized foreign labour to agriculture in the Okanagan Valley. Even before neoliberal hegemony, the federal government created other discursive and policy devices to diversify the pool of foreign temporary workers authorized to work in Canada. In 1973, in addition to the existing Seasonal Agricultural Worker Program, the federal government instituted the Non-Immigrant Employment Authorization Program. By 1982, there were 124,114 of these temporary workers in Canada. In the 1990s, the program was renamed Temporary Foreign Worker Program (TFWP). In 2002, a further bureaucratization of the TFWP instigated a pilot project that allowed Canadian employers to hire foreign migrant workers who fit the government's categorization of "low skill" (Sharma, 2006; Trumper & Wong, 2007). As in the case of the Seasonal Agricultural Worker Program, the low-skill label reinforces the material and symbolic segregation of racialized workers. Run by private contractors and not regulated by government-to-government agreements, the Agricultural Stream under this pilot project and the Lower Skilled Stream of the TFWP compete with the SAWP (Faraday, 2012) and exacerbate the precarious conditions of labourers. Private recruitment is, increasingly, bringing temporary foreign workers to Canada from Thailand, India, Guatemala, Peru, Honduras, El Salvador, and Philippines. Félix Martínez, of the Agriculture Workers Alliance, is of the opinion that although the Seasonal Agricultural Worker Program is, in many cases, most suitable for fruit growers, employers request workers under other temporary recruitment programs as a strategy to "motivate" their workers. In the Okanagan Valley, temporary workers from Guatemala and Peru perform farm work and fill fruit sorting and packing jobs (Hahn & Cohen, 2014). In 2012, around 1,000 temporary foreign workers came to British Columbia under these programs (see Table 9.1). It is estimated that 300 of them laboured in the Okanagan Valley.

The Emotional Workforce and Tourism

Today, agriculture in the Okanagan Valley has a stronger connection to tourism than ever before, as orchards, vineyards and wine, and local and organic farm produce have become essential to the new form of cosmopolitan tourism in the region (Tomic & Aguiar, 2006). Contemporary visitors find social meaning in the chic associated with drinking exquisite wines and eating superb foods in exclusive bistros and restaurants. Yet, because today's wine-drinking experience requires that patrons cultivate distinctive tastes, winery owners and operators hire and train servers to model the suave yet detached behaviour that suggests good judgment. The experience demands savvy, for an uneducated palate will not easily distinguish between the subtleties of wine flavours. Moreover, servers assist patrons in developing the savoir-faire to know which glasses are styled for particular kinds of wine and which foods are best paired with them. As Zembylas (2007) asserts, these trained servers have the skills not only to enact the classed ceremonies of wine drinking, but also to incite feelings of satisfaction in wine patrons from this enactment. These are emotional labourers.

In the 1980s, sociologist Arlie Hochschild pioneered the concept of "emotional labour," which she defined as "labour that induces or suppresses feeling in order to sustain the outward countenance that produces the proper state of mind in others" (1983, p. 7). Since Hochschild's early work, which analyzed the skills of Delta airlines crew members, her ideas have been widely used and developed in the study of workers in a varied range of occupations including bakeries, nursing homes, retail establishments, phone sex workers, and hairdressing, among others (Koch & Everke Buchanan, 2013; Wharton, 2009). Owners and operators of wineries employ such labourers to fill a crucial emotional workforce. Emotional labourers fill front-end occupations linked to tourism (Aguiar, Tomic, & Trumper, 2006). In the Okanagan Valley, a pool of mainly local young people, who take seasonal and poorly paid precarious employment in the wine industry, assume responsibilities for front-end activities and commodify their emotions as part of their roles (Aguiar, Tomic, & Trumper, 2006). The culinary experience is similarly organized. Restaurants that feature the pairing of wine and food also require servers who are conversant in sophisticated food language. Tour guides have also become increasingly crucial to Okanagan tourism; as experienced travellers in the region, their role is to take visitors to preferred wineries and assist them in cultivating appreciation for the bucolic scenery that brochures and websites have prepared them to experience.

The emotionally skilled worker interacts with tourists in situations as varied as food service in bistros and bed-and-breakfast establishments, where they ensure that the guests' experiences are exquisite and unique; in the taste rooms at wineries, where they help tourists to appreciate the wine they sample; and in spas, where those trained in massage or as aestheticians provide services for clients. The demands on such workers are considerable. For example, an advertisement to recruit employees for seasonal or summer work in the Okanagan's tourist industry described the position this way: "Retail sales associates are responsible for creating a positive winery experience by interacting with winery visitors and guests during tastings, tours, events and retail sales. Must be 19 years of age, willing to work weekends, evenings and holidays and hold a Serving It Right certificate. These positions are seasonal from April to October" (Castanet Classifieds, n.d.). In the Okanagan Valley, the prerequisite for emotional capital is, nonetheless, racial capital.

In British Columbia, as in the restaurant industry in other parts of the world (Jayaraman, 2013), a racialized division of labour places white workers in contact with customers, while people of colour are made invisible in kitchens and janitorial closets. Employers in the food and wine industry select their servers mostly from young, white, English-speaking workers whom they imagine have the capacity to cultivate the emotional capital necessary to interact with customers. Not surprisingly, the authors' recent visits to wine tasting rooms and upscale restaurants confirmed that the front-end workers were mostly white, were conversant in wine parlance, and ostensibly knowledgeable about food, especially organic produce grown on local farms. This group of mostly local young adults fills part of the 15,000 jobs required seasonally in the Okanagan's tourist industry (TOTA, 2012).

The Itinerant Professionals and Technicians

There is a smaller group of professionals and technicians who are instrumental in the production of a cosmopolitan Okanagan tourist experience: the wine makers, vineyard managers, chefs, sommeliers, hoteliers, restaurateurs, and other specialized professionals and technicians whose contributions serve to enhance the experience of tourism in the region. Standing (2011) calls these workers "proficians":

> This term combines the traditional ideas of "professional" and "technician" but covers those with bundles of skills that they can market, earning high incomes on contract, as consultants or independent own-account workers. The proficians are the equivalent of the yeomen, knights and squires of the Middle Ages. They live with the expectation and desire to move around, without an impulse for long-term, full-time employment in a single enterprise. The "standard employment relationship" is not for them. (pp. 7–8)

The owners of vineyards and wineries boast that their wine makers are highly reputed, internationally known, and capable of cultivating Okanagan wines to make them competitive at the global level. Moreover, restaurant owners make a point of announcing their hiring of chefs who have been trained in the most prestigious schools. Several upscale restaurants employ chefs whose culinary skills are sharpened to such a fine edge that they are able to satisfy the palates of even the most sophisticated patron. Such chefs prepare food with the freshest possible locally produced organic ingredients. Sommeliers add the "indispensable" pairing of food with wine. Equally vital is the wine critic, who establishes and disseminates taste by writing, acting, filming, and blogging. Proficians, as a distinct group of movable, well-paid, and confident individuals (Standing, 2011), have been essential in branding the Okanagan Valley as a cosmopolitan rural tourist destination.

Conclusion

Since the 1980s, the Canadian state has moved relentlessly to enforce neoliberalism. Concomitant with the surge of neoliberal economics and ideology, discourses of multiculturalism and tolerance have eroded, which has facilitated the consolidation of an economic, social, and cultural system that relies, in part, on temporary migrant labour to perform work at low wages that citizens and permanent residents refuse to undertake. As Goldberg (2009) points out, race is the silent concept that informs and organizes racial neoliberalism. In Canada, race has silently restructured and reorganized immigration policy to allow racialized workers to migrate to Canada to work and live in conditions tantamount to modern indenture. The Okanagan Valley's economy has also been, to a degree, restructured by racial neoliberalism. Building upon a history of agriculture that has helped represent the Okanagan Valley as a "four-season paradise" and of whiteness, orchardists and the wine and tourist industries have refashioned the landscape and modernized the practices of employing temporary, non-white workers for heavy seasonal work, while local power groups revitalized whiteness to serve a cosmopolitan tourist industry. The more than 100-year-old four-season paradise that was imagined by early land speculators to attract British upper classes to work and play in the Okanagan Valley has received a facelift that freshened its image to fit the conditions imposed by neoliberalism.

References

Aguiar, L., Tomic, P., & Trumper, R. (2005). Work hard, play hard: Selling Kelowna, BC, as year-round playground. *The Canadian Geographer/Le Géographe canadien, 49*(2), 123–139.

Aguiar, L., Tomic, P., & Trumper, R. (2006). New palate, new taste, new class: Wine tourism and the transformation of Kelowna and the Okanagan Valley. *CRWS News*, 29, 5–6.

Baines, D., & Sharma, N. (2002). Migrant workers as non-citizens: The case against citizenship as a policy concept. *Studies in Political Economy, 69*(Autumn), 75–107.

Barman, J. (1984). *Growing Up British in British Columbia: Boys in private school.* Vancouver, BC: University of British Columbia Press.

BC Cherry Association. (2014). Employment Information. Retrieved Feb. 4, 2015 from www.bccherry.com/employment/employment-details-information

Castanet Classifieds. (n.d.). Castanet Classifieds–Jobs–Browse the Latest Snapshot. Retrieved Feb. 4, 2015 from https://www.google.com/search?q=%E2%80%9CRetail+sales+associates+are+responsible+for+creating+a+positive+winery+experience+by+interacting+with+winery+visitors+and+guests%22&ie=utf-8&oe=utf-8

Central Okanagan Economic Development Commission. (2012). *2012 Economic Profile Regional District of the Central Okanagan.* Retrieved Feb. 4, 2015 from http://www.investkelowna.com/sites/default/files/uploads/2012_regional_economic_profile_final_2012-05-10.pdf

Cherries to China: How Growers are Building the Value Chain. (2014). *TheGrower.org* May, *64*(5), p. 5. Retrieved June 4, 2014 from http://www.thegrower.org/readnews.php?id=4h0k8g0r9g8s

Couture, H. (2009). *Les jeunes migrants québécois dans les vallées fruitières de la Colombie-Britannique: Ethnographie d'une forme de mobilité* (Unpublished master's thesis). Université Laval, Montreal, QC.

Day, R.F. (2000). *Multiculturalism and the history of Canadian diversity.* Toronto, ON: University of Toronto Press.

Dunae, P. (1981). *Gentlemen emigrants: From the British public schools to the Canadian frontier.* Vancouver, BC, and Toronto, ON: Douglas & McIntyre.

Employment and Social Development Canada. (2014). *Labour Market Opinions — Annual Statistics.* Retrieved from http://www.edsc.gc.ca/eng/jobs/foreign_workers/lmo_statistics/annual-agriculture.shtml

Fairey, D., Hanson, C., MacInnes, G., Tigar McLaren, A., Otero, G., Preibisch, K., & Thompson, M. (2008). Cultivating farmworker rights: Ending the exploitation of immigrant and migrant farmworkers in BC. Vancouver, BC: Canadian Centre for Policy Alternatives.

Faraday, F. (2012). *Made in Canada: How the law constructs migrant workers' insecurity.* Toronto, ON: Metcalfe Foundation.

Fowler, T. (Ed.). (2013). *From crisis to austerity: Neoliberalism, organized labour and the Canadian state.* Ottawa, ON: Red Quill Books.

Goldberg, D. (2009). *The threat of race: Reflection on racial neoliberalism.* Malden, MA: Blackwell.

Gould, S.J. (1996). *The mismeasure of man.* New York, NY: W.W. Norton.

Hackett, N. (1996). *Surprise success: Wine, tourists, and the woes of free trade.* Burnaby, BC: Centre for Tourism Policy and Research, Simon Fraser University.

Hahn, E., & Cohen, A. (2014). Letter: Temporary farm workers contribute to Okanagan economy. *Capital News,* Mar. 25.

Hira, A., & Bwenge, A. (2011). The wine industry in British Columbia: Issues and potential. *AAWE Working Paper No. 89.*

Hochschild, A. (1983). *The managed heart: Commercialization of human feeling.* Berkeley, CA: University of California Press.

Joy, A. (1982). *Accommodation and cultural persistence: The case of the Sikhs and the Portuguese in the Okanagan Valley of British Columbia.* (Unpublished doctoral dissertation). University of British Columbia, Vancouver, BC.

Jayaraman, S. (2013). *Behind the kitchen door.* Ithaca, NY: Cornell University Press.

Koch, G., & Everke Buchanan, S. (Eds.). (2013). *Pathways to empathy: New studies on commodification, emotional labor, and time binds.* Frankfurt-on-Main, Germany: Campus Verlag.

Koroscil, P. (2003). *British garden of Eden: Settlement history of the Okanagan Valley, British Columbia.* Burnaby, BC: Simon Fraser University.

Lanthier, M. (1984). The pattern: A history of social discrimination against farm-workers in the Okanagan-Similkameen, 1890–1983. A Report Prepared by Mario Lanthier, Backpackers and Orchards-Workers Support Association Kelowna, BC, Aug. 1. Kelowna Public Archives Doug Findlater fonds 2006.017.

Lanthier, M., & Wong, L. (2002). Ethnic agricultural labour in the Okanagan Valley: 1880s to 1960s. Report prepared for the Royal BC Museum. Retrieved June 10, 2014 from http://www.livinglandscapes.bc.ca/thomp-ok/ethnic-agri/british.html

Leibel, G. (2007). *The changing face of farm labour in British Columbia: Exploring the experiences of migrant Quebecois and Mexican agricultural workers in the Okanagan Valley* (Unpublished master's thesis). University of Victoria, Victoria, BC.
Norton's Okanagan Harvest: World Class Cherries. (n.d.). Retrieved Feb. 15, 2015 from www.Okanaganharvest.com/Employment
Osoyoos Times Staff. (2013, June 20). BC Fruit Growers bosses inform council about how working "nimbler and smarter" keeps them above competition from Washington State. *Osoyoos Times*. Retrieved July 5, 2014 from http://www.osoyoostimes.com/b-c-fruit-growers-bosses-inform-council-about-how-working-nimbler-and-smarter-keeps-them-above-competition-from-washington-state/
Primeau, M. (1982). *Backpackers' & fruit pickers' pocketbook: Welcome to Kelowna, BC.* Kelowna, BC: The Committee of Assistance to Transients and Fruit Pickers.
Rattansi, A. (2007). *Racism: A very short introduction.* Oxford, UK: Oxford University Press.
Roman, R., & Velasco Arregui, E. (2013). *Continental crucible: Big business, workers and unions in the transformation of North America.* Black Point, NS: Fernwood.
Russo, R. (2012). *Solidarity forever, Canadian never: SAWP workers in Canada* (Doctoral dissertation). University of British Columbia, Vancouver, BC.
Sharma, N. (2006). *Home economics: Nationalism and the making of "migrant workers" in Canada.* Toronto, ON: University of Toronto Press.
Standing, G. (2011). *The precariat: The new dangerous class.* London, UK: Bloomsbury.
Street Guide to the City of Kelowna. (1979). Kelowna, BC: Kelowna Public Archives.
Stueck, W. (2011, Oct. 14). Mexican labourers keep BC wine flowing. *Globe and Mail.* Retrieved July 7, 2015 from http://www.theglobeandmail.com/news/british-columbia/mexican-labourers-keep-bc-wine-flowing/article4179529/
Tomic, P., & Aguiar, L. (2006). *Wine snobbery: Re-inscripting taste in the Central Valley of Chile and the Okanagan Valley of British Columbia.* Paper presented at the XXVI International Congress of the Latin American Studies Association (LASA), San Juan, Puerto Rico.
Tomic, P., & Trumper, R. (2012). Mobilities and immobilities: Globalization, farming and temporary work in the Okanagan Valley. In P. Lenard & C. Straehle (Eds.), *Legislated inequality: Temporary labour migration in Canada* (pp. 73–94). Montreal, QC: McGill-Queen's University Press.
Tomic, P., Trumper, R., & Aguiar, L. (2005, Aug. 1). Reinventando Kelowna: Jubilaciones, tecnología, vino y turismo en una ciudad del hinterland de Canadá. *Scripta Nova: Revista Electrónica de Geografía y Ciencias Sociales, IX*(194) (77). Retrieved June 2, 2014 from http://www.ub.edu/geocrit/sn/sn-194-77.htm
Tomic, P., Trumper, R., & Aguiar, L. (2010). Housing regulations and living conditions of Mexican migrant workers in the Okanagan Valley, BC. *Canadian Issues/Thèmes canadiens*, Spring, 78–82.
TOTA. (2012). Embracing our potential: A ten-year tourism strategy for the Thompson Okanagan Region. Retrieved June 2, 2014 from http://www.totabc.org/corporateSite/regional-strategy/
Trumper, R., & Wong, L. (2007). Canada's guest workers: Racialized, gendered, and flexible. In S. Hier & B. Singh Bolaria (Eds.), *Race and racism in 21st century Canada* (pp. 151–170). Peterborough, ON: Broadview.

Walia, H. (2010). Transient servitude: Migrant labour in Canada and the apartheid of citizenship. *Race & Class*, *52*(July), 71–84.
Wharton, A.S. (2009). The sociology of emotional labor. *Annual Review of Sociology*, *35*(April), 147–165.
Wells, D. (1995). The impact of the postwar compromise on Canadian unionism: The formation of an Auto Worker Local in the 1950s. *Labour/Le Travail*, *36*(Fall), 147–173.
Wilson, W. (2005). *Kelowna: One hundred years of history, 1905–2005.* Kelowna, BC: Kelowna Publishers.
Wong, L. (1988). *Migrant seasonal agricultural labour: Race and ethnic relations in the Okanagan Valley* (Doctoral dissertation) York University, Toronto, ON.
WWOOF. (n.d.). Welcome to WWOOF Canada. Retrieved Feb. 4, 2015 from www.wwoof.ca
Zembylas, M. (2007). Emotional capital and education: Theoretical insights from Bourdieu. *British Journal of Educational Studies*, *55*(4), 443–463.

Contributors

GIANNA ARGENTO, BA (University of British Columbia), JD (University of Calgary, 2014), is a Crown prosecutor with Alberta Justice and Solicitor General. During law school, she attended courses at the European Academy (EURAC) for "Human Rights, Minorities and Diversity Management: Special Focus on Europe and Canada" (2012), and was founder and president of the Pro-Bono Students Innocence Project at the University of Calgary (2011–2014).

BOB BARNETSON is a professor of labour relations at Athabasca University. His research focuses on the political economy of workplace injury and the regulation of child, migrant, and farm work in Alberta. He is the author of *The Political Economy of Workplace Injury in Canada* (Athabasca University Press, 2010).

MICHAEL J. BROADWAY completed his PHD in geography at the University of Illinois, Urbana-Champaign. He is dean of the College of Arts and Sciences at Northern Michigan University. His research expertise focuses on the meatpacking industry's community impacts and he has studied small towns across the Great Plains and Prairies. He is a co-author with Donald Stull of *Slaughterhouse Blues: The Meat and Poultry Industry in North America* (2nd ed., Cengage 2013) and is a co-editor of *Any Way You Cut It: Meat Processing and Small-Town America*, published by the University Press of Kansas. In 2006, he was a visiting Fulbright Research Chair in the Department of Rural Economy at the University of Alberta, where he studied the impact of "mad cow disease" on a rural community, and the social changes accompanying the expansion of a meatpacking plant in Brooks, Alberta. He is the author of over 70 journal articles and book chapters that deal mostly with the meat industry.

JILL BUCKLASCHUK is a Social Sciences and Humanities Research Council of Canada postdoctoral fellow at the University of Guelph in the Department of Sociology and Anthropology. She recently obtained her doctorate from the University of Manitoba, where she completed a dissertation on lower skilled temporary migration in Manitoba. Based on years of community-based research experience, her work uses qualitative research methods to examine how non-permanent legal status impacts the social and workplace experiences of temporary migrants as they negotiate settlement in Canada.

DELNA CONTRACTOR, BA (University of British Columbia), JD (University of Calgary), is an associate at a national law firm in Toronto. In addition to her primary practice area of commercial litigation, Delna is passionate about human rights law and women's issues.

DARLENE A. DUNLOP dedicated herself, for more than a decade, to the emancipation of Alberta's farm workers. She worked as a migrant seasonal farm worker for 30 years in Alberta. In 2004, she became an activist and, with her spouse Eric Musekamp, co-founded the Farmworkers Union of Alberta as the vehicle for change for Alberta farm workers. In 2008, Dunlop co-wrote a paper, "'Harvesting Bread and Roses': Female Farmworkers in Alberta," with anthropologist Mary Kosta and presented it at the University of Lethbridge Women's Studies, Gender and Rural Migration Conference on International Women's Day. Dunlop and Musekamp's 15 years of lobbying the Alberta government finally yielded success when, on December 10, 2015, Premier Rachel Notley passed Bill 6: the Enhanced Protection for Farm and Ranch Workers Act.

BRYNNA HAMBLY (TAKASUGI), BA (Religious Studies, University of Calgary, 2007), JD (University of Calgary, 2014) is an associate at Carbert Waite LLP in Calgary, Alberta. Brynna practises in employment law, health law, and civil litigation. She developed a passion for employment law while completing her JD at the University of Calgary. Brynna has volunteered with several organizations as a lawyer, including Pro Bono Law Alberta's Civil Claims Duty Counsel project where she is a current volunteer.

ZANE HAMM'S background is in citizen engagement and rural-focused research. Her research includes dialogue and learning between generations, rural-urban migration and mobility, youth engagement, and community resilience and sustainability. Her current work with the Centre for Public Involvement focuses on maximizing citizen participation in municipal planning and decision making. Zane teaches citizen engagement and consultation, and MBA courses in community economic development. She has a PHD in educational policy studies, a specialization in adult education, and an MEd in international education. She grew up on a farm in Saskatchewan.

PAUL KENNETT is a lawyer at MacKay Real Property Law, where he practises residential real estate conveyancing and wills and estates. He received his Juris Doctor from the University of Calgary Faculty of Law in 2014 and was called to the Alberta bar in December 2015. He also attained the degree of master of arts in 2004, and bachelor of arts in 1999.

JENNIFER KOSHAN is a professor at the University of Calgary Faculty of Law. She led a constitutional clinical course in 2014 that developed arguments for a constitutional challenge to the exclusion of farm workers from labour and employment legislation in Alberta. Her research and teaching interests are in the areas of constitutional law, human rights, violence against women, and public interest advocacy. Jennifer was awarded the 2013 Canadian Association of Law Teachers Prize for Academic Excellence, which honours exceptional contributions to research and law teaching by a Canadian law teacher in mid-career.

C.F. ANDREW LAU received his Juris Doctor from the University of Calgary Faculty of Law in 2014. He articled at Sherritt Greene Barristers and Solicitors, an immigration law firm, in Calgary, Alberta, and is currently an associate at Parlee McLaws LLP with a focus in intellectual property law. Prior to law school, Andrew obtained his bachelor of science in electrical engineering at the University of Alberta in 2010. In addition to his primary practice area, Andrew has an interest in immigration law, environmental law, and human rights law, and he volunteers with Calgary Legal Guidance in immigration-related matters.

J. GRAHAM MARTINELLI, BAH (Queen's University), JD (University of Calgary, 2014), is an associate lawyer with Field Law LLP in Calgary. Prior to law school, Graham worked as a constituency assistant in his home federal riding of Skeena-Bulkley Valley while simultaneously employed as a haul truck driver at two copper mines in the region. He maintains a strong interest in natural resources and Aboriginal law, and he was one of four students to represent the University of Calgary at the 2013 Kawaskimhon National Aboriginal Law Moot.

SHIRLEY A. MCDONALD, PHD (University of Alberta, 2013), MA (University of Calgary, 2001) combines her research interests in Canadian literature and history in explorations of the life writing of Anglo-Canadian prairie settlers. She has received two Roger Soderstrom Awards of Distinction from the Alberta Historical Resources Foundation. She has articles in *Prairie Forum*; *The Australasian Canadian Studies Journal*; *English Studies in Canada*; *ARIEL: A Review of International English Literature*; *a/b: Auto/Biography Studies*; and *American Review of Canadian Studies*. She also has an invited publication in *Gary Geddes: Essays on His Works* (Guernica). Shirley teaches English at the University of British Columbia Okanagan.

ROBIN C. MCINTYRE is a criminal defence lawyer in Calgary. She earned her bachelor of science, majoring in biological sciences, from the University of Calgary in 2010, and her Juris Doctor from the University of Calgary in 2014, where she graduated on the dean's list and was ranked among the top 10 students of her class. She was called to the bar in 2015.

NELSON MEDEIROS, BA (University of Winnipeg), MEDes (University of Calgary), received his Juris Doctor from the University of Calgary Faculty of Law in 2014 and is practising as a lawyer for the City of Calgary. Nelson practised as an urban planner prior to law school, and he has a particular interest in municipal, property, and constitutional law.

KERRY PREIBISCH (1970–2016) was a feminist sociologist with research interests in gender, migration, and rural livelihoods; temporary migration programs, migrant rights, and development; im/migration and social change; and ethical food production. Her publications appear in *International Migration Review*; *International Migration*; the *Canadian Medical Association Journal*; the *International Journal of the Sociology of Agriculture and Food*; *Citizenship Studies*; the *Journal of Ethnic and Migration Studies*; and *Signs: Journal of Women in Culture and Society*, among others. She testified at human rights tribunal proceedings and in front of provincial, national, and international bodies, including the United Nations, advocating for better treatment and policies for migrant workers. She was given a César E. Chávez Black Eagle Award for her efforts. As a community-engaged scholar, she worked closely with migrants and their allies. Her most recent research traced the transnational migratory circuits of rural Guatemalan men and women to Canada and the United States as documented and unauthorized farm workers. Over the past two decades, Kerry undertook research in 20 different countries, mostly in the Americas, and was recognized internationally as an expert on temporary migration programs in North America.

HEIDI ROLFE received her Juris Doctor from the University of Calgary Faculty of Law in 2014. She also holds a bachelor of applied science in environmental engineering from the University of Waterloo and has a particular interest in environmental and regulatory law. After law school, Heidi completed a clerkship with the Federal Court of Canada and is currently practising in Vancouver, British Columbia.

PATRICIA TOMIC taught sociology at the University of British Columbia, Okanagan campus. Her areas of interest include the politics of language and the Latin American experience in Canada; tourism, wine, and migration in the Okanagan Valley; and the effects of neoliberalism in Chile (1973 to the present).

RICARDO TRUMPER taught sociology at the University of British Columbia, Okanagan campus. His research interests include migration, mobility, and neoliberalism. He is currently conducting research on mobility, disasters, and sports in Chile. He is also studying the repercussions of neoliberalism and neoconservative policies, global mobility, and migration in the Okanagan Valley.

KAY ELIZABETH TURNER, BA (McGill University, 2009), JD (University of Calgary, 2014) was called to the Alberta bar in 2015 and is currently practising corporate law at a national law firm in Calgary. Prior to her career in law, she worked in the not-for-profit and political sectors and has particular interest in governance, constitutional law, and issues of gender inequality.

Index

Other Titles from The University of Alberta Press

We Are All Treaty People
Prairie Essays
ROGER EPP

Provocative essays explore the poetry and political economy of life in Canada's rural West.

Heavy Burdens on Small Shoulders
The Labour of Pioneer Children on the Canadian Prairies
SANDRA ROLLINGS-MAGNUSSON

Pioneer children performed vital work to help their families on the Canadian Prairies.

Writing Off the Rural West
Globalization, Governments and the Transformation of Rural Communities
ROGER EPP & DAVE WHITSON, Editors

Some of the most intense effects of globalization can be seen in rural communities.

More information at www.uap.ualberta.ca

Farm Workers in Western Canada